CHILDREN OF CONFLICT

Children of Conflict

A Study of Interracial Sex and Marriage

FERNANDO HENRIQUES

E. P. Dutton & Co., Inc. / New York 1975

First published in the U.S.A. 1975 by E. P. Dutton & Co., Inc.

FIRST EDITION

10 9 8 7 6 5 4 3 2 1

CLOTH: ISBN: 0-525-07996-3
PAPER: ISBN: 0-525-47385-8
Library of Congress Catalog Card Number: 74-22057
Published in England under the title *Children of Caliban: Miscegenation*

CONTENTS

LIST OF ILLUSTRATIONS

ACKNOWLEDGEMENTS

The author and publisher would like to thank the following for permission to reproduce copyright photographic material: the collections of the Rare Book Division of the Library of Congress, Washington, D.C. (1); the Mary Evans Picture Library (4, 5); John R. Freeman & Co. (6); Wide World Photos (8).

Photograph 7 is reproduced from *Few Surprises or Comforts* by Eugene Richards by permission of The MIT Press, Cambridge, Massachusetts, © 1973 The Massachusetts Institute of Technology.

Introduction

Miscegenation – the mixing of races – has been a social and sexual phenomenon throughout the history of the world. In my view its importance and significance as a social catalyst has not been sufficiently recognized. A number of factors have contributed to this state of affairs. These are largely concerned with profound guilt feelings arising out of the sexual abuse which has been characteristic of the sexual relationships of the European and non-European. Thus the main purpose of *Children of Conflict* might be said to be an attempt to redress this neglect.

No single book could possibly survey all the manifestations of miscegenation on a global scale. What I have attempted to do is to take a number of specific cases – the United States, Britain, the Caribbean and Africa – and to analyse them in considerable detail both historically and sociologically. This analysis is preceded by a discussion of the social situations which precipitate sexual relationships between different ethnic groups. The main emphasis of the book is on such relationships between European and non-European. The last section of *Children of Conflict* is an analysis of miscegenation in the world today.

My interest in writing the book has been in part promoted by the fact that my own ethnic background is extremely diverse – African, Indian and European. Born in Jamaica, the greater part of my life has been spent in a predominantly white society – Britain. I am married to an Englishwoman, and have experienced the problems of creating a racially mixed family.

One of the most fascinating aspects of the phenomenon discussed is the variation and change, which can be seen in the historical dimension, of the European's social and sexual exploration of alien and exotic peoples. The evidence suggests that the notion of physical repugnance on the part of the European when faced by people totally dissimilar in appearance is no more than a myth. For example, there could be no greater physical antithesis than that between the Nordic-type Englishman and a female Australian Aborigine; yet sexual relationships have existed between these ethnic groups from the period of initial contact in the eighteenth century to the present day.

It has been often suggested that the European colonizer only turned to 'native' women because of the deprivation of his own womankind. The material presented in *Children of Conflict* destroys this idea. This is especially the case in regard to the historical situation of whites and blacks in the United States and in contemporary Africa.

It is essential for the student of miscegenation to appreciate the fact that contemporary manifestations of racial mixing have been very largely determined by the historical matrix of colonization. The latter, particularly when associated with slavery, gave opportunity to the colonizer to abuse sexually the indigenous inhabitants of the colony. It is very rarely that this opportunity was not realized. Clearly a number of factors affected this type of situation. The individual given power and authority over others is always tempted to abuse them. The colonizer is no exception. Personal and sadistic elements assisted him to his task. Possibly overriding these were political and psychological motivations concerned with denigrating the status of the males of a subject people by abusing their womenfolk. In some chapters I have tried to show that this was indeed the case.

It is clear that the vast majority of sexual contacts between Anglo-Saxons on the one hand and Africans and Asians on the other were confined to casual encounters and to concubinage. Marriage between races is a mark of equality. For the 'subject' race to achieve that equality meant the destruction of their servile status. Thus in almost all Anglo-Saxon colonial communities there existed penal legislation directed against legitimate unions. The Republic of South Africa is the sole surviving heir of this tradition. In that country not only is marriage prohibited between black and white but there is a total ban against sexual relations between the ethnic groups.

A theme which constantly occurs in the history of miscegenation is the fear of racial pollution. The notion here is that an ethnic group has almost a divine mission to maintain its racial purity. The consequences of this belief have produced immeasurable suffering in the world – Hitler's genocidal activities were only one of the more recent manifestations of this delusion. The myth may have had its origin at a time when societies were divided into communities based upon self-sufficiency and isolation. At such a period the attitude might have been justified. But to project the philosophy of primeval hunters and foodgatherers into the modern world as a rationale for racist theories is absurd. Dr Johnson once said that patriotism was the last refuge of the scoundrel. Today it might be said that racism is the last refuge of the deprived and socially immature.

Another aspect of miscegenation which is dealt with in *Children of Conflict* concerns the role of the white woman in the context of inter-racial concubinage. Frequently her position was most exposed and vulnerable. This is particularly the case where black slavery existed. Her reaction to neglect by her spouse was often an irruption of vindictive cruelty against female slaves. The following are typical examples from the eighteenth-century Caribbean:

> Mr Dalrymple was informed by a young woman slave, in Grenada, who had no teeth, that her mistress had, with her own hands, *pulled them out*, and given her a severe flogging besides, the marks of which she then bore. This relation was confirmed by several town's people of whom he inquired concerning it ...
>
> Lieutenant Davison states, in his evidence, that the clergyman's wife at Port Royal [Jamaica] was remarkably cruel. She used to drop *hot sealing wax* on her negroes, after flogging them. He was sent for as a surgeon to one of them, whose breast was terribly burnt with sealing wax. He was also called in to a woman slave, who had been *tied up all night* by her hands, and had been abused with *cayenne pepper, by the same mistress*, and in a way too horrid and indecent to mention ... He has often gone in remonstrated against her cruelty, when he has seen the negro women *chained to the washing tubs, almost naked, with their thighs and backs in a gore of blood, from flogging.*
>
> (Evidence to the Select Committee of the House of Commons 1790 and 1791 on the Part of the Petitioners for the Abolition of the Slave-Trade.)

The white woman protected by her husband from the advances of males of the 'subject' race, and at the same time neglected by her spouse who sought sexual relations with coloured women, has played an extremely significant role in determining the course of race relations. I have tried in the book to assess the importance of that role.

In the concluding section of *Children of Conflict* I have attempted an analysis of inter-ethnic marriage and sexual relations as they appear in the contemporary world. It is obvious that with the advent of the former colonial societies to the status of independent nations the whole climate and atmosphere of race relations has undergone a radical change. There are manifestations of exclusivity and separateness, as in the United States between black and white. My thesis here is that this is very much a temporary phenomenon, and that if the world is to solve the problem of inter-racial conflict the only sure foundation is inter-racial marriage.

The purpose of *Children of Conflict* is to examine the whole fabric of the concept we know as miscegenation, to examine notions of repulsion and attraction and to disabuse the reader of many of the notions which have, for so long a time, clouded our thinking on this phenomenon, which is probably one of the most crucial problems facing mankind at the present day. 'We must love one another or die.' (T. S. Eliot.)

The design of the book is such – it is fully annotated – that it is hoped that it will be of value to the serious student of miscegenation; at the same time the general reader may find that it will assist him to an understanding of this crucial problem.

CHILDREN OF CONFLICT

CHAPTER 1

A Personal Statement

In a book of this kind the writer's position must be made absolutely clear. What vitiates so much writing, not only about miscegenation, but concerning the whole field of racial contact, is the author's attempt to take an objective view although much of what he may have to say is governed by an unconscious bias. To put it another way, the white person who writes about racial problems knows, consciously or unconsciously, that he can always retreat into the unassailable security of a world in which, for the most part, the European is still dominant.

I have experienced, not only the role of the academic, in which I have discussed, hopefully with detachment, problems of race and colour, but also the inescapable role of the recipient of prejudice – the man of colour.

I am a West Indian. My family came to England from Jamaica just after the First World War when I was three years of age. Thus we have some claims to be regarded as the first of the immigrants, in the proper sense, from the Caribbean to Britain. My father was what was known as a produce merchant – that is someone who deals in spices and similar foodstuffs. He established himself in the City of London near to Mincing Lane, and his family in a succession of suburbs in North-West London. In this the family was no different from their English counterparts except in terms of colour.

My parents in Jamaica were regarded as being of 'good' colour. That is to say although coloured the actual colour was unobtrusive – they could have 'passed for white' in the United States. In Europe they were often taken as coming from the Mediterranean. Their ancestry was totally mixed. On my father's side there was a strong Portuguese-Jewish (Sephardic) element together with a Greek strain – Dimitrious was his mother's father's name. Colour, in the sense of the African, was not pronounced in his generation, but was very much apparent in that of his father's – his paternal uncle was as dark as I am. My mother's family appears to have been predominantly French and African from Haiti. My mother herself and her mother were of 'good' colour. Her maiden name was Meaux and she married a Delfosse. Such families in Jamaica trace their descent from refugees who fled the Haitian revolution of 1791.

For parents of 'good' colour in Jamaica to have dark children was not exactly a disaster, but certainly a subject for commiseration. I use dark advisedly, rather than black or African, for in fact my brothers and sisters have neither African features nor Negroid hair. My sisters have inherited the aquiline features of my mother but not her fair complexion. My brothers and myself exhibit, what are called in Jamaica, East Indian features – that is those of an Indian from India. With such a mixed racial background, and in the absence of accurate records, it is difficult to identify all the strains within the family. It is very possible that there is an East Indian component. An Amerindian element cannot be ruled out. Two of my own children, themselves the product of further mixing, my wife being Anglo-Irish and Scots, have an approximation of the Mongolian eye characteristic of the Amerindian. As regards myself, I think I must be numbered amongst the most thoroughly miscegenated individuals in the world.

In Jamaica my family occupied, as fair-coloured people, a comfortable, respected position in the colour-class hierarchy. As I have said, the advent of dark children was regretted but the family's position was not seriously affected. It is important to realize that fair-coloured people of my father's generation felt very little except contempt for black people. Their attitude was similar to that of the nineteenth-century upper middle class in Britain towards the proletariat – one spoke of peasants, the other of 'niggers'. Both dilated on the shiftlessness and ineptitude of the despised group. In the case of the Jamaican fair-coloured individual it was a conscious attempt to deny his heritage of colour. To be honest I am not entirely free of this prejudice and denial myself.

For such a family to venture into the Britain of 1919 was to exchange the circumstance of assurance for the uncertainty of the unknown. This was borne home to me when, at the age of seven, I went to my first boys' school after kindergarten. This was a Roman Catholic preparatory school. My stay there lasted exactly a day. It was obvious, even to me, that my colour was unsuitable. Clearly the school authorities had been misled by my parents' appearance and had assumed I would be similar to them.

My next attempt at schooling met with greater success. This was a large Catholic grammar school with a significant minority of foreign boys from South America and elsewhere. The most prominent of these was Henry O., the son of a Nigerian chief. He was a small, lithe and extraordinarily pugnacious creature. An excellent athlete and boxer, he dominated the school. I was expected to fulfil a similar role. This expectation was sufficient to protect me. It was then I began to realize that being coloured might have a positive as well as a negative aspect.

My parents had never entertained black people in Jamaica so that I knew that Henry's presence would have been unwelcome. On the other hand our home in Hampstead was constantly filled with the English friends of my brothers and sisters. We appeared to be accepted totally by them. Our joint experiences tended to make our colour recede.

As I began to move into adolescence inevitably relationships with girls began to develop. These were of an essentially fugitive nature. Hence there was no necessity to become involved with their families. Thus I was never confronted with parental hostility. With very little money to spend I could afford to go to only the cheapest cafés. I can recall no incident from those days before the war in which I suffered humiliation on account of my colour. Nevertheless, it was at this period in my life that other attitudes began to form in my mind, and which have remained with me until now. I began to feel instinctively that there were areas where I must try to penetrate. The simplistic explanation might be that I was so aware of my colour that I was seeking hostility and prejudice. This is far from the truth. Nine-tenths of the time I never thought of myself as coloured.

This attitude was coupled with another – that of avoidance of other coloured people. This was based on the idea that while my white friends accepted me their acceptance might not extend to those similar to me. As far as my own 'society' went I was completely part of it. The Black American would say that I thought white. With this was associated the contradiction that I did not want rivals of the same exoticism as myself, who might compete for my friends' attention.

When war was declared in September 1939 my immediate reaction was that I should join the armed forces. There was no thought that through my colour I would be thought to be outside the conflict. My experience at the recruiting centre in Central London was traumatic. An RAF sergeant told me quite bluntly that 'wogs', that is people of non-European descent, were not considered officer material. That of course was in 1939. A year later, as Britain became pressed, the situation became quite different. I cannot say that disgust invaded me totally at this rejection. It was rather like being confronted with hatred by someone you loved and thought loved you.

If I was not white enough to fly I was permitted to defend London in another capacity – I joined the National Fire Service in September 1939. I remained as a fireman for three years during which only one incident occurred which made me conscious of my colour. This was being told by an irascible officer that my quarters were too good for a 'nigger'.

Although constantly on the alert the Fire Service provided long periods of standing-by when I could study. This I did, and to the surprise of both my friends and myself obtained an Open Scholarship to Oxford. It had always been my ambition to go to that university, and I was determined to take advantage of every possibility while there. To become a graduate of Oxbridge in English eyes was to ensure that a living of some sort would be open to one. But I had an additional ambition. This was to become President of the Oxford Union Society. The Union at that time could have been regarded as an exclusive gentleman's club and debating society. Most of its ex-Presidents had subsequently become leading political figures in the country. Two West Indian ex-Presidents, Bahadur Singh of Trinidad and Cameron Tudor of Barbados, assisted me in my ambition. In time I succeeded in being elected President, and thus became a figure of a little significance on the Oxford scene.

As an undergraduate I had the usual experiences every student does. We lived within the charmed circle of the university as privileged people. My colour was an asset in my experiences with women. It was only when I attempted to carry a relationship to the point of seriousness and sought to meet the girl's parents that I encountered hostility. The father, luckily away at sea, was a naval petty officer. In the British Navy such individuals while having all the duties of ordinary officers can never aspire to the status of gentleman. Their position is essentially equivocal and this is represented in their behaviour. From the moment I entered the house in suburban Portsmouth I was met with frigidity. The mother refused to have her meals with us, and clearly was obsessed with the idea of what her neighbours would think at the idea of her entertaining a *black* man.

I had read history at the university for my first degree, and then deciding on an academic career became a post-graduate student in anthropology. For my field-work I resolved to return to Jamaica and make a study of a community in the area from which my family had come. In many ways this was a traumatic experience. West Indian society is probably one of the most colour-conscious societies in the world. Thus I was exchanging the measure of apprehension which always surrounded me in white society for the intricacies and subtleties of a community where one's shade of colour was supremely important.

I stayed with my brother who was the local judge, and very swiftly found that black people I met were not welcome in his house. The same applied to any friendships I formed with girls – only those of the 'right' colour met with approval. I was both attracted and repelled by what I found in the society. By comparison with the society I was used to,

Jamaica at that time appeared to be excessively parochial. The people, as all West Indians, possessed an insouciant charm which attracted me enormously but at the same time I missed the sophistication of Oxford. In a curious way my life in England had freed me of colour so that it never occurred to me that the literature and art of Europe was an expression of 'white' values as opposed to 'black' ones. I could never say with James Baldwin that Chartres Cathedral was meaningless to him because black people were not involved in its creation. My values were, and are, concerned with the *human* spirit and not with the colour of the body that contains it.

My work completed I returned to England and Oxford. Soon after my return I met my future wife. She came from an Anglo-Irish-Scots professional family – both her parents were doctors. Her father had died before the 1939 war so that the decision to accept me as a son-in-law was taken by her mother and an old family friend. I do not think that either my wife's family or myself have ever consciously thought that we were what is known as a 'mixed' couple. Subconsciously I may have been aware of the significance of my marriage in terms of miscegenation, but at the conscious level I only knew I was marrying the woman I loved.

It is difficult to convey my *lack* of colour consciousness. I can only ask the reader to remember that eighty-five per cent of my experience from early childhood was life in an almost exclusively white world. I was, to use the fashionable phrase, the apotheosis of the Black Anglo-Saxon or Afro-Saxon. I even reacted as an Englishman did to the sight of mixed couples in London streets – with aversion and distaste. This may have been because I felt unconsciously that they represented a threat to the careful invulnerability I had built up over the years.

Like society, no human being remains changeless in his ideas and behaviour. My identification with the black world was crystallized for me by attending the Black Power Conference in Bermuda in 1969. This, together with my later experience of the United States, added another dimension to my thinking about the relationship between the European and non-European.

Soon after my marriage I completed my doctorate at Oxford and was offered a job as a lecturer in anthropology at the University of Leeds. My acceptance there was absolute, and I can recall no occurrence which could be interpreted as colour oriented. My Sephardic connections enabled me to become familiar with the large Jewish community in the city. My research was concerned with mining communities in the North of England, and with the sociology of sexual behaviour. My children were born there, and again were fully accepted into the community.

The turning point in my career came with an offer to go to the new

University of Sussex to run a research centre concerned with the problems of multi-racial societies. So after a long period at Leeds I moved to Sussex some ten years ago. My work now involved a new connection with the Caribbean for, after a time, a branch research centre was created in Barbados. Up to the present time this has meant that I have been very much concerned with the new independent countries of the English-speaking Caribbean, and in South America with Venezuela and Brazil.

In 1970 I accepted an offer to be Visiting Ford Professor at the Massachusetts Institute of Technology. I had visited the States several times but only for brief periods. Now I was to live there for over a year. The experience I had not only of Cambridge and Boston but also of New York, California and Arizona gave me considerable insight into current black/white relationships in the United States. I realized that because of my background and of the way I speak the reaction of American whites to me was not the reaction they would have to a black American. At the same time my colour is so obvious that I presented a kind of problem. I was very much aware of the tension as when travelling with a white woman on the Boston subway I noticed a cop sitting opposite fuming at the sight of us. On the other hand inter-racial couples were a common occurrence on the streets of Cambridge.

I have tried in this brief personal statement to make the reader aware of who I am and what I am. I hope I have declared my bias. It is the bias of a black man who grew up in a white world, and whose major orientation lies with Europe, but who nevertheless can never escape the heritage of his colour, and who is a part of the process of miscegenation that he has tried to describe.

CHAPTER 2

The European Image of the Non-European

The Euro-American world is the contemporary equivalent of the Classical World. That is to say it dominates societies outside itself through its political and technological superiority in a manner very similar to that of the Graeco-Roman empires. Inevitably domination in both cases led, and has led, to a perception of the differences between themselves and those dominated.

But an important distinction can be made between these two worlds in terms of their perception of the outsider. In the case of Euro-America colour, that is skin colour, has become the main criterion by which the differences are assessed. Most authorities, however, agree that colour prejudice as we know it did not exist in Greece and Rome.[1] For the Greeks the matter was simple – anyone who was not Greek was a barbarian. Although a pejorative term, to be classified as a barbarian did not mean the individual's exclusion from the community of man. He could be held to be inferior by virtue of his physique, his culture and his customs. But he could also be admired and even borrowed from. The latter is particularly pronounced in the case of the borrowings from Egypt of religious deities and forms by the Greeks. Herodotus' view of the inhabitants of India and those of Egypt is illustrative of this:

> Eastward of these Indians are another tribe ... who are wanderers, and live on raw flesh. This tribe is said to have the following customs: If one of their number be ill, man or woman, they take the sick person, and if he be a man, the men of his acquaintance proceed to put him to death, because, they say, his flesh would be spoilt for them if he pined and wasted with sickness. The man protests he is not ill in the least; but his friends will not accept his denial – in spite of all he can say, they kill him, and feast themselves on his body. So also if a woman be sick, the

women who are her friends, take her and do with her exactly the same as the men. If one of them reaches to old age, about which there is seldom any question, as commonly before that time they have had some disease or other, and so have been put to death – but if a man, notwithstanding, comes to be old, then they offer him sacrifice to their gods, and afterwards eat his flesh ... All the tribes which I have mentioned live together like the brute beasts; they have also the same tint of skin, which approaches that of the Ethiopians.[2]

It is very noticeable in that passage that Herodotus remarks on the skin colour of the Indians almost as an afterthought. His revulsion is aimed at their cannibalism – something totally remote and disgusting from a Greek point of view. The reference to brute beasts concerns these people's apparent practice of having their wives in common. Again, something quite alien to the Hellene.[3] Herodotus also adds his belief that the semen of dark or black people is the same colour as their bodies as against that of Europeans which was white.[4] It was an opinion refuted by Aristotle in his *Historia Animalium* (iii, 22).

The respect for a non-Greek people reaches its height in Herodotus' opinion of the Egyptians:

The Egyptians were also the first to introduce solemn assemblies, processions, and litanies to the gods; all of which the Greeks were taught the use by them. It seems to me a sufficient proof of this, that in Egypt these practices have been established from remote antiquity, while in Greece they are only recently known ... With respect to the Egyptians themselves, it is to be remarked that those that live in the corn country [Upper Egypt], devoting themselves, as they do, far more than other people in the world, to the preservation of the memory of past actions, are the best skilled in history of any men that I have ever met ... Medicine is practised among them on a plan of separation; each physician treats a single disorder, and no more: thus the country swarms with medical practitioners, some undertaking to cure diseases of the eye, others of the head, others again of the teeth, others of the intestines.[5]

There is no doubt that the reputation of Egyptian medicine was renowned throughout the Ancient World. Homer speaks of this in the *Odyssey* (Book IV, 229): 'And in medical knowledge the Egyptian leaves the rest of the world behind.'[6] It is of some interest to note that although Herodotus has nothing but praise for the Egyptians he refers to them as 'black' (Book II, 57). In no sense is this to be construed as a derogation. He is merely pointing out the physical difference between the Greeks and

Egyptians. Through the process of miscegenation with surrounding Negro peoples, which appears to have always existed, the Egyptians in Greek eyes would appear darker than himself.[7]

The Roman view of those outside Italy, with the exception of the Greeks, was that they were barbarians. They condemned the northern Europeans for their lack of civilized ways. But their real obsession was with stature and physique. Tacitus writes of the Germans:

> In every household the children, naked and filthy, grow up with those stout frames and limbs which we so much admire. Every mother suckles her own offspring, and never entrusts it to servants and nurses. The master is not distinguished from the slave by being brought up with greater delicacy. Both live amid the same flocks and lie on the same ground till the freeborn are distinguished by age and recognized by merit.[8]

One can imagine how such living-conditions would have appalled the sensibility of the civilized Roman. With regard to physique, it does appear that Roman stature was inferior to almost all the Northern peoples, including the British, with whom they fought. Tacitus has frequent references to the prodigious size of the tribesmen against whom Rome battled.[9] Caesar wrote: '... practically all the Gauls despise our lack of height compared to their own stature.'[10] Strabo was of the opinion that the Britons, on average, were six inches taller than the average Roman.[11]

Despised as they were, those born outside Italy could overcome their natural disadvantages by becoming Romanized. In other words if they changed their way of life, thus recognizing the superiority of Rome, they could become identified with all that Rome stood for. This is seen in the numerous references in the literature to the barbarian habit of wearing trousers (braca) as compared with those, as in southern Spain and Gaul, who had given up trousers for the toga and were known as people of the toga.[12] Prejudice in fact stopped at the point where the person against whom it was directed adopted the way of life of those that despised him.

That there was awareness of colour in the Ancient World is apparent, but awareness did not lead to prejudice. Agatharchides, the philosopher, remarked that Ethiopians would create fear in the Greeks because of their martial qualities rather than their darkness. The general opinion seems to have been amongst both the Greeks and Romans that it was what a man did rather than his racial origins which governed your estimate of him.[13]

Dark skins were regarded in many instances as enhancing beauty. Naturally enough concepts of beauty varied a great deal in the classical period. The point, however, is that blackness was a positive rather than a negative attribute. Herodotus' opinion of the Ethiopians was that they '... are said to be the tallest and handsomest men in the world'.[14] Mythology supports this view in relation to women. In the legend of Perseus and Andromeda, Perseus, flying along the coast of Philistia (the contemporary Israeli coast), sees Andromeda chained naked to a rock in the sea to await death from a sea monster. Her beauty is so overpowering that he becomes immediately in love with her. He slays the monster and marries her. The point to note is that Andromeda must have been black as she was the daughter of the Ethiopian King and Queen of Joppa.

Poetry is also a witness to the fact that black women were found to be as attractive as those who were white. Ovid in *The Amores* (Book II, ix) speaks of his love for a black slave-girl: 'In return for these offices to you, dusky Cypassis, pay me today the sweet price of your caress!' Martial, after describing how he was pursued by a girl who was the apotheosis of all that was white, sought for himself a woman darker than night (*Epigrams*, I, 115, 4–5). But perhaps the most charming tribute to the beauty of blackness is in the following poem of Asclepiades:

She waved her branch, fair Didyme,
And waving stole my heart away;
And now like wax in fire, see,
I melt in swift decay.

If she is black, what's that to me?
This charcoal too is black, but yet
No rose more red can ever be
When once alight 'tis set.

(*Anthologia Palatina*, 5, 210)

The acceptance of the Negro or Ethiopian in sexual terms can be distinguished in other ways. The use of an effigy of the phallus as a protection against the evil eye is a well-known phenomenon in Mediterranean societies even in our own day. This was very apparent in classical times.[15] The theory was, and is, that the evil eye was so fascinated by the obscene that it could do the individual no harm. In this connection the phallus of the Negro was used. 'The phallus was ... a most potent charm against the evil eye and Jahn gives many illustrations of these Goethe grotesque which is not a humpback but a misshapen Negro with a large *membrum* who is also making with his right hand one of the best known signs against the evil eye.'[16]

It is of some interest to note that among the so-called obscene frescoes from Pompeii, now in the Museum of Naples, many depict black men engaged in copulation with white women.[17] This would appear to indicate an acceptance of this type of interracial sex. In fact the evidence suggests that there were no legal or social barriers to sexual relations and marriage between Europeans and non-Europeans, or indeed any type of racial mixing. Herodotus recounts how an Egyptian garrison left without supplies for some time decided to desert to Ethiopia:

> Psammetichus [the Egyptian King] informed of the movement, set out in pursuit, and coming up with them, besought them with many words not to desert the gods of their country, nor abandon their wives and children. 'Nay, but,' said one of the deserters with an unseemly gesture, 'wherever we go, we are sure enough of finding wives and children.' Arrived in Ethiopia, they placed themselves at the disposal of the king.[18]

Again, mythology is the source of tales which demonstrate that miscegenation was not abhorrent to the classical world. There is the story of Danaüs and his fifty daughters, seven of whom were born of an Ethiopian woman.[19] Aurora, or Eos, the goddess of the dawn, married Tithonus, an Ethiopian. Their son Memnon, described by many as black, was king of Ethiopia and was one of the defenders of Troy.[20] The famous oracle at Delphi was reputedly founded by Delphos, who was the son of Apollo and Melanis – a derivative of the word for black in Greek. Thus Delphos was a mulatto.[21] In Judaic tradition there is the same acceptance of miscegenation as being normal. Josephus in his *Antiquities of the Jews* tells the story of Moses, who during the Israelite captivity in Egypt became general of an invading force of Egyptians against Ethiopia. At the siege of Saba this incident occurred:

> Tharbis was the daughter of the Ethiopians [that is to say of their king]: she happened to see Moses as he led the army near to the walls, and fought with great courage ... she fell deeply in love with him; and upon the prevalency of that passion, sent to him the most faithful of her servants to discourse with him upon their marriage. He thereupon accepted the offer, on condition she would procure the delivering up of the city; and gave her the assurance of an oath to take her to his wife ... No sooner was the agreement made, but it took effect immediately; and when Moses had cut off the Ethiopians he gave thanks to God, and consummated his marriage, and led the Egyptians back to their own land.[22]

Miscegenation was not merely of mythological significance in the Classical World. It was so much a matter of the everyday that satirists and philosophers comment upon it. Juvenal suggests that were it not for abortion mixed offspring would be far more common:

> ... Things might be worse – just suppose
> She chose to stay pregnant, to swell her belly with frolicsome
> Infants: you might become some piccaninny's Papa,
> And find yourself making your will on behalf of a son and heir
> Whose off-black face was better not seen by daylight.
> (Satire VI, 599–602)

Martial writing on adultery cites black children as proof of it.[23] But there was also scientific interest in miscegenation. Pliny and Aristotle were both interested in the transmission of the physical characteristics of the descendants of mulattoes.[24] There is, however, no criticism in such authors of the fact of interbreeding. Further evidence of the social acceptance of race mixing is to be found in the visual arts (vase paintings and sculptures) depicting both Negroes and individuals exhibiting Negroid characteristics. It is very possible that, precisely because of the lack of barriers to racial mixture, in the course of time the Negro and his descendants would have been absorbed in the predominantly white population.

The Classical World's acceptance of colour in a way which is singularly lacking in our own is perhaps exemplified by the great statue of the many-breasted Diana in her temple at Ephesus – her face was black as were her hands. Or by these lines of Menander:

> ... Mother, if a man has a noble character
> Which prompts him to a good life, then he's of noble birth,
> Even if he's a black African ...[25]

In contrast to the acceptance and serenity of the Graeco-Roman World in relation to those differentiated from it by colour the attitude of its successor, Christendom, is far more complex and ambivalent. The belief in a Paradise from which man was driven led to the creation of a whole mythology which delineated the possibility of the existence of an earthly paradise which could be discovered on this earth. Ethiopia, which figures so largely in early Christianity, became the legendary locale of this paradise. It was known from a very remote period that this land was inhabited by people of dark or black skin. There are a number of references in the Old Testament.[26] There is no hint that such people are regarded as being inferior because of their skin colour – this only transpires at a later stage. Queen Bilquis of Sheba, described by Josephus as queen of Egypt and Ethiopia, is seen as more than the equal of Solomon. The Magi, elusive figures in the Gospel of St Matthew, have become in the course of centuries distinctive racial types. Only one is a European – Melchior – Caspar is African and black, Baltasar is associated with India.[27] The Negro is thus from an early period in the West virtually sanctified.[28]

It is not, however, only in Biblical tradition that the indifference to racial distinctions is to be noted. There is, for example, the extraordinarily long-lived legend of the Priest-King, Prester John. In both the popular and learned mind, informed by minimal geographical knowledge, Ethiopia and India were one, and this was Prester John's kingdom. He was virtually believed to be the monarch of the land which contained Paradise.

There was a practical basis for the preservation of the myth of Prester John. From the beginning of the eighth century Europe had been menaced by Islam. It was felt that an alliance with the black Redeemer-King in his kingdom so near to Paradise would enable the West to overcome the pagan might of the Moslems. One of the most fascinating aspects of the myth is the fact that it persisted for so many centuries – for nearly 500 years. In the twelfth century it was said that Prester John had written to the Byzantine Emperor at Constantinople. Two hundred years later his emissaries were believed to have visited the courts of southern Europe. In the year that he died, 1460, Prince Henry the Navigator of Portugal expressed a wish to visit the legendary kingdom and meet the great Priest-King.[29]

In the reality of the early Christian Church no distinctions appeared to have been made in terms of skin colour or ethnic origin. In the history of Egyptian monasticism it is quite clear that Ethiopians and Europeans lived and worked for God side by side.[30] The most remarkable of these black Fathers was undoubtedly an Ethiopian called Moses. Like many who felt the call of religion Moses in his early life had been guilty of many crimes, including brigandage. Once converted he devoted his whole being to serving God. His asceticism and his teaching made him famous throughout the monastic world.[31] This comes out very strongly in an anonymous account of his life:

> Neither to slave nor to evil-doer is the Kingdom of Heaven closed but within are they who have repented as they should and who have chosen to live rightly and according to God. Neither is the kingdom closed to Scythian or to Ethiopian ... This can be seen in the case of very many others but especially in the case of Moses the Ethiopian ... This man whose body was black had a soul more radiantly bright than the splendour of the sun.[32]

The real confrontation between European and non-European in the so-called Dark Ages was, however, not in terms of the conversion of

Ethiopians to Christianity but of a North African people, the Moors, as invaders of Europe. The story of their domination of Spain for nearly 800 years, and their incursions into other parts of Europe, is well known. What is of great significance is that this was the first time that the West had been exposed on such a scale and time dimension to peoples alien in religion, culture and appearance, and that this experience was one of subordination.

The term 'Moor' is somewhat imprecise. Originally it was used of the inhabitants of the Roman province of Mauretania. When applied to the invading forces which conquered Spain in AD 711, it includes Arabs, Berbers and people of Negro origin as well as intermixtures of the three. The Berbers in appearance are very similar to Western Europeans, blond hair and white skin colour. Blondness is rare among Arabs and their skin colour tends to be darker than the Berber. Both groups clearly belong to the ethnic Caucasoid category.[33] Contemporary Berbers in North Africa have a symbiotic relationship with Negroes in their villages. Negroes carry out traditional tasks such as ironwork, butchering and making music. Although the Berbers are apparently opposed to miscegenation there is little doubt that racial intermixing has taken place.[34]

Shortly after the conquests of the Moors the process of miscegenation between themselves and the Visigothic tribes began. This is typified by the marriage of Eligona, the widow of Roderick, the Visigothic King and the son of Musa, the Governor of Mauretania.[35] That there were blacks in the Moorish Army is very much borne out by *The Song of Roland*, the eleventh-century epic poem:

> Then first rides out a Saracen, Abisme,
> In all that host there was none more vile than he,
> ... And black he is as melted pitch to see.
> ... What help is that? Marsile [the Moorish leader]
> has taken flight,
> Yet there remains his uncle Marganice,
> That governs Carthage, Alfrere and Garamile,
> And Ethiope, a land accursed and vile.
> In his command are all the Negro tribes;
> Thick are their noses, their ears are very wide;
> Full fifty thousand are gathered in their lines,
> Boldly and fast and furiously they ride,
> Yelling aloud the Paynim battle-cry.
> ... When Roland looked on these accursed tribesmen –
> As black as ink from head to foot their hides are,
> With nothing white about them but their grinders – ...[36]

Miscegenation between Arab and Negro peoples had been common in the pre-Islamic period:

> Despite the value they attached to genealogy and superior stock, the Arabs, and especially the sedentary townspeople, did not keep their race pure ... the infiltration of Negro blood, which has spread to all parts of the peninsula [Arabia] and seems destined one day to change the appearance of the race completely, began in a very distant past. It started in the Yemen, which was in continual contact with Africa on account of its geographical position ... The same infiltration came slower and later in the Hejaz and the Nejd, but even there it took place at a far earlier date than is generally thought. Antar, the romantic hero of pre-Islamic Arabia, was a half-caste through his mother, and yet his totally African appearance did not prevent his marrying a princess from one of the tribes proudest of its nobility; this melanian mixing was so common, and had long been accepted in the centuries immediately prior to Mohammed ...[37]

Antar's father was an Arab warrior, Shaddad:

> He was the son of a black female slave called Zabiba. This blemish [sic] in his birth, however, he redeemed by his personal courage. He fell in battle against the Taiyi' tribe. His memory as the most popular Arab hero still lives on today through the *Antar Romance* and in many placenames.[38]

Evidence of this kind would suggest that alliances between Moors and Visigoths meant that in fact the admixture of Negro strains must have been considerable.

In the subsequent centuries from the European point of view there is less practical experience of the non-European world. The imagination was fed by travellers' tales, some fictitious, some real as those of Marco Polo. There is little here of disparagement – the emphasis is upon the exotic and wondrous. For the thirteenth-century Venetian, Marco Polo, the Great Khan's court outshines what Europe can provide. What changes this relatively benign picture radically is the advent of the Portuguese voyagers on the coasts of Africa in the fifteenth century. The first settlement in West Africa (1482) was made at Mine or Elmina in Ghana, where a great fortress, San Jorge, was built.

From the beginning sexual relations between Portuguese and Africans appear to have been entirely uninhibited though confined to concubinage. For example in the area of Upper Guinea, between Cape Palmas and the Senegal river, many Portuguese traders became totally absorbed in African life to the extent of discarding European clothing and tattooing their bodies. Living and eating like the Negroes they learned their languages and were admitted to the fetish cults. They were known as *tangos-maos*, or *lancados*. 'They acquired a special standing in the eyes of many of the Negro rulers and their peoples. Some of them were able to marry into the ruling families, while others made advantageous agreements with local chiefs.'[39]

The Portuguese who had 'gone native' together with his black wife and mulatto children was able to be a more efficient trader than his European rival. Trade meant the slave-trade of which the Portuguese were the initiators. Islands, such as those off Cape Verde and São Tomé in the Gulf of Guinea, became slaving entrepots or reception areas for slaves taken from the mainland. In the case of São Tomé a component of the colonists sent from Portugal at the end of the fifteenth century were forcibly baptized Jewish boys and girls. When they reached maturity, '... few of the women bore children of the white men; very many more bore children of the Negroes, while the Negresses bore children of the white men.'[40]

The degree of acceptance of European-African unions in this area is illustrated by a contemporary account of São Tomé in the early seventeenth century:

> They [the Europeans] all have wives and children, and some of the children who are born there are as white as ours. It sometimes happens that, when the wife of a merchant dies, he takes a Negress, and this is accepted practice, as the Negro population is both intelligent and rich, bringing up their daughters in our way of life, both as regards custom and dress. Children born of these unions are of a dark complexion and called Mulattoes, and they are mischievous and difficult to manage.[41]

An interesting comparison can be made here between the mainland where the Portuguese became Africanized, and São Tomé where the African was becoming Europeanized.

There is little doubt that the luxuriance and sensuality of life in the tropics inflamed the senses of the Portuguese colonizer. The same process occurred in his Anglo-Saxon counterpart but Protestantism acted as a barrier to the exuberant expression of his passions. The Portuguese in Brazil, Africa and the Far East, despite restrictions placed on the indigenous populations, entered freely into sexual liaisons and marriage with local non-European women. Contemporary sixteenth-century accounts indicate that carnality was a predominant feature of Lusitanian colonization.

A letter sent to St Ignatius Loyola by a Jesuit priest, Nicolas Lancilotto, in Goa in December 1550, deplores the sexual extravagance into which the colonizers have fallen:

> Your Reverence must know that the sin of licentiousness is so wide-spread in these regions that no check is imposed upon it, which leads to great inconveniences, and to great disrespect of the sacraments. I say this of the Portuguese, who have adopted the vices and customs of the land without reserve, including the evil custom of buying droves of slaves, male and female, just as if they were sheep, large and small. There are innumerable Portuguese who buy droves of girls and sleep with all of them, and subsequently sell them. There are innumerable married settlers who have four, eight, or ten female slaves and sleep with all of them, and this is known publicly. This is carried to such excess that there was one man in Malacca who had twenty-four women of various races, all of whom were his slaves, and all of whom he enjoyed. I quote this city because it is a thing that everybody knows. Most other men, as soon as they can afford to buy a female slave, almost always use her as a girl-friend [*amiga*] besides many other dishonesties in my poor understanding.[42]

Despite their licentiousness, which appeared to recognize no racial boundaries, it would be wrong to assume that the Portuguese were free of racial prejudice. Quite the contrary was the case. The Roman Catholic Church itself was concerned to preserve the priesthood from the contamination of those of mixed blood. In 1585 the head of the Jesuit missions to Asia, Alexandre Valignano, wrote in the following way:

> ... all these dusky races are very stupid and vicious, and of the basest spirits, and likewise because the Portuguese treat them with the greatest contempt, and even among the inhabitants of the country they are little esteemed in comparison with the Portuguese. As for the *mesticos* [mixed-bloods] and *casticos* [progeny of a European father and an Indo-European mother], we should receive [that is, into the Jesuit order] either very few or none at all; especially with regard to the *mesticos*, since the more native blood they have, the more they resemble the Indians and the less they are esteemed by the Portuguese.[43]

A trifling change of language, and the above could have been written by the most stalwart of Anglo-Saxon administrators in nineteenth-century Africa. The paradox is that in the case of the Portuguese uninhibited sexual activity did not lead to respect for the 'native' and the mixed blood.

There is a curious ambivalence inherent in the Portuguese attitude towards miscegenation. On the one hand there are official directives, such as those of Affonso de Albuquerque, Governor of Goa, which sought to encourage marriage between Portuguese and the female relatives of the Moslem defenders of Goa. The directives, however, make it quite clear that it is the fair-skinned and Christianized women who are to be sought out. Alliances with Dravidian – very dark – women from South India were to be avoided. The dilemma facing those who were anxious to preserve the racial purity of the Portuguese was the usual one of a paucity of European women in the new colonies. The acquisition of fair-skinned Moslem women represented a compromise between the realities of the situation and racial pride.

Albuquerque's policy dates from 1510. In the centuries following there appears to have been reluctance on both sides – Indian and Portuguese – to contract marriage. On the Indian side this is particularly the case with the Brahmin and other high castes favoured by the Portuguese. They were as racially conscious as the Portuguese. No such inhibitions applied to sexual relationships outside marriage. Concubinage in one form or another was the main channel of miscegenation. Despite the fulminations of the Church and legislative decrees the Portuguese soldiers and merchants were quite happy to enter into alliances of an extra-marital nature with Indian women and those of mixed race. A group which was especially favoured in the seventeenth and eighteenth centuries as a source of concubines was that of Nautch-girls. The latter were prostitutes attached to Hindu temples and were reputedly famous for their sexual expertise.[44]

The popular reputation of the Portuguese as colonizers is that they were singularly free from race prejudice as compared with other European nations. Examination of their record in this respect, as we have seen, does not really lend support to this view. It is true that in their extra-marital activities the Portuguese exhibited little prejudice, to say the least, but the choice of concubinage as against marriage is indicative of a belief in the inherent inferiority of the 'subject' people. The acceptance of inter-racial marriage is an indicator of equality between peoples whereas indulgence in concubinage serves to mark the sexual exploitation of the colonized.

The Anglo-Saxon view of miscegenation differs from that of the Latin peoples of Europe. Coming later as they did to the experience of colonization than the Portuguese the Anglo-Saxon reaction in the sixteenth century is based more on literary sources than on reality. Books such as *Mandeville's Travels*, William Waterman's *The Fardle of Facions* and Peter Martyr's *The Decades of the New World* were the inspiration of their image of the non-European.[45] This influence is very much apparent in the dramatic works of the age. The Moor from Africa is depicted as a savage, lustful creature – the villain of the piece – and is contrasted with the valorous, noble-hearted, white-skinned European. A distinction, however, is made between black Moors and those described as 'white' or 'tawny'. The latter are exemplified in the Prince of Morocco in *The Merchant of Venice*. Interestingly enough 'white' Moors are never wholly villainous.

Some instances will help to make clear the picture of the black man as seen by the Elizabethans and their successors. *Lust's Dominion* was published in 1657 and was attributed to Christopher Marlowe. Recent authorities give the authorship to Thomas Decker, Wharton and John Daye. In the play Eleazer, a 'black' Moor, has made the Queen Mother of Spain his mistress. All around him are subject to his power and violence. Despite this he is acutely aware of the hatred and antagonism that both his existence and sexual relationships arouse in the Spanish populace. Eleazer can describe himself thus to the father of his Spanish wife, Maria:

> The Queen with me, with me, a Moore, a Devill,
> A slave of Barbary, a dog; for so
> Your silken Courtiers christen me.
>
> (227–229)

Lust's Dominion is a play in which lust, treachery, intrigue and villainy are personified in Eleazer, the 'black' Moor. Part of his wickedness is that he can excite the sexuality of European women. This suggests that the myth of the potency of the black male, which we refer to elsewhere, goes back a long way.

The forerunner of Eleazer is the character of Aaron in Shakespeare's *Titus Andronicus* (*c.* 1589–90). Aaron is also a 'black' Moor and has a queen as his paramour. 'She [the Queen] had a Moor as revengeful as herself, whom she trusted in many great affairs and usually privy to her Secrets, so far that from private Dalliances she grew pregnant, and brought forth a Blackamoor Child ...'[46] It is this child which creates the racial atmosphere of the play. In Act IV. ii, a nurse presents the illicit offspring of the Queen and Aaron to the latter and the two legitimate sons of the Queen:

> A joyless, dismal, black, and sorrowful issue.
> Here is the babe, as loathsome as a toad
> Amongst the fairest breeder of our clime.
> The empress sends it thee, thy stamp, thy seal,
> And bids thee christen it with thy dagger's point.

The nurse's sentiments would not have been out of place in the antebellum southern United States.

Aaron's response is: 'Out, you whore! Is black so base a hue?' The brothers demand that Aaron gets rid of the proof of their mother's infamy.

It is possible that, in the speech now given by Aaron, Shakespeare is attempting to combat the prejudices of his day against miscegenation:

> Stay, murderous villains! will you kill your brother?
> Now, by the burning tapers of the sky,
> That shone so brightly when this boy was got,
> He dies upon my scimitar's sharp point
> That touches this my first-born son and heir …
> … What, what, ye sanguine, shallow-hearted boys!
> Ye white limed walls? Ye ale-house painted signs!
> Coal-black is better than another hue;
> In that it scorns to bear another hue;
> For all the water in the ocean
> Can never turn the swan's black legs to white,
> Although she lave them hourly in the flood.
> Tell the empress from me, I am of age
> To keep mine own; excuse it how she can.

Fourteen years after *Titus Andronicus* appeared *Othello* was presented on the London stage (1604). The plot is too familiar to dwell on here but the point to emphasize is that *Othello* represents a complete transformation of the 'black' Moor from a villainous and perfidious character into a man of nobility and principle. It is not evil which causes him to kill Desdemona but credulity. He is both to be pitied and admired. The fact that Elizabethan audiences were prepared to accept the dramatic presentation of black and white marriage shows that they were more enlightened than many of their descendants in North America.

Miscegenation on the stage at this period generally takes place between a non-European man – the archetypal Moor – and a white woman. There are, however, some plays in which the embodiment of lust is a black woman who seduces the European male against his better judgement. One is John Webster's *The White Devil.* Zanche is the heroine's maid. She panders to her mistress' appetites. But she is also lustful in her own right and more than that. 'This is Zanche the symbol; a constant reminder on the stage of the presence of evil, of sin, and particularly of the sin of lust from which springs much of the evil in the play. Unlike her mistress, however, she is openly what she is; she is the black foil against which the character of the white devil could be more clearly judged.'[47]

As with the 'black' Moor in *Othello*, Shakespeare raises the woman of colour – Cleopatra – to heights not only of passion but of nobility. At the beginning of the play her complexion is described as tawny. Of herself she says, 'Think on me, That am with Phoebus' amorous pinches black.' 'The suggestions of a dark complexion here would make Cleopatra's sensual character more readily acceptable to Shakespeare's audience.'[48] If this is the case here again are the roots of the myth of black sexuality which is so much part of the contemporary scene.

The main European view of the non-European in the sixteenth and seventeenth centuries was that of creatures which personified many of the European's own evil characteristics. Othello and Cleopatra stand out as magnificent exceptions. It is a view which lacks the actuality of experience – at this time it is only the Portuguese and Spaniards who have had that experience. Travellers' tales, legends and the mythical blackness of the devil combine to give a picture of the lustful black who preys upon the susceptibilities of the good and noble European.

It is, however, in the eighteenth century that there occurs a crystallization of the views of the European about the non-European. It is not our purpose here to enter into a detailed analysis of the concept of The Noble Savage as exemplified by Rousseau in his *Discourse on Inequality* (1754) – this has been brilliantly analysed by H. N. Fairchild in his *The Noble Savage* (1928) – but to touch upon some aspects which have a direct bearing on our theme.

In 1773 Thomas Day, a minor English writer and philanthropist, published in conjunction with one Bicknell a poem called *The Dying Negro*. It is the story of a Negro slave who kills himself rather than give up his love for a white woman. Of course, as in almost all cases of this kind, the Negro is a prince. *The Dying Negro* is clearly a lineal descendant of Mrs Aphra Behn's famous *Oroonoko*, the Royal Slave. He is cast in an essentially heroic mould. The poem represents his thoughts before his suicide in the course of which comparison is made between the African and the European to the detriment of the latter:

> No pangs like these my pallid tyrants know,
> Not such their transports, and not such their woe …
> … Damp'd by base lucre, and repell'd by fear,
> Each nobler passion faintly blazes here.
> Not such the mortals burning Afric breeds,
> Mother of virtues, and heroic deeds …
> … Nature has there, unchilled by art, impress'd
> Her awful majesty on every breast.
> Where'er she leads, impatient of control,
> The dauntless Negro rushes to the goal;
> Firm in his love, resistless in his hate,
> His arm is conquest, and his frown is fate.

Such effusions have to be seen against the background of eighteenth-century England in which the *exceptional* Amerindian, African and

Indian, preferably of real or imagined noble lineage, was lionized by 'society'. Individuals such as Olaudah Equiano from Nigeria were adulated in the literary salons of the day. The sentimentality with regard to the non-European was seldom put to the test of reality. It remained very largely on the imaginative level.

A more realistic approach, however, is to be discovered in the novel *Sandford and Merton* (1783–89) by the same author, Thomas Day. It was a book written for the instruction of the young. A wandering Negro helps to educate the young hero, Tommy, by comparing the virtues of Africans to the iniquities of the European including the enslavement of black people.

It must be remembered in connection with such writings that the same public which welcomed their appearance looked askance at 'white' West Indian families in which colour was perceptible. The brotherhood of man expressed as an idea in a drawing-room was one thing, to personally indulge in miscegenation was quite another. The attitudes are reminiscent of liberal whites in America who publicly advocate inter-racial housing but silently pray it does not occur in their suburb.

The intellectual and the literary were one source of the European's view of the non-European. Another was the discovery of the world of the Pacific in the sixties of the eighteenth century.

We do not intend to survey the very considerable literature concerning the advent of this new world of the Pacific into the consciousness of Europe but merely to indicate its importance for the formulation of ideas concerning the non-European. Captain Cook's description of the Tahitians can be taken as typical of the enthusiasm which the physical appearance of the Polynesian generated in the mind of the European:

> Their natural complexion is a fine clear olive, or what we call brunette; their skin delicately smooth, and agreeably soft. The shape of their faces is in general handsome, and their eyes are full of sensibility and expression; their teeth are likewise remarkably white and regular, and their breath entirely free from any disagreeable smell ... Their motions are easy and graceful, but not vigorous; their deportment is generous and open, and their behaviour affable and courteous ...[49]

Reports of the sexual customs of the Polynesians were also received with avidity. The fact that sexual interaction was not surrounded by the constraints normally accepted in Europe created the picture of an erotic paradise which, fostered by Hollywood, has survived to this day. In the brief interlude before venereal disease, alcohol, and corruption destroyed this world of sexual freedom, miscegenation was common between European men and local women. The most famous example was that of the mutineers of the *Bounty*, who founded their tiny nation on Pitcairn Island with women taken from the islands.[50] Sexual accessibility, the exotic attraction of 'brunette' skin colour and the ambience of the tropics all provided a context in which miscegenation flourished.

The sexual, romantic appeal of the Pacific was to persist throughout the nineteenth century. Writers as disparate as Baudelaire, and later Pierre Loti, Byron and Tennyson evoked the paradisaical quality of life in the South Seas and especially its erotic content. Tennyson can write in *Locksley Hall*:

> Droops the heavy-blossom'd bower, hangs the heavy-fruited tree –
> Summer isles of Eden lying in dark-purple spheres of sea ...
> ... I will take some savage woman, she shall rear my dusky race
> Iron jointed, supple sinew'd, they shall dive, and they shall run,
> Catch the wild goat by the hair, and hurl their lances in the sun;
> Whistle back the parrot's call, and leap the rainbow of the brooks,
> Not with blinded eyesight poring over miserable books ...

This may have been Tennyson in a weak moment, but the case is somewhat different with Byron. In *The Island* Byron rhapsodizes over the simplicity and ease of love between the mutineers of the *Bounty* and women of the South Sea. But in the nineteenth century there were other forces at work beside the lyrical and romantic which affected the image of the non-European.

There were many advocates of racist thought in the last century. Individuals who thought that all the ills of mankind came from a refusal to recognize the inherent superiority of the Caucasian.[51] Outstanding among these – they can be said to have laid the foundations of contemporary racist opinion – were Robert Knox and Count Arthur de Gobineau. The latter in his essay on *The Inequality of Human Races* (1853) divides man into three races – White, Black and Yellow. While postulating that there is no question of the intrinsic superiority of the White, he advocates race mixture as a means of progress. It must not, however, go too far as this leads to degeneration. The arguments are shot through with contradictions which nevertheless did not inhibit its wide circulation in intellectual circles of the day. Gobineau's remarks on the results of miscegenation are typical of his confused thinking:

> It may be remarked that the happiest blend, from the point of view of beauty, is that made by marriage of white and black. We need only put the striking charm of many mulatto, Creole, and quadroon women by the side of such mixtures of yellow and white as the Russians and Hungarians. The comparison is not to the advantage of the latter ...[52]

On the same page Gobineau writes: '... the peoples who are not of white blood approach beauty, but do not attain it ...'

Robert Knox, at one time Professor of Anatomy at the University of Edinburgh but who was forced to leave the University through his involvement in filching corpses for dissection, is an even more muddled thinker than Gobineau. His racism is naked – the black peoples are to be kept in subjection for their own good. To him their inferiority is self-evident:

> ... the grand qualities which distinguish man from the animal – the generalizing powers of pure reason – the love of perfectibility – the desire to know the unknown – and last and greatest, the ability to observe new phenomena and new relations; these mental faculties are deficient, or seem to be so, in all dark races. But, if it be so, how can they become civilized?[53]

In an appendix to his book, *The Races of Men*, first published in 1852, entitled 'An Inquiry Into the Laws of Human Hybriditie', Knox set his face resolutely against any form of miscegenation. He proved to his own satisfaction that the result of race mixture was always total degeneration. His views were fashionable for a time – he was in great demand as a lecturer to learned societies – and his influence must have been considerable, even extending to contemporaries such as Carlyle.

To these distinguished racists a third name can be added, that of Thomas Houston Chamberlain (1855–1927). His contribution, *Foundations of the Nineteenth Century*, was published in Germany in 1899. His fervent belief in the purity and destiny of the so-called Aryan race inspired many – in eleven years it went through nine editions and sold 60,000 copies. Hitler owed a great debt to it.

By the end of the nineteenth century the stage was set for the new racism based on what purported to be 'scientific' evidence unlike the philosophizing which had preceded it. The Noble Savage was a thing of the past. The intelligence tests used by the United States Army for admission and grading in the 1914 war became the touchstone for demonstrating the inferiority of coloured peoples. Eysenck, Jensen, Shurey and their associates are the lineal descendants of Knox and Gobineau. Their concern is to demonstrate that the non-European can be shown scientifically to be essentially inferior to the European in terms of intelligence. The inference to be drawn is obvious. Mixture of the two can only lead to degeneration. The controversy and miscegenation both continue.

CHAPTER 3

The Bastion of Racial Purity

'Almighty God created the races white, black, yellow, malay and red, and he placed them on separate continents. And but for the interference with his arrangement there would be no cause for such marriages. The fact that he separated the races shows that he did not intend for the races to mix.'[1] This was the opinion of the trial court judge in 1959 when sentencing a Negro–white couple for contravening the Miscegenation Statutes of the State of Virginia which prohibit marriage between Negroes and whites. The husband, Richard Perry Loving, a white construction worker, and his wife, Mildred Jeter, who was part Indian and part Negro, had gone to Washington, DC and there contracted a perfectly legal marriage. They later returned to Virginia and cohabited as man and wife. According to the State Laws the Lovings had been guilty of a felony.

The Virginia Code stated quite categorically that 'If any white person intermarry with a colored person, or any colored person intermarry with a white person, he shall be guilty of a felony and shall be punished by confinement in the penitentiary for not less than one nor more than five years' (Virginia Code, Section 20–59). The Lovings had attempted to evade the law by getting married outside the State. But there was also legislation to cover such a situation. Section 20–58 of the Code states, 'If any white person and colored person shall go out of this State, for the purpose of being married, and with the intention of returning, and be married out of it, and afterwards return to and reside in it, cohabiting as man and wife, they shall be punished as provided in Section 20–59, and the marriage shall be governed by the same law as if it had been solemnized in this State. The fact of their cohabitation here as man and wife shall be evidence of their marriage.'

The naïve might think that such legislation was contrary to the

Fourteenth Amendment of the Constitution of the United States which lays down *inter alia* that 'No State shall make or enforce any law which shall abridge the privileges or immunities of citizens of the United States.' There was, in fact, a long, complicated legal fight ahead before the Lovings were able to claim their rights as citizens to marry each other. That this was so illustrates the entrenched attitudes which still exist in the United States against the social and sexual mixing of Negroes and whites.

Before we analyse the case of the Lovings, it will be useful to look at the legal map of the USA relating to miscegenation. In 1955 it was stated that more than half the States of the Union had miscegenation laws on their Statute Books, and that no court in the land, except the California Supreme Court (*Perex* v. *Sharp*, 32 Cal. 2d 711, 198 P.2d 17 1948), had ever declared such legislation unconstitutional.[2] By the autumn of 1964 the number of such States had fallen to eighteen. These were Alabama, Arkansas, Florida, Georgia, Indiana, Kentucky, Louisiana, Maryland, Mississippi, Missouri, North Carolina, Oklahoma, South Carolina, Tennessee, Texas, Virginia, West Virginia and Wyoming. As might be expected only two of these bastions of racial purity – Wyoming and Oklahoma – are not in the South. As a result of the Supreme Court decision in the case of the Lovings, which we discuss below, Maryland repealed its anti-miscegenation laws in 1967. It must not be thought that such laws necessarily have the outmoded antiquity of the so-called Blue Laws of Massachusetts which made adultery a penal offence, and which although remaining on the Statute Book are virtually never invoked. The majority of these laws are Acts passed between 1950 and 1966 supplementing existing laws. So much for the oft-quoted changed attitude of the white towards the Negro.

It is, however, a fact that in the last eighteen years fourteen States repealed their anti-miscegenation Acts. These were Arizona, California, Colorado, Idaho, Indiana, Maryland, Montana, Nebraska, Nevada, North Dakota, Oregon, South Dakota, Utah and Wyoming. It is also a fact that only two of these States – Maryland and California – have sizeable Negro populations. The inference is an obvious one: legislators outside the South could afford to give up their prejudices as the likelihood of racial intermarriage was remote.

From 1871 to 1965 in a considerable number of the anti-miscegenation States the local Supreme Courts maintained the constitutional correctness of legislation prohibiting inter-racial marriage in the face of attacks based on infringements of the Fourteenth Amendment. In 1965 in the case of *Jones* v. *Lorenzen*, the Oklahoma Supreme Court 'felt constrained' to support the State's anti-miscegenation statute because no federal court had yet held such statutes unconstitutional. This demonstrates on the one hand a savage adherence to the letter of the law, and on the other a cynical disregard for humanitarian principles.

The United States Supreme Court must shoulder part of the blame for avoiding the responsibility of taking decisions in this crucial area. From the time of *Brown* v. *The Board of Education* (347 US 483, 1954) – a case which was concerned with segregation in public schools – the Supreme Court refused to review decisions concerning the validity of anti-miscegenation laws in particular States. The thinking may well have been that traditionally marital laws have been entirely the concern of the individual States and not of the Federal Government. Thus the age at which individuals can marry may be as low as twelve in Kentucky and as high as sixteen in California. Nevertheless a twelve-year-old Californian cannot feel that the rights given to him under the Fourteenth Amendment have been set aside because he cannot contract a legal marriage. Our view would be that any legislation which prohibits inter-marriage between racial groups is an infringement, not only of the United States Constitution, but of the UN Declaration of Human Rights.

It may be difficult to ascertain the reasoning process behind the US Supreme Court's negative attitude. It is not so with regard to that of State Courts. In the case of *Naim* v. *Naim* (197 Va. 80, 87 S. E. 2d 749)[3] the State Court of Virginia gave as its opinion that it was a proper function of the State 'to preserve the racial integrity of its citizens ... to prevent the corruption of blood, [the creation] of a mongrel breed of citizens [and] the obliteration of racial pride ...' Virginia is obviously the spiritual home of Mr Enoch Powell.

Having been convicted, the Lovings made an appeal, in 1966, to the Supreme Court of Appeals of Virginia.[4] Mr Justice Carrico stated that the sole ground of appeal made by the defendants was that Virginia's anti-miscegenation laws were a violation both of the Constitution of the State, and that of the United States. That they were in fact denied due process of law and equal protection of the law. The problem was not a new one to the Court. About ten years earlier (1955) in the case of *Naim* v. *Naim* these laws had been thoroughly reviewed and their constitutionality upheld. The defendants maintained that the *Naim* decision relied on *Plessy* v. *Ferguson* (163 US 537, 16 S.Ct 1138, 41 L.Ed, 256, 1896) and that the *Plessy* decision was reversed in *Brown* v. *The Board of Education.* (We cited this case above.) This was not convincing as the *Plessy* case was concerned with a Louisiana Act requiring separate railway carriages for white and coloured. This was upheld under the 'separate but equal' doctrine. Whereas in the *Brown* case the Federal Supreme Court had ruled that this doctrine had no place in the field of public education.

In the opinion of the judge the *Plessy* case had been quoted in *Naim* to demonstrate that the US Supreme Court had not taken a decision which contradicted an earlier one by the Tenth Circuit Court of Appeals (*Stevens* v. *United States*, 146 F.2d 120). This had stated that 'a state is empowered to forbid marriages between persons of African descent and persons of other races or descents. Such a statute does not contravene the Fourteenth Amendment.' Further in the *Plessy* case it was enunciated that 'Laws forbidding the intermarriage of the two races ... have been universally recognized as within the police power of the state.'

Mr Justice Buchanan in the *Naim* case had pointed out that the *Brown* case had demonstrated that the opportunity to acquire an education was 'a right which must be made available to all on equal terms'. But this could not support the contention that racial intermarriage must be available on the same terms. (There would seem to be an element of sophistry in this argument.) Mr Justice Carrico then stated that the US Supreme Court had itself indicated the decision reached in *Brown* did not have the effect on anti-miscegenation laws which the defendants claimed. Six months after that decision, in November 1954, the Supreme Court had denied a writ of certiorari – that is, refused the right of appeal – in the case of *Jackson* v. *State of Alabama*. That case had been concerned with a Negro appellant who claimed 'her constitutional right and privilege of intermarrying with a white male person', and that the Alabama statute forbidding racial intermarriage denied her her constitutional rights under the Fourteenth Amendment. The Supreme Court by its action of denial had upheld the constitutionality of the Alabama statute.

The defendants also said that the opinion given in *Naim* was based upon that of *Pace* but contended that the US Supreme Court had overruled the latter in *McLaughlin* v. *State of Florida* (379 US 184, 85 S.Ct 283, 13 L. Ed. 2d 222).

> The *Pace* case, decided in 1883, involved an attack upon the constitutionality of an Alabama statute imposing a penalty for fornication between a white person and a Negro. Another statute provided a lesser penalty 'If a man and woman live together in adultery or fornication'. A white woman and Pace, a Negro, were convicted and sentenced under the first statute 'for living together in a state of adultery or fornication'. Pace appealed, claiming that the statute under which he had been convicted was violative of the Fourteenth Amendment. The Court rejected this claim, holding that 'whatever discrimination is made in the punishment prescribed in the two sections is directed against the offense and not against the person of any particular colour or race'. (106 US, at p. 585, I S.Ct, at p. 639, 27 L. Ed., at p. 208.)

In the *McLaughlin* case, which was decided in 1964, the US Supreme Court had reviewed a Florida statute under which it was unlawful for a Negro and white person not married to each other to 'habitually live in and occupy in the night time the same room'. The presumption here would seem to be that in the eyes of the law sexual intercourse could only take place at night. The statute in question required a different burden of proof and penalty than other statutes relating to fornication and adultery in general. It must be said that the laws of the United States relating to sexual behaviour display a positively medieval conception of sexuality. The Court ruled the Florida statute invalid. In the judge's view, however, 'The *McLaughlin* decision detracted not one bit from the position asserted in the *Naim* opinion.'

Both parties in the *McLaughlin* case cited the Florida statute which made marriage between Negroes and white, illegal:

> McLaughlin contended that the miscegenation statute was unconstitutional because it prevented him from asserting, against the cohabitation charge, the defense of common law marriage. Florida argued that it was necessary that its cohabitation statute be upheld so as to carry out the purposes of its miscegenation statute which, it contended, was 'immune from attack under the Equal Protection Clause'. The court ruled that it was unnecessary to consider McLaughlin's contention in this respect because the court was holding in his favour on the cohabitation statute. As for Florida's contention, the court said that, for purposes of argument, the constitutionality of the miscegenation statute would be assumed and that it was deciding the case 'without reaching the question of the validity of the State's prohibition against inter-racial marriage.' (379 US at p. 195, 85 S. Ct, at p. 230.)

The judge continued that the defendants had directed his attention to a great number of federal decisions in the sector of civil rights but in his view none of these decisions dealt with miscegenation statutes nor '... curtails a legal truth which has always been recognized – that there is an over-riding state interest in the institution of marriage'. He then quoted from the decision of the US Supreme Court in *Maynard* v. *Hill* (125 US 190, 8 S.Ct 723, 726, 31 L. Ed. 654, 657): 'Marriage, as creating the most important relation in life, as having more to do with the morals and civilization of a people than any other institution, has always been subject to the control of the legislature.'

Going even further, Mr Justice Carrico made this important statement – to take into account the arguments in favour of miscegenation made by sociologists, biologists and anthropologists as grounds for reversing the judgement given in the *Naim* case would be to make the court the legislative body: 'Such arguments are properly addressable to the legislature, which enacted the law in the first place, and not to this court, whose prescribed role in the separated powers of government is to adjudicate, and not to legislate.' Montesquieu's responsibility for the doctrine of the separation of powers, due to a misunderstanding of the British Constitution, and which was the basis of the US Constitution, is more than considerable.

The judge saw his function precisely:

> Our one and only function in this instance is to determine whether, for sound judicial considerations, the *Naim* case should be reversed. Today [1966], more than ten years since that decision was handed down by this court, a number of states still have miscegenation statutes and yet there has been no new decision reflecting adversely upon the validity of such statutes. We find no sound judicial reason, therefore, to depart from our holding in the *Naim* case. According that decision all of the weight to which it is entitled under the doctrine of *stare decisis*,[5] we hold it to be binding upon us here and rule that the Code, Sections 20–58 and 20–59, under which the defendants were convicted and sentenced, are not violative of the Constitution of Virginia or the Constitution of the United States.

The sentences given to the defendants were held by them to be unreasonable. It actually amounted to banishment. They had been ordered to leave the county and State 'at once and do not return together or at the same time to said county and state for a period of twenty-five years This has a fine medieval ring about it. This was in lieu of serving a period in prison. In other words their sentences had been suspended provided they left the State. An interesting interpretation was given by the judge – that although it had been held in a North Carolina case that banishment was against public policy (*State* v. *Doughtie*, 237 N.C. 368, 74 S.E. 2d 922) this punishment was not in fact banishment. Although they had been ordered to leave the State they could return at any time, provided they did not return together, or at the same time. His ruling was, nevertheless, that the conditions of sentence were unreasonable. Suspension of sentence was to secure the rehabilitation of the offender. This meant they should not cohabit as man and wife in Virginia. This they could do without having to leave the State. Thus the sentence was unreasonable.

The Lovings' conviction was affirmed by the court, the validity of the sentence meted out was reversed, and they were remanded for further proceedings.

In April 1967 the Lovings appealed to the Supreme Court of the United

States. It was the decision taken in that case which has been of enormous importance to the American laws relating to miscegenation.

It is interesting to note that the Lovings were not alone in their fight for inter-racial justice. A number of briefs of *amici curiae*[6] were filed – the National Catholic Conference for Inter-racial Justice, the National Association for the Advancement of Colored People and the NAACP Legal Defense and Educational Fund, Inc. – urging reversal of their conviction. On the other side a similar brief was filed on behalf of the State of North Carolina, which possesses similar legislation to that of Virginia concerning miscegenation, advocating affirmation of the conviction.

Chief Justice Warren in the course of his summing up reviewed those parts of the Virginia Code concerning the sexual relations of black and white individuals. Several extraordinary facts emerged which illustrate the depth of irrational emotion and feeling which characterize the attitude of white Southerners towards miscegenation. The absolute refusal to countenance the legality of a mixed union is exemplified in the Virginia Code, Section 20–57: 'All marriages between a white person and a colored person shall be absolutely void without any decree of divorce or other legal process.' The full implications of this statute were experienced by Negro servicemen who returned to Virginia after the war with European wives. Their marriages legally contracted elsewhere could not be sustained in the Commonwealth of Virginia.

Lest there should be any doubt in the minds of potential offenders the Code defines with great exactitude the meaning of the terms white, coloured and Indian:

> It shall hereafter be unlawful for any white person in this State to marry any save a white person, or a person with no other admixture of blood than white and American Indian. For the purpose of this chapter, the term 'white person' shall apply only to such person as has no trace whatever of any blood other than Caucasian; but persons who have one-sixteenth or less of the blood of the American Indian and have no other non-Caucasic blood shall be deemed to be white persons. All laws heretofore passed and now in effect regarding the intermarriage of white and colored persons shall apply to marriages prohibited by this chapter. (Virginia Code Ann. Section 20–54 1960 Repl. Vol.)

In the United States the attitude towards the American Indian is essentially ambivalent. On the one hand there is the somewhat belated recognition that he is after all the First American despite the efforts made to destroy him in the past, and the hatred directed against him. On the other he cannot be admitted to equal terms with the white as clearly he is inferior, which is demonstrated by his way of life. The latter view forgets, in a convenient manner, that this way of life has been imposed by the white. The predominance of either view varies according to the white's proximity to the Indian. Thus the whites of Vermont, the majority of whom will probably have never seen an Indian, would tend to idealize him. The whites of the State of Washington, where there are Indian settlements, tend to be relatively hostile towards their own First Americans. In the case of Virginia the concession given to people with less than one-sixteenth of Indian blood is not entirely what it appears to be. According to a pamphlet issued by the Registrar of the Virginia State Bureau of Vital Statistics it was due to the following: '... the desire of all to recognize as an integral and honored part of the white race the descendants of John Rolfe and Pocahontas ...'[7]

The condescension implied in that statement is overwhelming. The story of Rolfe and Pocahontas is a romantic one – the daughter of an Indian chief, Powhatan, she saved Captain John Smith from death at the hands of her tribe. She subsequently married him and produced a son, John Rolfe. The latter played an important part in the early history of Virginia. Historically minded Virginians still make the pilgrimage to Greenwich parish church outside London, where she is buried, to pay their respects. It would appear that historical miscegenation in terms of the Indian can be tolerated by Virginian racists, but not the contemporary manifestation.[8]

Section I–14 of the Virginia Code lays down that 'Every person in whom there is ascertainable any Negro blood shall be deemed and taken to be a colored person, and every person not a colored person having one fourth or more of American Indian blood shall be deemed an American Indian; except that members of Indian tribes existing in this Commonwealth having one fourth or more of Indian blood and less than one sixteenth of Negro blood shall be deemed tribal Indians.'

The situation with relation to the definition of an Indian is obviously complicated. Clearly tribal Indian represents a purer form of Indian. But an individual who possesses an admixture of Negro is still classified as an Indian so long as his Indian blood is more than a quarter. Indulgence in racism can lead to extravagant niceties of definition and classification – there is Hitler's fictitious category of 'Honorary Aryan' invented for the benefit of his wartime allies the Japanese, and the tragic farce in South Africa where families can be reclassified as white or coloured overnight.

The existence of prohibitions against an activity can be taken to indicate the existence of that activity. It is certainly the case that miscegenation of the type prescribed by Virginian law has occurred in the State for generations. Over forty years ago A. E. Estabrook and I. E. McDougle published a book entitled *Mongrel Virginians*. This was a biological and sociological study of a group of people in a remote part of the State, known as the Win Tribe:

> They are described variously as 'low down' yellow negroes, as Indians, as 'mixed'. No one, however, speaks of them as white. The Wins themselves in general claim the Indian descent although most of them realize they are 'mixed', preferring to speak of the 'Indian' rather than of a possibility of a negro mixture in them. A few claim to be white. ... All these people lived on or near Coon Mountain ... their children intermarried with each other, with a few of the white families nearby and a few matings, of an illegitimate nature, took place with the negroes, some who were slaves and some free ...[9]

The origin of these people appears to be eighteenth century. Their persistence into our own times is, for the racial purist, a permanent reminder of that which must not be allowed to happen. There is little doubt that there are the equivalent of 'Win' tribes all over the south of the United States – in fact wherever anti-miscegenation laws are to be found. As we have suggested elsewhere if peoples of different ethnic origin inhabit the same area, whatever restrictions may be in force, sexual unions are inevitable.

Before considering the judgement of the Supreme Court in the *Lovings* appeal it will be helpful to look at the details of another case which we have mentioned, *McLaughlin*, which came on appeal to that court in October 1964.

The area of vagueness surrounding the definition of race has a crucial effect in cases brought under miscegenation statutes. This transpired in the *McLaughlin* case. In their appeal the appellants claimed that their convictions violated their right, under the Fourteenth Amendment, of due process on the grounds either that there was no proof of McLaughlin's race, or that the State of Florida's definition of a Negro was unconstitutionally vague. The Statute in question (Section I.01 [6]) states: 'The words "negro", "colored", "colored persons", "mulatto", or "persons of color", when applied to persons, include every person having one-eighth or more of African or Negro blood.' This is more precise than the Virginia stipulation: 'Every person in whom there is ascertainably any Negro blood shall be deemed and taken to be a colored person.' At the first trial of McLaughlin one of the arresting officers was permitted, although the defence objected, to give his opinion as to the race of each of the defendants on his observation of their physical appearance. It was argued before the Supreme Court that the Florida definition was circular in that it provided no independent means of assessing the race of a defendant's ancestors, and that evidence based on physical appearance was not permissible because not related to any objective standard.[10]

A consideration of how States, other than Florida and Virginia, attempt to define a Negro demonstrates the jungle of uncertainty which surrounds such attempts. Indiana follows the Florida pattern. Maryland classifies as Negro all persons of Negro descent to the third generation. Arkansas and Kentucky do not trouble to define; to them a Negro is a Negro. Arizona was in the same category until 1942 when the legislature amended this defect. It has been pointed out that: 'These varying definitions mean that a person can find himself a white person in one state and a Negro under the statute of another state.'[11]

It must not be thought that it is only the Negro and the Indian who are affected by racist legislation. The range of non-Caucasians with whom the Caucasian may not mingle his seed is very wide – Mongolians (Mississippi), Chinese and Japanese (Georgia), Malayans (Maryland), Asiatic Indians (Virginia), Mulattoes (Delaware), Ethiopians (Nevada prior to the repeal in 1962), Koreans (South Dakota prior to repeal in 1957), Mestizos and half-breeds (South Carolina). One wonders if there were any practical grounds for this highly idiosyncratic choice – was there a period when Maryland was subjected to a sudden invasion of Malayans bent on destroying the racial purity of the State? Did an expedition of Ethiopians ever penetrate the fastnesses of Nevada there to rape and pillage? The truth may very well be that legislators merely thought of ethnic groups they most actively disliked. The racist path is unpredictable.

The real heights of absurdity were reached in the State of Colorado before the repeal of its anti-miscegenation statute in 1957. Citizens of the State could only be subject to the statute if they lived in certain parts of the State as the law only applied to those sections of the State which had not been acquired from Mexico. Clearly the application of the law in areas where the population was already mixed would have been even more absurd – proceedings might have had to be taken against a majority of the people. The distinction between different parts of the State was upheld at law.[12]

Lack of precision in the definition of a Negro can be to the advantage of an accused. Missouri makes provision for the defendant to appear on the witness-stand so that the jury can decide what race he belongs to. A number of other States have a similar test. The ignorance of the jury of racial characteristics, for even the physical anthropologist confronted with the infinite gradations of race mixing is hard put to give a definite opinion, may well benefit the accused. Association with a racial group has been admissible as proof of the individual's ethnic group in the Carolinas.[13]

The public racial reputation of a person has also been accepted.[14] Proof must be established beyond reasonable doubt as to the individual's race before there can be a successful criminal prosecution. Thus with obviously black people there is no doubt, but the fair-skinned mixed blood with European-like features and hair stands a fighting chance of being regarded as white.

It is perhaps important to realize that all American legislation of the type we are discussing is designed to prohibit marriage or sexual relations between white and non-white. No State has made laws whose aim is to prevent such relationships between non-whites. Thus for example anywhere in the United States it is legally permissible for an Hindu to cohabit with a Negro providing they do not offend against local fornication regulations. The USA must be one of the few civilized countries which still possess restrictions of this nature. In Florida fornication has its price – 'If any man commits fornication with a woman, each of them shall be punished by imprisonment not exceeding three months, or by a fine not exceeding thirty dollars' (Florida Stat. Ann. Section 798.04). Public sexual morality would appear to be a matter for great concern in the Sunshine State. The section (798.02) of the Florida Statutes under the heading 'Lewd and Lascivious Behaviour' – this has a splendid fulminating ring to it – states the following: 'If any man or woman, not being married to each other, lewdly and lasciviously associate and cohabit together, or if any man or woman, married or unmarried, is guilty of open and gross lewdness and lascivious behaviour, they shall be punished by imprisonment in the state prison not exceeding two years, or in the county jail not exceeding one year, or by a fine not exceeding 300 dollars.' There are a number of possible interpretations of the effects of this statute. Either there are innumerable prisons full to capacity in the State; or the State Treasury has a sizeable income from prosecutions under this section; or perhaps, as is most likely, the statute is never invoked except when it is a matter of racial preservation. But questions persist in the mind – are topless waitresses guilty of lewd and lascivious behaviour?

The penalties for violating anti-miscegenation laws vary considerably. It is a serious criminal offence, a felony in Alabama, Georgia, Oklahoma, Tennessee and Virginia; a lesser crime, a misdemeanour, in Arkansas, Delaware, South Carolina, West Virginia and Wyoming. Punishments also vary from thirty days (Delaware) to ten years' imprisonment (Florida, Mississippi and North Carolina). Generally the statutes do not distinguish between marriage and cohabitation. As marriage itself is prohibited, violation of the fornication and cohabitation restrictions is inevitable. It follows logically that infringement of inter-racial cohabitation regulations cannot be avoided by a subsequent marriage. If the racial factor is not present, however, this is a good defence for infringement of the fornication laws by white people. Legislation in Mississippi makes this quite clear. In that State a person or a corporation can be prosecuted for urging or supporting any form of miscegenation. To issue a licence for marriage, or to marry, a mixed couple is a criminal offence in Georgia, Kentucky, South Carolina and Wyoming.[15]

Normally there must be criminal intent present in order for there to be a legal violation of anti-miscegenation laws. That is to say the couple must be aware of their racial status. If real lack of knowledge can be demonstrated this may constitute a successful defence. In the light of what we have stated above regarding the equivocal nature of racial classification this is not as fanciful as it sounds. Louisiana is quite specific on this point: 'Miscegenation is the marriage or habitual cohabitation with knowledge of their difference in race between a person of Caucasian or white race and the person of a colored or Negro race' (Louisiana Revised Statutes 14:79). Ignorance of racial status can of course bear hardly on a couple who may all at once discover that they are not legally married. Marriages of this kind are void *ab initio*, that is from their inception, not merely voidable. For example in English law a marriage can be discovered to be illegal – there may be an impediment such as the non-dissolution of a former marriage which both parties were unaware of at the time of the marriage – this is voidable but does not necessarily set aside all the legal rights which obtained during the course of such a marriage. In the American case – that is when the marriage is void *ab initio* – all such rights are destroyed.

The situation is further complicated by the fact that a couple legally married in one State may enter another where the marriage is void. The accepted view has been that a State may refuse to recognize any union which is repugnant to its stated policy. The individuals who leave a State, which prohibits their marrying, with the avowed intention of contracting a legal marriage elsewhere, and then return cannot evade the prohibition.[16] This in fact was the basis of the *Lovings* case. Some States, such as Virginia, do not merely rely on traditional practice but declare their intention in statutory form. As we have seen, Virginian law not only prohibits Negro–white marriages but also those between whites and Mongolians. In the *Naim* case the pair had gone to North Carolina where the latter unions are valid. Upon their return to Virginia they were prosecuted, and the Virginia Supreme Court of Appeals held that their marriage was invalid.

Complexity increases when natives of a State which recognizes their marriage move to a State which does not. This creates a special problem which is reflected in the division among the States which possess anti-miscegenation laws. Arkansas, Indiana, Kentucky and Wyoming uphold such marriages. Delaware, Louisiana, Mississippi, Tennessee and Texas declare them invalid. Both groups have statutory authority for their actions. A much larger number of States, including Alabama, Florida and Maryland, have no directive in their statutes as to the course to be adopted. The hardship inflicted upon mixed couples by legislation of this kind does not need to be dilated upon.

The writer, as a coloured West Indian, has often speculated as to the train of events which would ensue if he travelled to, and took up temporary residence in, say, Mississippi, if he were accompanied by his English wife. After twenty years of marriage would he be prosecuted for fornication and 'lewd and lascivious behaviour'? It is possible that cases have occurred involving African officials at the UN who are married to European women. Such individuals may have been invited to address black universities in the South. In most instances the length of stay would be short, and thus the easiest course for the authorities to adopt would be to give the individual the status of 'Honorary Aryan' for the duration of his visit. In other words ignore his existence. In my own case if I were to intimate that my visit would be for several months this might create a severe problem for the upholders of racial purity. My appearance is such as to not lend credence to any fictional, Caucasian status over a long period. If we were prosecuted this might lead to international complications as we are both British citizens. Readers can speculate on the variety of pressures which might be brought to bear to persuade us that our sojourn in the South was not in our own interest.

That such a state of affairs could arise would seem to be an indictment of a nation which claims to be a bulwark of democracy in the free world.

Until the *Lovings* case (1967), the Supreme Court of the United States had refused to rule on the constitutionality of anti-miscegenation laws. This is not to suggest that it was the avowed policy of the Court throughout its existence to avoid responsibility, or that it believed in doctrines of racial purity. A more reasonable interpretation of the Court's reluctance to pronounce on such matters is that it was a reflection of its concern with the rights of States *vis-à-vis* the Federal Government. Such an interpretation of course leaves out any consideration for the plight of the individual as the victim of monstrous acts of inhumanity. The ordinary citizen in any civilized state believes that the law is there for his protection and to enable justice to be done. Can it be said that these purposes are fulfilled by anti-miscegenation laws?

The review we have attempted to give of the contemporary legal background to anti-miscegenation legislation was considered necessary in order to appreciate fully the overwhelming significance of the Supreme Court's decision in the *Lovings* case – 'There can be no doubt that restricting the freedom to marry solely because of racial classifications violates the central meaning of the Equal Protection Clause [of the Fourteenth Amendment].'

Chief Justice Warren stated that: 'Penalties for miscegenation arose as an incident to slavery and have been common in Virginia since the colonial period.'[17] The current anti-miscegenation statutes dated from the passing of the Racial Integrity Act of 1924 during a period of intense 'nativism' in the years immediately following the First World War. The statutes absolutely prohibited a 'white' person marrying anyone but another 'white' person. A marriage licence could not be obtained until the appropriate official was satisfied that the applicants' statement as to their race were correct. It was the duty of local and state registrars to keep certificates of 'racial composition'. The appropriate comment here is that the reader should remember that only one other society has ever had similar legislation – Hitler's Germany.

The State of Virginia did not contend that its powers to regulate marriage were unlimited notwithstanding the commands of the Fourteenth Amendment. Its argument was that the meaning of the Equal Protection Clause was that State penal laws containing '... an interracial element as part of the definition of the offence must apply equally to whites and Negroes in the sense that members of each race are punished to the same degree'. In other words it was the classical Southern argument against desegregation. The further contention of the State was that as its statutes punished equally both white and Negro partners in a mixed marriage they did not despite their reliance on racial classifications 'constitute an invidious discrimination based upon race'.

If this interpretation by the State, that the Equal Protection Clause did not outlaw anti-miscegenation statutes, was correct the question of unconstitutionality before the Court was whether there was any rational basis for a State to treat mixed marriages differently from other unions. Scientific evidence on this point was doubtful therefore the Court should 'defer to the *wisdom* of the state legislature in adopting its policy of discouraging inter-racial marriages'. (My italics.)

The Supreme Court rejected entirely this argument that mere equal application of penalties to white and Negro was sufficient to remove racial classifications from 'the Fourteenth Amendment's prescription of all invidious racial discriminations'. The State argued further that the Congressional Record at the time (1868) of the Thirty-ninth Congress indicated that the framers of the Fourteenth Amendment did not intend to make unconstitutional the anti-miscegenation laws of the individual States. In the view of the Court, however, 'The clear and central purpose of the Fourteenth Amendment was to eliminate all official state sources of racial discrimination in the States.'

There was no doubt in the minds of the Court that these particular Virginia laws rested entirely upon distinctions drawn according to race. In fact they proscribed generally accepted conduct if carried out by people of different races. In the case of *Hirabavashi* v. *United States* (320 US 81m 100 [1943]) the Court had stated: '... distinctions between citizens solely because of their ancestry [is] odious to a free people whose institutions are founded upon the doctrine of equality ...' If such distinctions were to be upheld it would have to be shown that they were necessary for the accomplishment of a permissible State objective which was independent of the very racial discrimination which was the object of the Fourteenth Amendment to eliminate. Two members of the Supreme Court had already given their opinion in *McLaughlin* v. *Florida* that they 'cannot conceive of a valid legislative purpose ... which makes the color of a person's skin the test of whether his conduct is a criminal offence'.

What it auounted to was that the Virginia Statutes, based on racial classifications, must be their own justification as means designed to maintain white supremacy. Was this a permissible State objective?

The Chief Justice ended his judgement as follows:

> ... The freedom to marry has long been recognized as one of the vital personal rights essential to the orderly pursuit of happiness by free men. Marriage is one of the 'basic civil rights of man', fundamental to our very existence and survival ... To deny this fundamental freedom on so unsupportable a basis as the racial classifications so directly subversive of the principle of equality at the heart of the Fourteenth Amendment is surely to deprive all the State's citizens of liberty without due process of law. The Fourteenth Amendment requires that the freedom of choice to marry, or not marry, a person of another race resides with the individual and cannot be infringed by the State.
>
> These convictions must be reversed.
>
> *It is so ordered.*

It is just over a hundred years – 1868 – since the Fourteenth Amendment was passed by the Thirty-ninth Congress. The interpretation of it given by Chief Justice Warren could have been made at any time in the last hundred years. The fact that such an interpretation was not made has meant that a very large number of the individual States, as we have seen, were able to create legislation of the most violent racist character. That this was so is not, in our view, only a tenderness and solicitude for States' rights but betrays the basic attitude of intolerance and inhumanity concerning the Negro which is characteristic of so many white Americans. They are willing, if only reluctantly, to desegregate schools, public places of entertainment, restaurants, housing areas and so forth, but engraven on their hearts is the question – 'What would you do if your daughter married a Negro?'

The young, white middle-class girls who joined the Freedom Marchers in the South in the fifties, and who virtually prostituted themselves to Negroes, were expiating the intolerance of their parents. Perhaps their children will not have to do the same for them. Meantime we should remember that despite the Supreme Court decision the Lovings cannot, if they so desired, move to Mississippi without risking imprisonment. It is not that any significant number of whites or Negroes wish to intermarry, but rather that so long as anti-miscegenation laws exist in a society they are an intolerable affront and insult to the dignity of the human state.

CHAPTER 4

Race Mixture in the United States - The Historical Background, New England and Pennsylvania

In endeavouring to trace the history of race mixture between Negro and white in the United States it is necessary to make an important distinction between the South and New England. It is a distinction which first of all can be seen in demographic terms. For example, the slave population of Massachusetts in 1776 amounted to 5,249, or 1·5 per cent of the white population of 343,845. The number of slaves in Virginia in 1782 was 270,762 against a free population of 296,852.[1] But we also have to see this distinction as a difference in ethos between the North and the South.

Colonial New England was essentially a society based upon Puritanism with its emphasis on the patriarchal family. The rigidity of behaviour of the slavemaster was extended to the slave. He was expected, and forced, to observe the same strict code of sexual morality that bound the free, white population. Illicit unions between any members of the community, whether slave or free, were punishable at law. Sexual relations prior to marriage met with severe penalties.[2] Sexual crimes such as sodomy, bestiality, rape and adultery were subject to the death penalty.[3] Control of the Negro slave in all respects was much easier than it was in the plantation economy of the South. New England was essentially a farming community with dimensions of seafaring and manufacture. Farms were small, and the owners could seldom afford to have more than two or three slaves. Inevitably, working with the family in the fields or the home, the slave was easily subject to the restrictions imposed by his owner.[4] There were exceptions to this general pattern, such as the Narragansett Country in southern Rhode Island, where farms varied from 300 to thousands of acres and produced cattle and dairy products,[5] but the general picture which emerges is that of small-scale farming in which both family and slaves were the producers. A pattern similar in many respects to that of South Africa at the beginning of the nineteenth century.

Thus both religion, and the code of sexual morality stemming from it, in the social and economic context of New England created a situation in which the Negro slave was the overt mirror of his master. Cohabitation among slaves was forbidden unless they were legally married. This was in dramatic contrast to the situation in the South. A Negro marriage in New England observed exactly the same forms as that for the free white population – banns were published a fortnight before the marriage.[6]

It would be wrong to assume, however, from this image that marriage for the Negro was identical in substance with that of his master. Pressures against proper fulfilment of such unions were considerable. The simplest were cases where slaves of different owners wished to marry. Agreement had to be made between the owners as to the way in which the husband would support the wife, or indeed where they should cohabit.[7] Whatever the situation, the interests of the owner remained paramount. In the published notices of slave marriages the description is merely by the Christian name followed by Negro. Thus marriage did nothing to alter their status as slaves.[8] Clergymen were aware that slave unions were not the same as others, and tended to use a different form of words from those of the ordinary marriage service. 'Slaves were licensed to be conversant and familiar together as husband and wife ...'[9] That such marriages were a mockery, merely promoted to satisfy the conscience of the slaveholder, is quite evident. However strong the conscience the economic motive nearly always prevailed. Thus the marriage did not prevent the slave-husband being sold away from his wife, or given to another owner by his master.[10] There was a tendency for mother and children to be regarded as an entity for the purposes of sale. Advertisements in newspapers of the period make this point clear.[11]

The economy of New England in the eighteenth century was such that to own too many slaves was an economic embarrassment. This affected slave families for it meant that children were frequently sold or *given away* by the owner. If there was no work on the farm for them they were only extra mouths to feed. A typical advertisement illustrating this took the following form: 'A Negro child soon expected of a good breed, may be owned by any person inclining to take it away.'[12] Wives were even sold because they were too fertile.[13]

The Puritan code of sexual behaviour, so strict in its punishment of infractions, led to the murder of children by their mothers. For both black and white the penalty for illicit sexual intercourse – the proof being the birth of a bastard child – the penalty was a fine and up to twenty lashes. Infanticide carried the death penalty. At least at the level of fornication there was equality between the female slave and her mistress.[14]

That the slave was aware of the disrupting and demoralizing effects of servitude upon his family is apparent in the petition presented to the Massachusetts Government in 1773:

> ... The endearing ties of husband and wife we are strangers to for we are no longer man and wife than our masters or mestesses [mistresses] thinks proper ... Our children are also taken from us by force and sent many miles from us wear [where] we seldom or ever see them again there to be made slaves of for life which sometimes is vere short by Reson of Being dragged from their mothers Breest. How can a slave perform the duties of a husband to a wife or parent to his child? How can a husband leave master and work and cleave to his wife? How can the wife submit themselves to there husbands in all things? How can the child obey their parents in all things ...[15]

Needless to say this plea had no effect whatsoever. To have accepted its argument would have been to destroy the whole edifice of slavery.

Marriages took place not only between slaves, but between slaves and free blacks. If a freeman married a slave-woman the children belonged to her master, which the law demanded. If, however, the woman was free and married a slave the children were free. It was possible for a free Negro to purchase a slave in order to marry her.[16] Naturally enough the same privilege of matrimony extended to the union of free blacks. In such cases it is clear the factors of disruption so common among the slaves did not occur. From the records it appears that distinguished members of the community, such as Cotton Mather, as magistrates, were willing to perform the ceremony.[17]

So far we have discussed sexual union between black people, but the process of amalgamation or miscegenation between Negroes and other ethnic groups in the New England colonies occurred from an early period. One dimension of this was the marriage between Negroes and Indians. It must be remembered that in these colonies not only had there been Negro slaves from before the middle of the seventeenth century, but that Indian slavery was of the same antiquity. There is some debate about the actual date when Negro slavery began in New England but most authorities agree that the year 1638 can be regarded as the time of its inception.[18] For Indian slavery the date is 1637.[19] Co-existent with slavery was the institution of indenture. The latter was the system whereby an individual either bound himself, or was forcibly bound, to be a bond servant to a master for a specified period of time – seven to fourteen years. In many instances the condition of such servants was little different from that of the slaves. Indenture applied not only to whites, probably the largest category, but to Indians as well. Both the latter could be, and were enslaved but only rarely did a white person become a slave. This only came about if the individual behaved in a vicious criminal way, or as an indentured servant assaulted his master.[20] White indentured servants were sent from Britain into all the North American and Caribbean colonies throughout the seventeenth century. This was particularly true of the period after Monmouth's abortive rebellion against James. Transportation to the colonies through indenture continued to be a method of punishing criminals in Britain well into the nineteenth century. The foundation of the economic prosperity of the Australian State of New South Wales can be attributed largely to the existence of indentured labour.

Unions between Indians and Negroes were common. Evidence from Rhode Island and Massachusetts indicates that the dilution of the Indian through such unions was extremely apparent. In one case at Gay Head in Massachusetts, of 142 individuals classified as Indians only less than ten could be described as racially pure – 'the rest are largely intermixed, chiefly with Negroes ...'[21] The participants in these alliances varied. A black slave might marry an Indian slave. Free Indian women might marry black slaves. In other cases both parties might be free.[22] At times the three ethnic groups – white, black and Indian – were present in an union. This occurred when a mulatto, or an even more diluted mixture, such as that of an octoroon (someone with an eighth of Negro blood), married an Indian. The most famous example is that of Crispus Attucks, the coloured hero of the American Revolution.[23]

The evidence would suggest that there was no basic antipathy between Negroes and Indians as regards marriage. They both suffered the same servile status according to the slave codes of all the New England colonies. This in itself must have constituted a bond between the two groups. This community of feeling was assisted by the imbalance of males and females amongst black slaves. There were far more males than females – of 2,674 Negro slaves over sixteen in Massachusetts in 1755 only 855 were women.[24] In some counties there were three times as many males as females.[25] Reasons for the imbalance are apparent. There was a greater demand for Negro men, for their capacity for work was greater than that of women, as was their ability to survive the dreadful voyage of the Middle Passage from Africa. Slave-traders were even given instructions to this effect: 'Buy no girls and few women but prime boys and young men ...'[26]

There is no question that Negro–Indian marriages took place freely and frequently, especially in Connecticut.[27] From the black side a shortage of women, and a community of interest, were the most powerful factors creating this situation.

A point at which New England would appear to be very much opposed to the South was in relation to intermarriage between white and black. Until the early eighteenth century there was no anti-miscegenation statute in Massachusetts. The statute itself was repealed on 6 March 1840.[28] Interestingly enough in such marriages the male partner was most often the Negro. They were in fact rare. 'Intermarriages between whites and blacks are very rare, oftner between black men and white women than on the contrary ...'[29] It is likely that the context of this type of union was the friendship of a free Negro for a white female bond servant who had served her indenture, though there is no record of this being the case. On the other hand it is extremely doubtful that a white woman of any position or status in the community would have contracted marriage with a black. There are possible exceptions to this. An outstanding example is that of Lemuel Haynes, the first Negro clergyman in North America to preach to white congregations; a mulatto, the son of a white woman and a Negro, he married a white woman.[30]

The area, however, in which miscegenation took place on a significant scale was not that of marriage, but that of illicit sexual relations. The expression of sexuality cannot be controlled by law. Man may define and narrow the dimension of such expression, but despite such efforts individuals will circumvent the laws. Historically all such attempts to exercise control of sexual behaviour have failed, including the most recent, that of South Africa, which has the most stringent anti-miscegenation laws. The Puritans of New England were no different. The law demanded complete sexual rectitude. Only in marriage was man to express his sexual nature. Their catastrophic failure is evidenced by the innumerable cases of fornication and rape which came before the courts.[31] As we have said, the same laws governing sexual behaviour applied to both black and white. Thus fornication for either sex or ethnic group was punished by whipping. This is very far removed from the apparently unbridled and unpunished promiscuity of the Southern plantation. If a woman in New England had an illegitimate child she might have to pay a fine as well as undergoing chastisement.[32]

Looked at from the stand-point of today the early colonists in New England appear to have been obsessed with sexuality. The evidence suggests that both prurience and sadism played their part in the acting out of their obsession. It is clear their ideas were not engendered by the context of a new environment – they had possessed them in Britain. But in New England for the first time they had power to enact their own laws and penalties. It may occur to the student that for a people so given to piety the Puritans exhibited a remarkable appetite for fornication. Such activity is essentially clandestine so that cases before the courts, as a result of informers' actions, would not necessarily indicate the actual incidence. For example, the Middlesex Court of General Sessions in Massachusetts between 1726 and 1780 sentenced 523 spinsters and 160 couples for fornication.[33] There must have been many more such cases which never came before the courts.

As early as 1642 Governor William Bradford of Plymouth Plantation is lamenting the sins of the colonists:

> ... Marvilous it may be to see and consider how some kind of wickednes did grow and breake forth here, in a land wher the same was so much witnesed against, and so narrowly looked unto, and severely punished when it was knowne; as in places more, or so much, that I have known or heard of ... And yet all this could not suppress ye breaking out of sundrie notorious sins (as this year, beside others, gives us too many sad presidents and instances), espetially drunkennes and unclainnes; not only incontinencie between persons unmaried, for which both men and women have been punished sharply enough, but some maried persons also. But that which is worse, even sodomie and bugerie (things fearfull to name,) have brook forth in this land, oftener than once ...[34]

Bradford, clearly an extremely intelligent man who knew his countrymen, was aware that the severity of the laws against sexual misconduct was itself an incentive to the same misconduct. But he was also aware that an evil leaven had entered the body politic of the colonists:

> ... But it may be demanded how it came to pass that so many wicked persons and profane people should so quickly come over into this land, and mixe themselves amongst them? seeing that it was religious men yt begane ye work, and they came for religious sake ... it is ever to be remembered that where ye Lord begins to sow good seed, thr ye envious man will endeavore to sow tares. Men being come over into a wilderness, in which much labour and servise was to be done aboute building and planting, etc., such as wanted help in yt respecte, when they could not have such as ye would, were glad to take such as they could; and so many untoward servants, sundry of them proved, that were thus brought, both men and women kind ... An other and a maine reason herof was, that men, so many godly disposed persons willing to come into these parts, some begane to make a trade of it, to transporte passengers and their goods, and hired ships for that end; and then, to

> make up their fraight and advance theor profite, cared not who ye persons were, so they had money to pay them. And by this means the cuntrie became pestered with many persons, who, being come over, crept into one place or another ... so allso they were sente by their friends some under hope yt they would be made better; others that they might be eased of such burthens, and they kept from shame at home yt would necessarily follow their dissolute courses. And thus, by one means or another, in 20. years time, it is a question whether ye greater part be not growne ye worser ...[35]

That must be one of the earliest references to that scourge of the old British Colonial Empire – the remittance man, the individual who shipped to the colonies and lived there on money received from home. There is some substance to Bradford's argument – that the purity of the original group of settlers had been corrupted by others not professing the same ideals. On the other hand surely the sexual ethics of Puritanism should have been proof against such assaults? An argument could be advanced that the necessity which impelled the imposition of such severe restrictions indicates an active desire for sexual transgression. The refusal to recognize the essential carnality of man caused the Puritans infinite distress. Their error may have been inspired by their predecessors – the Early Fathers of the Church who took refuge in the Egyptian desert away from the temptation of women, only to be pursued by visions of erotic splendour on an heroic scale. Their belief may very well have been that of St Jerome – 'Regard everything as poison which bears within it the seeds of sensual passion.'[36]

Error may be condoned; prurience, however, is another matter. Whippings were a public affair for the edification of the faithful. There can be little doubt that as much as the spectacle was edifying it also yielded a type of sexual pleasure. The parallel is with the flagellation mania which was such a strong characteristic of public schools and brothels in nineteenth-century England. That this was indeed the case appears from the extraordinary debates which took place concerning the death penalty for sodomy and adultery:

> As, for instance, in ye case of adultrie (if it be admitted yt is to be punished with death, which to some of us is not cleare), if ye bodie be not actually defiled, then death is not be inflicted. So in sodomie, beastialitie, if therebe not, penetration ... because, though ther be not penetratio corporis, yet ther may be similtudo concubitis muliebris ... Because something else might be equivalent to penetration wher it had not been, viz. ye fore mentioned acts with frequencie and long continuance with a high hand, utterly extinguishing all light of nature;

besides, full intention and bould attempting of foulest acts may seeme to have been capitall here ...[37]

Even the so-called Permissive Society does not (yet) debate in public what constitutes penetration of a woman's vagina. It is of some interest that the Puritans did not actually impose the supreme penalty for adultery but were content with fines and whippings. No doubt this was not due to squeamishness but to fear of depleting the population.

The sexual offender in New England had to face not only the courts and their punishments, but the wrath and penalties of the Church. The latter were formidable. The Church's attitude was put by Cotton Mather:

'... If any of our society defile himself with *Fornication*, wee will give him our *Admonition*; and so debar him from the Meeting, at least *half a year*; nor shall hee return to it, ever any more, without exemplary Testimonies of his becoming a *new Creature* ...'[38] This meant excommunication. Being cut off from the Church was not only a matter of spiritual deprivation but entailed becoming a social pariah whom everyone avoided. The procedure for reconciliation involved public confession before the pastor and the congregation. The Church itself was as obsessed with sexual infringements as the laity. One authority states: 'The prohibition of adultery furnished the basis of more ecclesiastical prosecutions than any other provision in the Decalogue ... A majority of all sexual offenders and a plurality of all church members dealt with for violations of their religious obligations were charged with fornication ...'[39]

Prurience could be excused by a concern for practicality. In numerous instances fornication was followed by the birth of an illegitimate child. Such children could become a charge upon the county. Thus to penalize fornication, it was thought, would lessen the taxpayers' burden. It does not appear to have been a successful policy. 'Richard Prior, for fornication with Mary Williams, was committed to prison until he gave security in 30ri. to save the town of Ipswich harmless from all charges about the child ...'[40]

It must not be thought that such matters were only of concern in the early days of the New England colonies. The case of Mrs Baldwin of Pittsfield occurred as late as 1851 – she was arraigned before the investigating committee of Pittsfield Church on a charge of adultery. 'You stand charged with receiving visits of the said Dodge in your chamber, sometimes two or three times a day ... when your husband was away, and that one evening when he was out of town, and Mr Dodge was with you in the chamber your door was found locked, and it was nearly an hour after that before he came downstairs and left the house ...'[41] The point to note is that it was as late as the middle of the nineteenth century that the Church still felt it incumbent upon itself to prosecute in such matters.

Sexual intercourse between Negro slaves and white indentured servants can be explained in terms of their condition of life being very similar, but it does not explain the development of liaisons between master and slave. There are a number of problems to be considered here. Was it always a question of the slave-owner being able to exert his authority to compel a Negro woman into his bed? To what extent did the prestige of the white assist the compliance of the slave? What part did physical attraction play in such associations? It would appear that authority, white prestige and attraction were all factors affecting black-white liaisons. There is no question that the slavemaster had practically the power of life and death over his property – his slaves. This undoubtedly extended to the sexual field. The Negro's acknowledgement of white superiority was reinforced by his view of the mulatto, who frequently attained his freedom and while a slave was apt to be favoured by whites against the Negro. Of attraction there can be no doubt whatsoever from Cape Cod to New Orleans. The clandestine, the forbidden, combined with a series of myths to turn the Negro female into a black Aphrodite that the white man experienced difficulty in resisting.

The difficulty lies in attempting to assess the relative importance of these factors. Whatever analysis is made the fact remains that miscegenation between black and white was widespread throughout New England. What was said of Rhode Island applied to all the colonies: '... illicit intercourse between white men and coloured women in Rhode Island marked a numerous progeny ...'[42] In bastardy cases the court was sometimes reluctant to convict the white man responsible – he was merely given a nominal fine – but inevitably his coloured partner was both whipped and fined.[43]

Adultery was another area which contributed to intermixture of the ethnic groups. Interestingly enough many divorce cases concerned adultery between slaves and white women. In birth controlless days it was difficult to deny the evidence of a mulatto child.[44] Divorces were also granted to white women for the misconduct of their husbands with Negro women, who had borne their bastards.[45] Despite the severe penalties consequent upon black-white fornication and marriage, the number of mulattoes continued to grow. So much so that it was felt, particularly in Massachusetts, that their existence might endanger the existence of slavery as an institution. The mulatto in fact represented a bridge between the races, and the emotional and other bonds developed through their progeny hit at the very heart of the institution. But it was only in Massachusetts that these feelings were translated into penal action to stem the benign tide of intermixture.

In 1705 the Government passed special legislation for the 'better preventing of a spurrious and mix't issue ...' The Bill passed had a number of sections. Negroes and mulattoes in the first section were to be whipped, and sold out of the province if they committed 'fornication with an Englishwoman or a woman of any other Christian nation'. The white female offender had to support any child borne to her as a result of her misconduct. Inability to do so meant that she would be indentured as a servant for as long a period as the magistrates thought necessary for the support of the child.[46] This section was balanced by another which prohibited all white men from having sexual relations with Negro or mulatto women. Defiance of the prohibition brought severe whipping for the man and liability for the support of any ensuing children. The woman in question would be sold out of the province.[47] For the Negro slave the latter was regarded as little better than the death penalty. Stories were rife of the terrible conditions of slavery in the Caribbean, just as in the West Indies the slaves believed that life on the mainland was intolerable.

The most remarkable section of the Act reversed the state of affairs whereby all members of the community, slave and free alike, were permitted to intermarry. The law of 1705 stated no English or Scottish subject might enter into marriage with a Negro or mulatto. The individual who defied the law by performing such a marriage was to be fined £50 to be divided between the Government and the person who laid the information. On the other side the slave-owner was enjoined not to deny the right of the Negro to marry one of his own kind.[48]

There were a number of reasons why this stringent law failed to be effective. In the first place although the person who officiated at a white-black marriage was subject to fine the marriage itself was perfectly legal.[49] Provided a willing minister or magistrate could be found, and the money was available for the fine, a couple could defy the prohibitive law. But perhaps where the whole attempt to control miscegenation broke down was in the attitude and behaviour of the slave-owner. If his own concupiscence governed his behaviour then he could rely on his colleagues to help him conceal his liaison with a slave-girl, as they could rely upon him to do likewise. With regard to his slaves' sexual irregularities with white people in general his cupidity was greater than his principles, or respect for the law. If a slave were convicted he might suffer the permanent loss of his services. A prison sentence meant that he had to pay for the slave's keep while incarcerated. In addition he had to pay the costs of prosecution. It is understandable that in these circumstances masters were apt to ignore the existence of miscegenating couples.[50]

The other colonies in New England did not follow the Massachusetts example as we have said, and the mulatto population continued to grow quite freely. Rhode Island in 1782 had a total population of nearly 52,000. Seven point three per cent were classified as black. Of these 464 were described as mulattoes. In one Rhode Island town, Westerly, there were even more mulattoes than blacks.[51] In a comparison with the South it appears that the economic framework of New England did not favour the mulatto against the black as was the case of the South.

Pennsylvania exhibits in the colonial period several points of similarity with New England, and Massachusetts in particular. The economy of the areas was not entirely dissimilar. The characteristic of Pennsylvania was small-holdings associated with fairly large estates, and the existence of ironworks in the towns. An individual estate might employ as many as thirty Negro slaves, but the general pattern of slave-holding was similar to that of New England – three or four living on homesteads.[52] William Penn and his fellow Quakers had arrived in what was to become Pennsylvania to find Negroes already there and slavery established. The new Government lost no time in ratifying the state of affairs. Penn himself became a slave-master in a small way. To be fair it does appear that the Quakers were by no means totally enamoured of the institution. The reasons may have been in part religious, but also due to the presence of a considerable white labour-force both free and indentured. Many of these were of German origin, and as penniless immigrants had sold themselves into indenture. On arrival in Philadelphia they were sold off as so much cattle, or blacks. At times for lack of money parents had to sell their children. '... Parents must sell and trade away their children like so many cattle ...'[53]

The condition of these white immigrants was deplorable, and in many instances there was little to distinguish them from the slaves. They could not marry without their masters' consent, and if they bore illegitimate children their term of indenture was extended. It was almost inevitable that they should form sexual associations with Negroes. From an early period such associations were forbidden at law. The following entry appears in the Chester County Court, Pennsylvania, Records for 1698: 'For that hee ... contrary to the lawes of government and contrary to his masters consent hath ... got with a child a certain molato woman called swart Anna ...' The 'hee' refers to a white indentured servant.

Liaisons appear to have existed both between white men and Negro women and between white women and Negro men as the following case demonstrates:

David Lewis Constable of Haverford returned a negro man of his and a white woman for haveing a baster childe ... the negro said she intised him and promised to marry him; she being examined confest the same ... the court ordered that she shall receive twenty-one lashes on her beare backe ... and the court ordered the negro man never to meddle with any white woman more upon paine of his life ...[54]

There does not seem to have been the same kind of honeymoon in Pennsylvania with regard to racial intermixture as occurred in New England. The Quakers do not appear to have possessed the original magnanimity, and anxiety for the marriage of all, that inhabited the New Englander. On the other hand they were just as concerned about the iniquities of the flesh, with as little success as their fellow colonists further north. The City of Brotherly Love (Philadelphia) lived up to its name, for a contemporary wrote of unbridled kissing and loving-making within the city.[55]

For the Quaker concupiscence was a grave sin. But how to control it was beyond their powers. A Grand Jury in 1741 arraigned those who attempt '... to excell in all lewdness and obsenity which must produce a general corruption of such youths [apprentices, etc.] if not timely remedied ...'[56] But it was like attempting to stop a torrent with a sponge. Adultery was as common as it was in Massachusetts despite the severity of the punishment. An individual found guilty '... shall for the first offence be publicly whipped and suffer one whole year's imprisonment in the house of correction at hard labour, to the behoof of the publick and longer if the magistrate see meet ...'[57]

The danger of miscegenation was felt to be acute so that from 1700 onwards there are laws prohibiting sexual intercourse and marriage between black and white. A law of 1700 is reminiscent of similar legislation in the South in the same period. It laid down that a Negro who buggered or raped a white woman was to be executed. For attempted rape the penalty was milder – merely castration.[58] By 1725, despite such penal sanctions, matters were regarded as being extremely serious – there had been a clandestine marriage between a Negro and a white woman.[59] A petition was presented to the Assembly, and legislation was passed accordingly in 1725–1726. This categorically prohibited the union of black and white in any circumstances whatsoever. If such a marriage were performed the clergyman in question was to be fined £100. The white partner to the marriage was to be fined £30, or could be made an indentured servant for a period not exceeding seven years.[60] While this may have had an effect on legal unions – such marriages were in fact quite rare[61] – it did nothing to stem the growth of miscegenation. The marriage, as in New England, if legally performed, could not be declared void.

On 1 March 1780 an 'Act for the Gradual Abolition of Slavery' in Pennsylvania was passed. As a result of this the sanctions against ethnic intermarriage fell into abeyance. A contemporary writes of the effect this had in the succeeding years:

> I solemnly declare, I have seen more white women married to, and deluded through the arts of seduction by negroes in one year in Philadelphia, than for the eight years I was visiting [in the West Indies and the South] ... There are many, very many blacks, who ... will not be satisfied unless they get white women for wives, and are likewise exceedingly impertinent to white persons in low circumstances ... I know a black man who seduced a young white girl ... who soon after married him, and died with a broken heart; on her death he would not disgrace himself to have a negro wife, and acted accordingly, for soon after he married another white woman ... There are perhaps thousands of white women thus fascinated by black men in this city, and there are thousands of black children by them at present ...[62]

Perhaps the writer, Thomas Branagan, was exaggerating. He obviously felt that miscegenation was a blot on the escutcheon of the Anglo-Saxon, but betrays a certain naïvety in his last sentence above. The 'thousands of white women' were clearly not of his opinion. But these halcyon days did not last. This 'debauching' of the flower of Pennsylvanian womanhood aroused male white racist sentiment:

> ... After a while a strong feeling was aroused, so that in 1821 a petition was sent to the Legislature, asking that mixed marriages be declared void, and that it be made a penal act for a negro to marry a white man's daughter. In 1834 such a marriage provoked a riot at Columbia; while in 1838 the subject caused a vehement outburst in the Constitutional Convention then assembled. Three years later a bill to prevent intermarriage was passed in the House, but lost in the Senate. From time to time thereafter petitions were sent to the Legislature, but no action was taken; the obnoxious marriages continuing to be reported, and even being encouraged by some extreme advocates of racial equality. Nevertheless what the law left undone was largely accomplished by public sentiment and private action. As time went on marriages of white people with negroes came to be considered increasingly odious, and so became far less frequent. When a case occurred, it was usually followed by swift action and dire vengenance. The fact that a white man was living with a negro wife was one of the causes of the terrible riot in Philadelphia in 1849 ...[63]

It is to the credit of Pennsylvania that after 1780 it never reintroduced anti-miscegenation statutes, despite the type of agitation described above. Many authorities have suggested that the intermixture of European and Negro only took place because of the sexual deprivation suffered by the early colonists through their being very largely a male community. Clearly a case can be made out for this, but it is a case which does not cover Pennsylvania. As we have mentioned above, almost from the beginning of the colony there was a steady inflow of white immigrants of both sexes. Such authorities find it difficult to conceive that the very difference of colour and appearance may act as a powerful source of sexual attraction.

At the end of the nineteenth century, and the beginning of our own, the rate of intermarriage between Negro and white was very low:

> Although the law against inter-marriage in Pennsylvania was repealed more than a century ago, there has been little marriage between blacks and whites. According to the records of the city of Philadelphia, there were during the years, 1901, 1902, 1903, 1904 only twenty-one marriages of this kind. In 1900 there were six cases of inter-marriage out of 633 marriages. Three Negro men ... married three white women ... and three white men ... married three Negro women ... There were more inter-marriages when there were fewer Negroes than there are today ... In Pittsburg the number is estimated at fifty. In other places in the State where the Negro population is smaller, there is an aggregate of less than sixty cases. The number of known cases is small. The so-called mixed marriages are not approved by either the white or Negro group. Negro women especially object. When, however, such marriages are consummated in spite of Negro public opinion, the couple is almost always ostracized by the Negroes ...[64]

The low incidence of such marriages is not necessarily an indication of the rate of intermixture:

> Though there is but little contact between the races at the top, there is but little to keep them apart in the lower world. In the lowest stratum, the blacks and whites meet in prostitution and vice. There are in the slums both of Pittsburg and Philadelphia, and to an extent, in the smaller cities, frequent cases of cohabitation chiefly of white women and Negro men, less frequently of white men and Negro women. It is impossible to give the number of cases ...[65]

At this period conditions do not seem to have been so very different from what they were in the colonial era. Then cohabitation between white and black was common, as we have seen, at the level of the slave and the indentured servant.

The official rate of intermixture through marriage was considerably higher in New England at the turn of the nineteenth century. In 1900 the black population of Philadelphia was 62,613, but there were only six cases of intermarriage. The Negro population of Boston in the same year was 11,591, and in the period 1900–1904 there were 143 mixed marriages.[66] In Massachusetts as a whole there were fifty-two such marriages in 1900.[67] Writing in the 1890s, an avowedly racist critic of the Negro, F. L. Hoffman, stated that fifty-eight mixed unions occurred in Rhode Island.[68] The same author comes to a similar conclusion, with relation to the level in the society at which intermixture is most prevalent, as was the case of Pennsylvania – the level of the deprived.

A discussion of New England and Pennsylvania is not only of interest in itself with regard to miscegenation but it provides a vivid contrast with the essentially slave-holding States of the South.

CHAPTER 5

Race Mixture in the United States - The Ante-Bellum South

Miscegenation both in the South and New England can be regarded as three-dimensional. That is to say three racial groups were involved – Negro, white and Indian. The last, although only sporadically enslaved, enjoyed a servile status similar to that of the Negro. The difference between the Indian and the Negro was that, when not in servitude, he was frequently at war with the European. During the colonial period the attitude of the Anglo-Saxon towards the Indian was essentially equivocal. This is seen very clearly in the case of the Pocahontas-Rolfe marriage. A colonist in 1757 was able to write:

> ... we ought to have intermarried with them, which would have incorporated them with us effectively, and made them stanch friends ... but this our wise politicians at home put an effectual stop to at the beginning of our settlement here, for when they heard that Rolfe had married Pocahontas, it was deliberated in council, whether he had not committed high treason in so doing, that is, marrying an Indian princess; and had some troubles not intervened which put a stop to the enquiry the poor man might have been hanged up for having done the most just, the most natural, the most generous and polite action that was ever done on this side of the water. This put an effectual stop to all intermarriage afterward. Our traders have indeed their squaws, alias whores, at the Indian towns where they trade, but they leave their offspring like bulls or bears to be provided for at random by their mothers ...[1]

The current Virginia Code (Ann. Section 20–54 1960 Repl. Vol.) states that '... persons who have one-sixteenth or less of the blood of the American Indian and have no other non-Caucasic blood shall be deemed to be white persons ...' As we have noted (Chapter 3) in a pamphlet published by the Virginia State Bureau of Vital Statistics it is stated that this section of the Code was due to '... the desire of all to recognize as an integral and honored part of the white race the descendants of John Rolfe and Pocahontas ...'[2]

Unlike the French colonist, who took Indian women to his bed both as wife and mistress, the Anglo-Saxon, who would never contemplate marriage, was however reluctant to allow the law to curtail his promiscuity with relation to the Indian.[3] That a great opportunity was missed here is apparent from contemporary accounts:

> They had now made their peace with the Indians, but there was one thing wanting to make the peace lasting. The natives could by no means persuade themselves that the English were heartily their friends so long as they disdained to intermarry with them. And in earnest, had the English consulted their own security and the good of the colony, had they intended either to civilize or convert these gentiles, they would have brought their stomachs to embrace this prudent alliance. The Indians are usually tall and well proportioned, which makes full amends [*sic*] for the darkness of their complexions. Added to this, they are healthy and strong with constitutions untainted with lewdnes (unlike the Anglo-Saxon), and not enfeebled with luxury. Besides morals and all considered, I can't think the Indians were very much greater heathen than the first adventurers, who, had they been very good Christians, would have had the Charity to take this only method of converting the Natives to Christianity. For, after all that can be said, a spritly lover is the most prevailing missionary that can be sent among these or any other infidels. Besides, the poor Indian would have had less reason to complain that the English took their Lands, if they received it by way of a marriage with their daughters. Had such affinities been contracted in the beginning, how much bloodshed had been prevented, and how populous would the country have been, and consequently, how considerable. Nor would the shade of the skin have been any reproach at this day; for if the Moor may be washed in three generations, surely the Indian might be blanced in two ...[4]

There are a number of points to be noted in that quotation. It is probably a truism to state that the absence of legal miscegenation is an excellent indicator of the presence of prejudice and discrimination. Thus whatever the colonist might protest to the Indian he would feel and be aware that he was not considered the equal of the white. Colour itself obviously alarmed the writer (Colonel William Byrd, an aristocrat of aristocrats in Virginia). He takes refuge, in his defence of intermarriage, by extolling their virtues which, as it were, made up for their pigmentation, or indeed in facetiousness, that the Indian would be whiter in a couple of generations. There is a sense here that colour may be *the* determining factor in the relationship of races.

But there were eighteenth-century figures who appreciated the Colonel's argument, and wished to put it into action. Patrick Henry was one of these. In 1784 he presented a Bill to the Virginia Legislature which provided that:

> ... every white man who married an Indian woman should be paid ten pounds, and five for each child born of such a marriage; and that if any white woman married an Indian she should be entitled to ten pounds with which the county court should buy them livestock; that once each year the Indian husband of this woman should be entitled to three pounds with which the county court should buy clothes for him; that every child born to the Indian man and white woman should be educated by the state between the ages of ten and twenty-one years ...[5]

Sad to relate the Bill never passed its final stages to become law.

Although white-Indian marriage was frowned upon this did not in any way inhibit either promiscuity or concubinage between the two racial groups. To say, as some commentators did, that '... there is a degree of repulsion between the Anglo-Americans and the Indians which prevents their intermixing ...' is a gross absurdity.[6] Intermixing in sexual terms took place wherever there was contact between the races. This was specially true of the frontier region where criticisms of promiscuity by one's fellow Anglo-Saxons were few. A pattern approximating to the custom of sexual hospitality appears to have occurred in some areas. The white man, on arriving for a stay in an Indian settlement, would approach the parents of a girl to seek for her domestic and sexual services. An arrangement having been made he would set up his hut, and the girl lived with him during his stay.[7] Children subsequently born remained with the mother, and totally adhered to her people. In time many of these so-called half-breeds became leaders of war parties against the colonists.[8] Proper recognition of such unions, and the mixed blood, would undoubtedly have been to the advantage of the colonist, as it was in the case of the French in Canada, and the Portuguese in Brazil.

There is little doubt that the white man, through alcohol and the satisfaction of his lust, managed to achieve the debauching of the Indian over a period of time. 'All they [the Indians] know of us in relation to morals has been learned from those that have been among them, and painful to relate from this source they have learned nothing but the most libidinous and abandoned licentiousness.[9] Sexual attraction there undoubtedly was, but if this is the case it is difficult to explain the denial of social equality unless the denial is seen in terms of the Indian as a threat to the colonial society. What is surprising is that men of integrity and honour – it was not merely the agent or trapper who succumbed to the flesh – could treat Indian women much in the way a sailor treats a whore in any port in the world. If colonization is equated with war then clearly it was a right of conquest to abuse the women of the defeated. Yet there remain question-marks.

As was the case wherever the Indian or the Negro was to be found in the United States, Virginia enacted legislation to prohibit both marriage and fornication between whites and non-whites. The first enactment was in 1691:

> ... for the prevention of that abominable mixture and spurious issue which may hereafter increase in this dominion with English, or white women, as well as by their unlawful accompanying with one another. Be it enacted ... that for the time to come whatsoever English or white man or woman being free shall intermarry with a Negro, mulatto, or Indian man or woman, bound or free, shall within three months thereafter be banished and removed from the dominion forever ... and be it further enacted ... that if any English or white woman shall have a bastard child by a Negro or mulatto, she shall pay the sum of fifteen pounds sterling, within one month after the child is born, to the wardens of the parish, where she shall be delivered of such child, and in default of such payment, she shall be taken into possession of the said church wardens and disposed of for five years ... and such bastard child shall be bound out as a servant by the said church wardens until he or she shall attain the age of thirty years.[10]

Prior to this an Act of 1662 had laid down that if an Englishman indulged in fornication with a black woman any offspring inherited the status of the mother – that is, automatically became a slave. This was supposed to act as a deterrent to the compliance of the woman. It is clear that from the beginning there was a great fear of miscegenation. Slaves were first landed at Jamestown in 1619. Barely ten years later two white men, Hugh Davis and Robert Sweet, were held guilty of fornication with Negro women. One was '... bound and whipped before an assembly of negroes and others ...' The other had to perform public penance in church for '... lying with a Negro ...'[11] It cannot be said that fear of racial intermixture had a moral basis, for sexual immorality amongst the white community was not treated seriously.

The evidence suggests that in white eyes there was no difference between the Indian and the Negro – both had been reduced to servile status, and the notion that marriage was possible with them was unthinkable. Rejection of intermarriage with the Indian co-existed with unrestrained promiscuity with Indian women. The reduction of the Indian from his free status before the arrival of the colonists to that of a slave or quasi-slave engendered a community of thought and feeling with the Negro, who from the moment of his arrival was in servitude. This led to an extremely high degree of intermixture. So much so that the cessation of Indian slavery can be attributed to the absorption or amalgamation of the Indian with the Negro. This was true of all the slave States in the South.[12]

Throughout the nineteenth century there are frequent references to the extreme dilution of the Indian through intermixture. The Pamunky Tribe of King William County, Virginia, are thus described in 1854: 'Few of them deserve the name of Indians, so mingled are they with other nations by intermarriage. Some are partly African, others European, or rather, I should say Virginian ... it [the settlement] is inhabited by the most curious intermixture of every color and class of people ...'[13] Forty years later an official Government report states: 'No member of the Pamunky tribe is of full blood. While the copper colored skin and straight coarse hair of the aboriginal American shows decidedly in some individuals there are others whose Indian origin would not be detected by the ordinary observer. There has been considerable intermixture of white blood in the tribe, not a little that of the Negro.'[14]

The Pamunky Tribe are a typical example of the process of Indian-Negro miscegenation. That it was leading to obliteration of the Indian as such and to the creation of a dangerous category of free people of colour is apparent in a Petition presented to the state legislature by the white inhabitants of King William County in 1843. This was concerned with the ownership of lands which had been granted to the Pamunky Tribe. Its burden was that the Indians had become so diluted by mixture with Negroes that they can no longer be regarded as such:

> The claim of the Indians no longer exists ... his blood has so largely mingled with that of the Negro race as to have obliterated all the striking features of Indian extraction. Your petitioners express the general voice of the free white inhabitants of the county and as slave-holders they protest against this dangerous and anomalous condition, for it has assumed all the features of a legally established body of free negroes, the general resort of free negroes from all parts of the country ... the harbour for runaway slaves ...[15]

There were several similar cases concerning other tribes of Virginian Indians which had virtually become black.[16] It was a pattern – the dilution of the Indian through admixture with the Negro – that was repeated in the Carolinas and Tennessee.

Exceptions existed to this pattern amongst some Indian groups. In the territories of the southwest amongst the Chickasaw and Cherokee, white attitudes towards the Negro were apparent. The area was much settled by whites from the slave States. They brought with them all their racist notions concerning Negroes, intermarried with the Indians, and even introduced slave-holding to them. The situation is described in a letter from a Cherokee to the US Secretary of War:

> The census of this division of the Cherokees – has been taken within the current year, and the returns have been made thus – Native citizens, 13,563; white men married in the nation 147; white women 73; African slaves 1,277 ... White men in the nation enjoy all the immunities and privileges of the Cherokee people ... In the computation of the present year you will perceive that there are some Africans among us. They have from time to time been brought in and sold by white men; they are, however, generally well treated ... There is hardly any intermixture of the Cherokee and African blood ...[17]

It would be reasonable to suggest that if white settlement had not taken place in the area, and a free relationship had been able to develop between Indian and Negro, as it did elsewhere, the Cherokee would not have exhibited racial antipathy. Unfortunately the privileged position of these Indian-white groups has not been maintained, and they have fought desperately against the accusation of possessing Negro blood.[18]

The Cherokee and the Chickasaw remain exceptions to the general configuration of sexual relationships between Indian and Negro. Where white influence did not extend, as amongst the Seminole in Florida, both sexual and social relationships of the two ethnic groups are characterized by loyalty. As a result of intermarriage there developed numerous half-breed children. These were regarded as the rightful prey of white slave-holders – following the rule that children of a slave mother inherited her status. The country of the Seminole in Florida had become the refuge of the runaway slave. Many attempts both military and peaceful were made by Government to achieve the return of these people, but the Seminole protected them. It has even been suggested that the Seminole War was due to the desire of the Indian fathers to protect their mixed offspring.[19]

In general it can be said that when the Indian was on equal terms with the Negro – that is to say suffered the same condition of servitude – or met in a free situation, no racial antagonism was exhibited but quite the contrary as in the Seminole instance. What is far more difficult to explain is the attitude and behaviour of the white towards the Indian in general, and in regard to miscegenation. No hypothesis would seem to cover the range of behaviour in question. On the one hand there is the identification with the Cherokee and Chickasaw cited above. On the other there is the Virginia Act of 1691 which we have quoted above, and which penalized sexual relations between whites and both Indians and Negroes. Hoetink's theory of somatic distance – the nearer the European is in physical appearance to the non-European the greater the possibility of a benign relationship – is not borne out by the facts of the situation.[20] The Indian is undoubtedly closer physically to the European than the Negro. Thus the barriers against miscegenation should have been far less intense than in the case of the Negro. However, in the slave States we can assume, in the light of anti-miscegenation statutes, despite the exception of the frontier situation, that the racial antipathy against the Indian was as great as that directed against the Negro.

It is correct to assume that the situation of the conqueror, or of the slave-master, leads to sexual abuse of the conquered or the slave. The aftermath of the Second World War in Europe and elsewhere is proof of the first category. With regard to slavery it has to be remembered that the slave was in fact a chattel wholly owned by the master. The evidence from the south of the United States demonstrates that ownership led to the most gross violation of the natural rights of the slave as a person, of which sexual abuse was a major part. That is not to say that all slave-owners were monsters of libidinousness – many could claim that they had never polluted themselves in this way. But when one considers the growing volume of mulattoes throughout the period of slavery it is difficult not to accept that there were an equal number of the not-so-pure. To debate whether the white man or the black female was the sexual aggressor, as some authorities have done, is irrelevant.[21] It is clear that many slave-women realized the advantage of becoming the concubine of a white man – amelioration of her slavery and possible advantages for the children. It is equally clear that the white man did not wait upon this realization:

> Approximately a century and a quarter ago, a group of slaves were picking cotton on a plantation near where Troy, Alabama, is now located. Among them was a Negro woman, who, despite her position as a slave, carried herself like a queen and was tall and stately. The overseer (who was the plantation owner's son) sent her to the house on some errand. It was necessary to pass through a wooded pasture to reach the house and the overseer intercepted her in the woods and forced her to put her head between the rails in an old stake and rider fence, and there in that position my great-great-grandfather was conceived.[22]

There could be no complaint, no redress, the degradation of the woman was complete. If she resisted at the time, punishment could assume terrifying proportions:

> Thomas James, Jep's second son, had cast his eye on a handsome young negro girl, to whom he made dishonest overtures. She would not submit to him, and finding he could not overcome her, he swore he would be revenged. One night he called her out of the gin-house, and then bade me and two or three more, strip her naked; which we did. He then made us throw her down on her face, in front of the door, and hold her whilst he flogged her – the brute – with the bullwhip, cutting great gashes of flesh out of her person, at every blow, from five to six inches long. The poor unfortunate girl screamed most awfully all the time, and writhed under our strong arms, rendering it necessary for us to use our united strength to hold her down. He flogged her for half an hour, until he nearly killed her, and then left her to crawl away to her cabin.[23]

Such incidents are common in the slave reminiscences of the period. They are obviously the result of the extreme power possessed by the masters, and also of the sadistic sexual component which may be more readily found in racial groups with excessive sexual pudeur such as the Anglo-Saxon. (The reputation of the Englishman in nineteenth-century European brothels was that of the extreme pervert.[24]) It did not require an overtly sexual context for sadism to be expressed:

> On the estate I am speaking of, those women who had sucking children suffered much from their breasts becoming full of milk, the infants being left at home; they therefore could not keep up with the other hands: I have seen the overseer beat them with raw-hide, so that the blood and milk flew mingled from their breasts. A woman who gives offence in the field, and is large in the family way, is compelled to lie down over a hole made to receive her corpulency, and is flogged with the whip, or beat with a paddle, which had holes in it; at every stroke that labour was brought on, and the child was born in the field. This very overseer, Mr Brooks, killed in this manner a girl named Mary: her father and mother were in the field at the time ...[25]

Clearly the whole context of slavery fostered the expression of cruelty much as war does.

The fact that many slave-women were willing to risk extreme punishment rather than submit to the sexual demands of their masters, and even to suffer rape, destroys the myth of the natural libidinousness of black women. This is an Anglo-Saxon myth applying to both male and female

Negroes, and which is still current in the United States. Apart from mutual attraction, which we discuss below, what motivated the black woman to engage in sexual relations with whites on the plantation? Fear undoubtedly was a factor. Some women must have been too fearful to resist the advances made to them. Others, although such action was opposed to their own feelings, would submit in the hope of attaining freedom, or privileges.[26] Those of a strong religious character, or those inspired by regard for their slave-mates, formed the category of the raped and maltreated.

The 'husband' of a slave who became the target of the master's attentions was in a position of extraordinary difficulty. If he allowed what might be called his natural feelings to prevail and reacted violently his punishment might be unendurable. If on the other hand he accepted the situation, his stature as a man was greatly diminished. In the latter case the psychological damage to his personality might be irreparable. It could be suggested that contemporary black sexual relations are still informed by the memory of such behaviour. There is considerable evidence of both compliance and defiance on the part of black 'husbands'.[27]

The position of the female slave employed in the plantation house can be likened in some respects to that of the female domestic servant in a middle-class household in mid-nineteenth-century Britain. From a sexual point of view both were at risk. To refuse the advances of the master meant whipping for the one, and dismissal for the other. But in both cases there was the possibility of genuine attraction for the master, and vice versa. One of the paradoxes of the whole complex of this type of miscegenation was that despite the torrent of public invective directed against intermixture there were many white men who entered into enduring unions, the basis of which was mutual attraction, with slave-women.[28]

The practical implications of the bonds of affection and sentiment which developed between master and concubine were that he was concerned for her freedom and that of his mulatto children. Freedom was associated with having a competence to live in terms of property. The incidence of concubinage is in part indicated by the very large number of cases which came before the courts in which the bequests made by a slave-owner to his concubine and children in his will are disputed by his legitimate white family. The pattern was for the master to instruct his executors to sell part of his property and make provision for his illicit coloured family in a slave-free State. Public reaction to such behaviour was violent in its condemnation. Reaction of the family concerned was even more so – both their pride and their pockets were affected.

A South Carolina case of 1856 illustrates the lengths to which the enraged white family would go in order to defeat such bequests:

> Elijah Willis, by will, dated 1854, bequeathed Amy [his slave mistress], her seven children [some of whom were his own], and their descendants to his executors, directing them 'to bring or cause such persons, and their increase, to be brought to ... Ohio, and to emancipate and set them free'. He also bequeathed and devised to his executors all the rest of his property, from the sale of which to purchase lands in one of the free states for said slaves, to stock and furnish the same, and to place said persons in possession thereof ... His heirs-at-law contended that the will was void under the act of 1841, and also 'undertook to show insanity, fraud, and undue influence, by proving ... that the deceased was often under gloomy depression of spirits – avoiding society because of his connection with Amy, by whom he had several children; that he permitted her to act as mistress of his house; to use saucy and improper language; that she was drunken, and probably unfaithful to him; and that she exercised great influence over him in reference to his domestic affairs ...'[29]

Amy appears to have acted like many ordinary wives. Courts, however, did not always uphold the plea of outraged white relatives in such cases. The judgement given in a Kentucky case of 1831 is as follows:

> The fact that the deceased evinced an inclination to marry the slave, Grace, whom he liberated, is not a stronger evidence of insanity than the practice of rearing children by slaves without marriage; a practice but too common, as we all know, from the numbers of our mulatto population. However degrading, such things are, and however repugnant to the institutions of society, and the moral law, they prove more against the taste than the intellect. *De gustibus non disputandum.* White men, who may wish to marry Negro women, or who carry on illicit intercourse with them, may, notwithstanding, possess such soundness of mind as to be capable in law, of making a valid will and testament.[30]

The court showed both acumen and discernment in indicating the inherent hypocrisy of white society with regard to its sexual behaviour.

Some writers have suggested that it was the more uneducated and debased of the whites who sought sexual intimacy with black women. For example, R. B. Flanders states concerning Georgia: '... An absolute master [the overseer] on a plantation the owner of which was far removed, and having full control over the bodies of the female slaves, it would be rather difficult for an ignorant, intemperate, and morally weak individual not to take advantage of his position. *Even* [my italics] owners themselves were subject to liaisons with attractive mulatto slaves.'[31] Undoubtedly such men had easy access to slave-girls, but that they constituted the major part of their abusers cannot be maintained. The evidence is entirely the other way – that the plantation owner himself and his male kindred were far more prominent in the promotion of miscegenation. Numerous cases before the courts support this view.[32] It is of course evident in the initial colonial period, both in the North and the South, that there was a large dimension of liaisons between white indentured servants and black people, as we have shown in other chapters. But the total absolution of the planter class from this activity given by J. H. Russell in *The Free Negro in Virginia* (Baltimore 1913) would appear to be unwarranted. He writes: 'Illegal marriages and associations of whites with free Negroes was so disreputable and disgraceful that they were entered into by the vilest white persons at the price of chastisement by privately organized bands of white persons supported by community sentiment ...'[33] If this was really the case then the restraint of the Virginian planter, compared with his fellows elsewhere in the South, would seem to have been of heroic proportions.

The real situation is reflected in the socio-sexual life in many of the great cities of the South in the middle of the nineteenth century. The peak of miscegenation was probably reached in New Orleans. It is here that the female of mixed blood – mulatto, quadroon, octoroon – really comes into her own. Frederick Olmstead, that acute Northern observer, has left us a vivid picture of conditions in that city:

> I refer to a class composed of the illegitimate offspring of white men and coloured women (mulattoes or quadroons), who, from habits of early life, the advantage of education, and the use of wealth, are too much superior to the negroes, in general to associate with them, and are not allowed by law, or the popular prejudice, to marry white people. The girls are frequently sent to Paris to be educated, and are very accomplished. They are generally pretty, and often handsome. I have rarely, if ever, met more beautiful women, than one or two of them, that I saw by chance, in the streets. They are much better formed, and have a much more graceful and elegant carriage than in Americans in general, while they seem to have commonly inherited or acquired much of the taste and skill, in the selection and arrangement, and the way of wearing dresses and ornaments, that is the especial distinction of the women of Paris. Their beauty and attractiveness being their fortune, they cultivate and cherish with diligence every charm and accomplishment they are possessed of.
>
> Of course, men are attracted by them, associate with them, are captivated, and become attached to them, and, not being able to marry them legally, and with the usual forms and securities for constancy, make such arrangements 'as can be agreed upon'.

According to Olmstead to form such a liaison the white suitor would approach the mother of the girl formally, and would have to make arrangements with her that she regarded as suitable for her daughter. Given security that he would guarantee to support the girl in a proper manner, that she should have a sum for future support, and adequate money for children, the matter was allowed to proceed:

> The wealth, thus secure, will, of course, vary – as in society with higher assumptions of morality – with the value of the lady on the market; that is, with her attractiveness, and the number and value of other suitors she may have, or may reasonably expect. Of course, I do not mean that love has nothing at all to do with it; but love is sedulously restrained, and held firmly in hand, until the road of competency is seen to be clear, with less humbug than our English custom requires about it. Everything being satisfactorily arranged, a tenement in a certain quarter of the town is usually hired, and the couple move into it and go to housekeeping – living as if they were married. The woman is not, of course, to be wholly deprived of the society of others – her former acquaintances are continued, and she sustains her relations as daughter, sister, and friend. Of course, too, her husband (she calls him so – why shouldn't she?) will be likely to continue, also, more or less in, and form part of, this kind of society. There are parties and balls – *bals masqués* – and all the movements and customs of other fashionable society, which they can enjoy in it, if they wish. The women of this sort are represented to be exceedingly affectionate in disposition, and constant beyond reproach.
>
> During all the time a man sustains this relation, he will commonly be moving, also, in reputable society on the other side of town; not improbably he marries, and has a family establishment elsewhere. Before doing this he may separate from his *placée* (so she is termed). If so, he pays her according to agreement, and as much more, perhaps, as his affection for her, or his sense of the cruelty of the proceeding, may lead him to; and she has the world before her again, in the position of a widow. Many men continue for a long time, to support both establishments – particularly, if their legal marriage is one *de convenance.* But many others form so strong attachments, that the relationship is never discontinued, but becomes, indeed, that of marriage, except that it is not legalized or solemnized. These men leave their estate, at death, to their children, to whom they may previously have given every advantage of education they could command. What becomes of the boys, I am not informed; the girls, sometimes, are removed to other countries, where

their color does not prevent their leading reputable lives; but, of course, mainly in the same society and are fated to a life similar to that of their mothers ...[34]

Clearly one is a long way away from the degenerate overseer and the raping of slave-girls. New Orleans in the mid-nineteenth century with regard to sexual relationships between Negro and white was probably the most civilized part of the South.

There are a number of points to comment on in Olmstead's description. He brings out very clearly the apparent superiority of the mulatto over the black. There is little doubt that the free mulatto probably had distinct advantages of education and background as compared with the free Negro. In terms of the system of concubinage which existed this was inevitable. Sentiment and affection would impel a white father to educate his mulatto children. The significance of France in this connection is important. It is true to say that the French in North America had an infinitely better record in race relations than the Anglo-Saxon. This in fact was not difficult of achievement considering the latter's history of prejudice and discrimination. There was still a considerable bias towards France and things French in New Orleans in the 1850s. This comes out in the use of the term *placée*, which the French also left as a legacy in Haiti, and the whole institutionalization of the complex of man and mistress, which is so typical of metropolitan France.

Olmstead praises the appearance and good looks of the mulatto women. This would seem to rebut the ancient racist arguments of the South that the intermingling of the races produced a spurious, degenerate issue. Perhaps the most important point made by the writer is that concerning the existence of a coloured or mixed 'society' in which both white men and their mistresses were able to participate. Such a 'society' existed in parallel with the main white society. This manifestation occurred at the same period in other Southern towns, such as Charleston. The creation of coloured 'societies' as distinct from black in the North and Mid-West did not have the essential feature of the Louisiana model – a meeting ground for mulatto and white. The latter came into being in order to fulfil the need of a social milieu for inter-racial sexual and domestic relationships. It can be said that if this partial process of amalgamation in New Orleans had been carried out elsewhere in the United States the racial problem would not have assumed the proportions it has today. The French settlers in Louisiana did not have the advantage of an Old Testament religious upbringing as did their fellows in Virginia.

In 1609 a sermon was delivered to the planters of Virginia based on Genesis xii, 1–3:

> Abrams' posteritie [must] keepe to themselves. They may not marry nor give in marriage to the heathen, that are uncircumcized ... The breaking of this rule, may breake the necke of all good successe of this voyage, whereas by keeping the feare of God, the planters in shorte time, by the blessing of God, may grow into a nation formidable to all the enemies of Christ ...[35]

It was adherence to tenets such as these which formed the basis for so much of the racist attitudes of the South.

Above, we suggested that there was a parallel between the black female slave in the South with relation to sexual behaviour and that of the mid-nineteenth-century domestic servant in Britain. The parallel can be taken further. A considerable dimension of illicit white–black sexual relations was concerned with adolescent activity. The young sons of the master would seek out encounters with attractive slave-girls. In the same way the son of the house in Britain would attempt to seduce his father's servant-girls. For both groups of adolescents it was a method of sexual induction at hand. The psychological effects of this in the case of the South are considerable. The fact that the primary sexual experience was with a black woman must have a profound effect on subsequent such experiences. Must, indeed, have influenced their attitudes and behaviour towards women as a whole. It is a pattern which is repeated under Brazilian slavery.[36]

The sexual abuse of the slave, which was so characteristic of the South, appears to be part of a much wider pattern of socio-sexual relationships. It can be put in this way – wherever there are relationships of superiority/inferiority there is always the possibility of the superior group sexually exploiting the inferior. There are large numbers of examples apart from the two quoted – female promotion in the contemporary Western World in many instances depends on the willingness of the individual to make herself sexually accessible to her boss or superior. In such cases there is an element of choice, the woman can refuse. There was hardly such an alternative available to the slave.

The impression has sometimes been given that, apart from the heyday of the white indentured servant, the responsibility for black-white miscegenation is very largely that of the white man. The passionate gyneolatry of the Ante-Bellum South has obscured the fact that white women of the planter caste, and others of a lesser status, made a considerable contribution to the pattern of intermixture. Such women appear to have been just as susceptible to the sexual attractions of the Negro as their husbands. A review of Virginian divorce cases for the period 1800–1850 substantiates this view.

Petition after petition presented to the Virginia Legislature contains information of the following kind:

> ... That on the 11th day of May, while your petitioner was absent from home on business, his wife was delivered of a child, which on your petitioner's return and to his inexpressible grief and astonishment [*sic*] proved to be a mulatto, and which she shortly after confessed was the child of a negro slave ... Your petitioner further begs leave to state that from the time of the above mentioned distressing event his affections have been totally alienated from the said Lydia, and he has resolved never to cohabit with or acknowledge her as his lawful wife ...[37]

For a Southern gentleman to discover that his wife had cuckolded him with a Negro was indeed too much to bear. He could only take refuge in 'astonishment'. The usual double standard of sexual morals prevailed – for a man to have a Negro paramour was merely a sign of weakness, for a woman to act in a similar fashion was unspeakably heinous.

Before their fall from grace white women are always of unspotted character:

> ... he intermarried with a certain Elizabeth ———, a woman descended from honest and industrious parents, and of unspotted character so far as your petitioner heard, or had any reason to believe. Your petitioner lived with the said Elizabeth, with all the affection and tenderness that could possibly exist between husband and wife, for about four months, when to the great astonishment and inexpressible mortification of your petitioner, the said Elizabeth was delivered of a mulatto child, and is now so bold as to say it was begotten by a Negro man slave in the neighbourhood ...[38]

That his wife after months of marriage could actually have *preferred* to have had sexual intercourse with a Negro was obviously too terrible a thing to bear thinking about.

Sometimes there were obvious flaws of character in the wife – she may have wanted things from her husband he could not give her, a situation not entirely unknown in our day:

> ... that your petitioner and the said Elizabeth continued to live together in the strictest love, friendship, and happiness, about three years after their marriage. But at length your petitioner discovered with most heartfelt grief and sorrow, that his said wife Elizabeth was of a lewd, incontinent, profligate disposition and practice. But being so much attached to her person, having from his first acquaintance with her cherished the most ardent, tender affection, love and regard for her ...

admonished her repeatedly of the wickedness of such a course, and of the infamy and disgrace which must result from it, and that if persisted in a separation would take place. But alas! All this produced a contrary effect and your petitioner discovered at two different times her and the partner of her crime (a certain James Watts) a man of colour in bed together. He resolved to leave her ... determined never more to have any connection with a woman who so basely disgraced herself and dishonored her husband ...[39]

It is difficult to tell if the unfortunate woman only became profligate because of her discovered liaison with a man of colour, or was naturally promiscuous. From the husband's point of view the latter was clearly infinitely preferable.

A more naïve approach is detected in the following:

... But your petitioner not being willing to lend too favorable an ear to reports prevalent in the neighborhood, determined to see for himself and it is now with painful recollection that he states, that on his return home, at a late hour of the night, on entering his house he found the said Elizabeth, undressed, and in bed with a certain Aldrige Evans, a man of color ...[40]

But it was not only married women who were guilty of what was publicly held to be infamous conduct. The code of the South refused to recognize that a white woman could give herself freely, through desire, to a black man. Sexual intercourse could only be an act of rape. Some sixty cases of this kind came before the Virginian courts in the period 1789 to 1833. In no less than twenty-seven of these, after conviction but before sentence by the governor, representations were made by members of the community on behalf of the condemned Negro.[41] These were concerned to point out that the white women in question were of dubious character, and clearly had encouraged the Negro, if not seduced him. The following is a typical example:

... he [a Negro] was condemned on a charge of having ravished a woman named Sands. I am of the opinion, and several others amongst whom were some of the members of the court that sat upon his trial, that he should be transported rather than executed. The woman I learn from a variety of sources is under a very infamous character. She has lived as a concubine for some time past with a man named Vaughan, in whose house this Negro I am informed was as intimate as any white man. The woman appears large and strong enough to have made considerable resistance if she had been so disposed, yet there was by her own confession no mark of violence upon any part of her.[42]

It could well have been that attractive Negroes were at risk from such white women.

Some writers in the nineteenth century commenting on the situation in the South remark on the rarity of the *mésalliance* of white women and black men:

> ... although many white men have a wonderful inclination for black women, I could never learn but of one instance where a white woman was captivated by a Negro, and this was said to have been in Virginia; a planter's daughter having fallen in love with one of her father's slaves, had actually seduced him; the result of the amour was the sudden mysterious disappearance of the young lady ...[43]

But the weight of evidence is very much on the other side. Outspoken local critics, such as John Rankin in Kentucky, could write: 'Were it necessary I could refer you to several instances of slaves actually seducing the daughters of their masters. Such seductions sometimes happened in the most respectable families ...'[44] Even more compelling is the evidence from census returns. In one county of Virginia, Nansemond, in the return of 1830, a number of Negroes are listed as having white wives.[45] Again, there are numerous references in the Archives of States in the South to the sexual alliances of white women and Negro slaves or freemen.

> ... Sir: A Negro slave called Ben has lately been apprehended and brought before me. It appears that he has come into the state contrary to the act of the Assembly concerning slaves, free Negroes and mulattoes. A white woman who was with the fellow late at night claims him as her property. She declares that it was her design to emancipate and fix him here, that she then intended to return herself to North Carolina, from whence she came. It is the opinion of those who apprehended them that improper connection exists between them ...[46]

Our point here is that although Negro-white miscegenation was basically promoted by the action of white men in relation to black women, a far larger dimension than is popularly believed of white women were involved in this process. The notion of white womanhood beloved by Southerners was such that they were compelled to attribute such cases as could not be concealed to weakness and depravity. They could not accept that their own womenfolk could be moved by the same passions as themselves – the real and imagined sexuality of that which was black. So convinced were the planters of the imperviousness of their wives to male black charms that it was common for Negro boys to wait at table half-naked so that their sexual organs were fully visible.[47] May be such obtuse indelicacy was necessary for the perpetuation of the myth of white female chastity – the virgin-wife.

The most brilliant and perceptive analysis of the white woman in the South has been given by W. J. Cash in his *The Mind of the South* (NY 1941). But there are certain contradictions which continue to baffle the student. The establishment of slavery as an institution demanded certain imperatives in terms of rationalization for those who perpetuated the system. These were largely concerned with the inherent inferiority of the Negro, and his bestial habits. The converse of this was the ever-present fear that the Negro would revolt, and thus destroy the edifice of exploitation. To mark the essential inferiority of the black man it was necessary to deny him *all* natural rights as a man. This is symbolized by confronting him with the ironclad inaccessibility of the white woman. The sexual act between a man and a woman can be the most profound sharing of what it is to be human. If a whole category of persons is denied sexually to an individual this serves to emphasize his inferiority to her caste.

It is not as if the Southern woman lived in purdah, removed from the sight of the Negro. As a slave the Negro was involved in the domestic arrangements of the planter's household. His wife or female relative was the wet-nurse, the black mentor of the slave-master's children. Subject to the sight and sound of sexual titillation of white women the Negro was also more than aware that his own womenfolk were subject to the sexual abuse of his master. It was a situation of consummate degradation. To act otherwise than to accept invoked the terrible sanctions of castration, death or transportation. The Southern woman was fully conscious of her inimitable situation. And it gave rise to the most extraordinary sexual fantasies.

The notion of rape – the forcible overcoming of the denial – was the pivot of many fantasies. The basis of reality was small. In Virginia, for example, as we quoted above, sixty alleged cases came before the courts in a forty-four-year period from 1789 to 1833. In more than twenty-seven of these there was more than an element of doubt. The reality of statistics did not inhibit the fantasizing. The white imagination dwelt more easily on the apparent promiscuity of the Negro among his own kind.

The possibility of rape was no doubt connected with the unashamed view that both white men and women had of the Negro's genitalia while he waited at table, as we noted above. 'I am surprized this does not hurt the feelings of this fair Sex to see these young boys of about Fourteen and Fifteen years Old to Attend them, this whole nakedness Expos'd and I can Assure you it would Surprize a person these d——d black boys how well they are hung.'[48] It should be remembered, however, that Southern women did not possess a monopoly of fantasies concerning rape – their descendants today, as well as women from elsewhere in the United States, indulge in them, and indeed invite the act, on vacation on Caribbean and European beaches. The same phenomenon has been observed in connection with contemporary Englishwomen on holiday in Europe. The sexually dangerous is connected with differences in appearance, language and culture – sexual fantasies about black immigrants in Britain are common. It is possible that such erotic myth-making is characteristic of Anglo-Saxons who, until recently, enjoyed a high degree of sexual repression.

Connected with these ideas in the South were other myths concerning the size of the Negro penis, and the corollary that this connoted exceptional virility. The latter – the equation of size and virility – is a common belief amongst all European peoples. Recent research by Masters and Johnson would appear to demonstrate that there is no correlation between size of genitalia and sexual performance.[49] The myth of size itself is another matter. Here is what appears to be essentially debatable ground. From the earliest contacts that the European had with the African this impression of the inordinate size of the Negro penis appeared. Fifteenth-century maps depict figures extremely 'well hung'.[50] By the eighteenth century the notion was firmly implanted in the contemporary scientific and literary mind. The latter would no doubt in time have affected the thinking of the ordinary man. An outstanding example of scientific support for this thesis is to be found in the work of the German anthropologist Johann Blumenbach:

> It is generally said that the penis in the Negro is very large. And this assertion is so far borne out by the remarkable genitory apparatus of an Ethiopian which I have in my anatomical collection. Whether this prerogative be constant and peculiar to the nation I do not know. It is said that women when eager for venery prefer the embraces of Negroes to those of other men. On the other hand, that Ethiopian and Mulatto women are particularly sought out by Europeans. The cause of this preference may be various, but I do not know what it is.[51]

Lieutenant Feltman, whom we quoted above regarding half-naked Negro boys waiting at table, might very well have agreed with Blumenbach.

The latter did not have the advantage of some nineteenth-century anthropologists, that is of direct observation. One such could write:

> It was amongst the Malinkés of Kita [West Africa] that I found the most developed penis, and notably one of the maximum dimensions, being nearly twelve inches in length, by a diameter exceeding two and two-fifths inches. This was a terrific machine, and except for a slight difference in length, was more like the yard of a donkey than that of a man.[52]

The persistence of this myth into our own time is remarkable. John Dollard, the anthropologist, who did field-work in the South in the thirties wrote:

> There is a widespread belief that the genitalia of Negro males are larger than those of whites; this was repeatedly stated by white informants. One planter, for example, said he had had visual opportunity to confirm the fact; he had gone to one of his cabins, and on entering without warning, found a Negro man preparing for intercourse. Informant expressed surprise at the size of the penis and gave an indication, by his arm and clenched fist, of its great length and diameter. It was further said that this impression was confirmed at the time of the draft examination at the Southerntown Courthouse in 1917.[53]

Dollard also quotes Geoffrey Gorer, the English anthropologist, to the effect that in his observations in West Africa he was not aware of any disproportion between African and European male genitalia. My own observations amongst the coloured population in the Caribbean would confirm this.[54] More recently, it is quite apparent that contemporary pornographic books tend to emphasize the great size of the Negro penis as the symbol of outstanding virility.

There have been relatively few properly scientific studies of a comparative kind concerning white and black male genitalia. On the whole they have indicated that there is a disproportion in favour of the Negro.[55] I feel that considerably more research would have to be conducted amongst both American and African black populations to determine whether there is a true basis of fact for the extremely widespread mythology which has been built up in this connection.

We have devoted some attention to this aspect as it can be regarded as central to the conception of the Southern white woman, and her attitudes and behaviour. The matter can be summed up in this way. Whether or not there was biological confirmation of these fantasies there was psychological confirmation. The white Southerner, male or female, saw what he or she wanted to see, and believed what they wanted to believe. The result, for the male, entrenched his woman as the centre of a religion of gyneolatry. She might be adulated publicly – 'Woman!!! The centre and circumference, diameter and periphery, sine, tangent and secant of all our affections!' – in geometrical or trigonometrical terms, but what was the reality of this worship?

For the reality we have to turn to what was frequently her common circumstance. An extreme example from Virginia illustrates how public adulation could turn to everyday humiliation:

> The Negro woman named Milly of whom the said husband became possessed by intermarrying with your petitioner, the said husband was criminally, unlawfully, and carnally intimate with, and kept her the said Milly, from the time your petitioner first married him until she was from necessity compelled to leave him ... he the said ———, from his own confession not only in the presence of those affiants, but also in the presence of his said wife Ellen, had repeated carnal knowledge of the said Negro woman Milly, and moreover acknowledged that he perpetrated that diabolical act against which every generous and virtuous principle of the human soul revolts, he took her in his own wife's bed and there carried out his licentious designs, and those affiants further sayth, that the said Negro woman has since been delivered of a mulatto child.[56]

It seems clear that the husband in question delighted in causing this kind of humiliation to his wife. Yet in all probability, publicly, he would have upheld the honour and virtue of white women as the sacred symbol of the South.

Sometimes the petitioner is so carried away by the awful circumstances of a black woman supplanting her that the affectation of language characteristic of early nineteenth-century funerary monuments is used to address the legislature:

> Scarce had the first few weeks of her ill-fated marriage passed, when the mark of hypocrisy in which her vile and profligate husband had too successfully hidden his real character was thrown aside, and the ardent, tender lover became the cold, senseless, hard-hearted tyrant. But had this been the only cause of complaint, she would have submitted without a single murmur to her fate, in the fond hope that an affectionate, meek, and dutiful wife would in time have conquered his indifference and restored her to love and happiness. But the cup of misery was yet undrained; she had to learn the dreadful, heart-rending truth that she possessed no place in his heart; that another had usurped her empire over him, and that other (shameless truth) his own slave ...[57]

A very sad and heartrending case. But what it brings out is the inability of the privileged white woman to understand that a mere slave-girl could be a serious rival to her. Was she not the one praised and almost worshipped by her menfolk? How could a slave, a degraded creature, a thing not a person, be a source of attraction to her husband? What escaped her understanding was that the gyneolatry she enjoyed was very much akin to that which obtained in mid-Victorian England. There the middle-class wife was the guardian of the hearth, and mother. For sexual pleasure and feminine relaxation the husband went elsewhere – depending upon his means and station – to prostitutes of different kinds. The wife considered herself a childbearing machine with no thought, or indeed idea, of sex being a pleasure for both man and wife. She, admired and respected as a wife-mother, could leave such degrading habits to the prostitute. The situation was in many ways similar in the South. The difference, however, as we have seen from the cases quoted, was that the Southern gentleman apparently lacked the sensibility of his English counterpart. The latter would almost always create a separate establishment for his mistress and rarely subject his wife to the indignity of confrontation with his whore.

Herein was the flaw in the whole Southern conception of the white woman – in creating the image of the female *sans pareil* they also succeeded in creating an asexual paragon devoid of warmth, sexuality and affection. All these were to be found in the Negro woman – the slave, the totally despised. The paradox was that white society was determined at all costs to maintain the institution of slavery. To that end the slave was denied all rights as a human being. Marriage between white and black, but particularly of white women and black men, was prohibited – marriage can be regarded as the fundamental criterion of racial and social equality between groups. To safeguard the bastion of racial purity white women were turned into virginal automata. In such a situation miscegenation was both necessary and inevitable.

CHAPTER 6

Black and White Sexuality

> ... in the core of the heart of the American race problem the sex factor is rooted; rooted so deeply that it is not always recognized when it shows at the surface. Other factors are obvious and are the ones we dare to deal with; but regardless of how we deal with these, the race situation will continue to be acute as long as the sex factor persists. Taken alone, it furnishes a sufficient mainspring for the rationalization of all the complexes of white superiority. It may be innate; I do not know. But I do know that it is strong and bitter; and that its strength and bitterness are magnified and intensified by the white man's perception, more or less, of the Negro complex of sexual superiority.[1]

In that quotation James Weldon Johnson sums up what was the position in the United States up to our own time. Johnson's view is corroborated by the extraordinary omission of the sexual factor from so much of twentieth-century literature dealing with the Negro. An outstanding example is the *Daedalus* volume on 'The Negro American', which appeared in 1965. None of the eminent contributors make any mention of this crucial area of Negro-white relationships. There are many other instances of this pudeur.[2] It is very similar to the reluctance, until comparatively recently, in Britain, to discuss openly the problem of prostitution – in his *Social History of England* G. M. Trevelyan devotes half a page to this major social problem of the nineteenth century. In the case of Negro-white sexual relationships there is no question that this is invested with guilt feelings on the part of the white stemming from his role under slavery of sexual depredator. I feel with Johnson that unless the problem is understood and discussed there can be no hope for the resolution of the general social conflict between black and white in the United States. The alternative is to become a kind of sociological ostrich, pretending that integration in the public domain is the only proper solution.

There are difficulties in the way of combating the refusal of some authorities in the field to discuss the problem. What can be made of the following statement by two eminent sociologists in terms of an appreciation of the problem?

> The nature of the race-caste line in the United States is sharply indicated by the fact that we do not allow mixed families. Intermarriage is always frowned upon, and in some states is illegal. But interbreeding occurs, with or without marriage. In all such cases the family is assigned to the Negro race. When a couple consisting of a white man and a Negro woman have children the resulting family has traditionally consisted only of the mother and children. The father was not part of it. It was necessarily a matriarchal family. If, as happens sometimes in the North, the husband is a Negro and the wife white, the wife becomes, in effect, Negro with her children. All mixed families are Negro. So strong is this rule that white women who marry Negroes are generally – if their families cannot get them declared insane, as a middle-class family will try to do – read out of their families.[3]

Throughout the book (*Where Peoples Meet*, 1952) from which the quotation was taken there is no attempt at an analysis of the situation stated, no information is given regarding the systematic debauching of Negro women by white men throughout the history of slavery and its aftermath. For the reader with slight acquaintance with the American scene such information gives the impression that the authors are stating something which is an irreversible part of the general ethos of the American people. As we have shown in another chapter, the Supreme Court has recently held that the anti-miscegenation laws of the State of Virginia offend against the Fourteenth Amendment and are thus unconstitutional. This is clearly a denial of the attitude so blandly stated above.

As we shall see, the views of the authors of *Where Peoples Meet* could have been propounded in the middle of the last century.

It has been suggested that skin colour is an important factor in mate selection amongst Negroes.[4] That is to say a majority of Negro men choose brides of a lighter colour. This was the traditional pattern as exemplified by Herskovits' researches in Harlem over thirty years ago. In his sample of marriages 56·5 per cent were composed of female spouses who were lighter than their husbands.[5] This is in fact a phenomenon observable all over the New World.[6] Why this pattern should have been established is not difficult to elucidate.

Slavery imposed a number of patterns on the enslaved African. Foremost among these was the fact that the white became the ultimate symbol of authority, became the exemplar of all that was free and powerful in life.

In addition, through the system of concubinage which grew up under which the mulatto progeny of the planter and his concubine were favoured as against the black field slave, the mulatto attained to a status inferior to that of the white but nevertheless superior to that of the black. It was by no means an empty status. All over the South communities of free coloured people came into existence. Some, as in Louisiana, formed virtually an aristocracy of *gens de couleur* who sent their children to France to be educated just as their opposite numbers did in Haiti. Others were at great pains to distinguish themselves from both freed and slave Negroes:

> The free Negroes of Charleston, who organized the Brown Fellowship Society in 1790, admitted only *brown* men. This society provided for the education of the free people of color, assisted widows and orphans, and maintained a club-house and a cemetery for its members. They identified themselves as far as possible with the interests of the white slave-holding aristocracy and did not even permit a discussion of slavery among their members. Although they were not white, they could thank God that they were not black.[7]

For the black slave, while the position of such individuals could not be equated with that of his white master, nevertheless he could see that their condition was different from his own. Thus lightness of colour was inevitably associated with the beneficial in life. His own African values were denigrated and destroyed, and in their place he acquired white values. Skin colour symbolized the whole white world.

There is considerable evidence to suggest – we have cited this in other chapters – that the process of miscegenation between black and white occurred almost from the inception of slavery in North America. From the beginning, as we have seen, there developed a whole mythology concerning the sexuality of the Negro, both male and female. This is concerned with accrediting to black people a potency and virility far exceeding that of the European. In the male Negro the myth concentrates on an exaggeration of the size of the genitals. In the female on her excessive lubricity. The Negro individual becomes a symbol of sexual freedom which is denied to the white in his society. Thus, in a manner of speaking, he is the lineal descendant of Rousseau's 'Noble Savage', the child of nature, the uncivilized one, the slave yet the liberated one. Thomas Jefferson in his *Notes on Virginia* wrote: 'Negroes are more ardent after their females; but love seems with them to be more an eager desire, than a delicate mixture of sentiment and sensation ...' One can almost detect a sense of regret that the same ardent quality was lacking in the European.

The myth, as we have seen in other chapters, is still extraordinarily compelling. Its foundation may be in the much more open approach to sex which characterizes many African peoples. Another factor is possibly that it was a rationalization for the debauchment of black women by whites – that the former's overwhelming sexuality ensnared the white man against his better nature. This is a view propounded by L. J. Ragatz with reference to the Caribbean.[8] Simultaneously with this there grew up, because of the guilt engendered by the spoliation of Negro women, the myth that black men were endowed by nature with sexual organs and a virility far exceeding that of the European. Thus white women had to be protected against black rapists.

Even academics were, and are, infected by the myth. Arthur W. Calhoun, the famous historian of the American family, writes in the following manner:

> At the opening of the twentieth century, the point where the Negro American was furthest behind modern civilization was in his sexual mores. Immodesty, unbridled sexuality, obscenity, social indifference to purity were prevalent characteristics. Children of ten to twelve knew a hundred vile songs; they were sung in many homes without thought of impropriety. Masturbation was common among the children of both sexes, and intercourse was begun shortly after or even before puberty.[9]

A tremendous indictment after 300 years of slavery and the systematic sexual degradation inflicted by the white slave-master.

The mythology not only became embedded in white social mores but it affected the thinking of black people as well. Thus William Hannibal Thomas, a Negro author, was able to write at the turn of the century:

> But, while the Negro is thoroughly imbruted with lascivious instincts, there are many contributory causes, which accelerate libidinous acts. For instance, the practice of masturbation is common among children of both sexes, and the physical desire awakened and stimulated by organic manipulation inevitably leads to sexual intercourse. It is, therefore, almost impossible to find a person of either sex, over fifteen years of age, who has not had actual carnal knowledge. But not only do the young Negro girls who grow up in idleness become prematurely old in viciousness, but even those better reared are amazingly yielding to licentious overtures ... such girls are not easily deterred from following their inclinations ... Innate modesty is not a characteristic of the American negro woman. On the contrary, there is observable among them a willing susceptibility to the blandishments of licentious men.[10]

Thomas' book, *The American Negro*, was published in New York in 1901. It belongs to the same genre as the work of anti-semitic Jews – there is a conscious endeavour not only to seek out and exaggerate the weaknesses of his own people less than forty years after emancipation, but also a complete acceptance of the inherent superiority of the white. His strictures on the sexual nature of the Negro could have been written by any literate, myth-driven, white Southerner.

A point to note is that both at the time Thomas was writing and at the present time, there were, and are *white* communities in remote parts of the United States, such as the Appalachians, which exhibit characteristics closely resembling those imputed to the Negro. The novels of Erskine Caldwell, such as *Tobacco Road*, describe this type of community.

Even if we accept that there is evidence to suggest that Negro genitalia are in fact larger than those of the European – we have cited this evidence in other chapters – the myth suffers from a further fallacy. This is the correlation between size of penis and sexual performance. This is an age-long belief which has no scientific basis. It is interesting to note that in the American pornography of the seventies the Negro no longer appears as a kind of despised sexual machine but is admitted as an equal with his white counterparts, and also that a white woman having sexual intercourse with a Negro is accepted as being normal. But in the pornography – a new assertion of the myth – his genitalia are always of tremendous size. The following is taken from Harold Horton's *Swappin With the Honkies* (California, 1970). A white woman is describing her black neighbour:

> ... But when she saw it, she almost stopped breathing. When he dropped his shorts, he revealed the biggest *donkey* [penis] on record. At least, on her record! What he had hanging between his legs would have made two or more of what Jerry [her husband] had. It was certainly nothing she could laugh off, although her voice came up in a kind of warm, bubbling gasp of awe.

It could possibly be interpreted as an index of improving race relations in the United States that pornography has now given its imprimatur to inter-racial sex.

Masters and Johnson in their pioneering study, *Human Sexual Response*, refute this ancient belief of a correlation between size and performance:

> Another widely accepted 'phallic fallacy' is the concept that the larger the penis the more effective the male as a partner in coital connection. The size of the male organ both in flaccid and erect state has been presumed by many cultures to reflect directly the sexual prowess of

> the individual male ... The delusion that penile size is related to sexual adequacy has been founded in turn upon yet another phallic misconception. It has been presumed that full erection of the larger penis provides a significantly greater penile size increase than does erection of the smaller penis. This premise has been refuted by a small group of men selected from the study-subject population for clinical evaluation.[11]

The establishment of the fact that fallacies are inherent in a myth does little or nothing to affect its efficacy. Notwithstanding scientific evidence people will continue to believe that the black man's penis is larger, and thus his sexual performance greater, than his white counterpart. The behaviour of American and Canadian female tourists in the Caribbean provides ample proof of this contention.

So far we have been considering the sexuality, real or imagined, of the black man from a white point of view. When the Negro woman is considered the myth does not represent her as having physical characteristics which are necessarily more sexually stimulating than those of the white woman. Her endowment from the myth is a capacity for sexual response far greater than her Caucasian sister. Combined with this is her ability to allure the unfortunate white man, even against his will, into the paths of concupiscence. In fact no white man is safe from her devastating wiles. The archetypal Negro woman bears a resemblance to Circe – in satisfying the white males' appetites she turns them into swine. In a more practical way she occupies very much the same position in relation to the white man as that of the prostitute in England occupied in relation to Victorian middle- and upper-class males – a font of sexuality and release not to be found in the bosom of the family.

The following quotations from Calhoun's *Social History of the American Family* bear out the contention that the unfortunate white man was at the mercy of that embodiment of sexuality – the black or coloured woman: 'The heaviest part of the white racial burden [in slavery] was the African woman, of strong sex instincts and devoid of sexual conscience at the white man's door, in the white man's dwelling.' 'Under the institution of slavery, the attack against the integrity of white civilization was made by the insidious influence of the lascivious hybrid woman at the point of weakest resistance. In the uncompromising opposition of the white mother and wife of the upper classes lay the one assurance of the future purity of the race.' '... There are many pure and virtuous men in the South, who are, and who have been so, even from their childhood; but ... they labour under a temptation greater than persons who occupy the same social position in the free states. It is admitted, by truthful men in the

South, that slavery is a source of unbounded licentiousness ... It is with pain that I express the conviction that one of the reasons why wicked men in the South uphold slavery is the facility which it affords for a licentious life.'[12]

The last quotation suggests that it may not have been entirely the fault of the lubricious black woman that white men were ensnared – they may also have desired ensnarement. There is little doubt, as we pointed out in the chapter on the South, that there were innumerable cases where extreme coercion was used by the master to force a slave-woman into his bed. To suggest that the black woman's charms were so irresistible that no man could stand against them is merely another rationalization for a situation in which the white male was the guilty exploiter and debaucher of the Negro woman.

Frank Harris, that astute and clever Irishman, fell a victim to the myth when he was a young man. He encounters a coloured girl, Sophy. He writes of her in the following way:

> As I touched her sex, she wound her arms round my neck and kissed me greedily with hot lips. To my astonishment her sex was well formed and very small: I had always heard that Negroes had far larger genitals than white people; but the lips of Sophy's sex were thick and firm ... Sophy was the pearl of all the girls I met in this first stage of my development and I only wish I could convey to the reader a suggestion of her quaint and enthralling caresses. My admiration of Sophy cleansed me of any possible disdain I might otherwise have had of the Negro people, and I am glad of it ...[13]

Unfortunately white manhood in the United States does not appear to have followed Frank Harris' example – it certainly seeks such encounters, as we have seen, but they do little to diminish white disdain of Negro people.

In the contemporary world the myth of black sexuality still persists. It has been given many interpretations which confuse the reality of Negro sexual behaviour. One fact, however, does stand out. The constraints imposed upon the black male by the white society in which he lives have affected his attitude towards his own sexuality:

> ... yes, he was a good lover. But I think he was good because I was white and he had to prove to me that he was better than any white man. This was an added stimulus to his love making, I think. And, too, the very fact that I'm white and sort of forbidden works on a black man psychologically and excites him more sexually than he might be with a black girl. It doesn't matter how many white girls a black man has slept

with, he still finds that white skin super-exciting and he has to prove that he's better in bed than a white man. Sometimes he tries so hard to give the girl a good time that he cheats himself.[14]

The above quotation gives an insight into one of the components of what might be termed the black erotic ethos. In one sense the individual is trying to fulfil the myth both for the white woman's satisfaction and his own. There is a certain subtlety in this. It is not the case however in experiences which appear to be far commoner:

I got to admit I was too busy wondering if I'd live up to *her* fantasies about black men ... We saw each other for a couple of months and she told me about the fantasies, how she believed all the myths about black men being sexual savages who could rape a woman and make her love it. And how a black man – any black man – could make love longer and better than any white man. And of course she was surprised that my penis was no different than a white man's, except it was darker. She told me she'd expected a black man's penis to be enormous, maybe bigger than she could take.[15]

In a study by two white psychiatrists, first published in 1951, the myth of black virility is put firmly in its place:

The most surprising fact about the sex life of the Negro – of all classes – lies in its marked deviation from the white stereotypes that exist on the subject. The Negro is hardly the abandon-sexual hedonist he is supposed to be. Quite the contrary, sex often seems relatively unimportant to him ... Masculinity is closely tied to power in every form in our society. The male is the much the more vulnerable to socioeconomic failure. He unconsciously interprets it as a loss in masculinity, i.e. as femininity. The inability to function successfully in the male sexual role can be one of the outcomes of this interpretation ...[16]

Such findings relate back to a number of sociological studies which demonstrated the instability of Negro families in the United States, and the much larger number of black families than white in which the woman was the head of the household.[17] For example, in 1962 8·6 per cent of white families had female heads as against 23·2 per cent of black families. Such figures can be related to the fact that black unemployment in the USA in the last ten years has been almost twice that of whites.[18] Such information provides the background for the statement quoted above by Kardiner and Ovesey concerning the sense of inadequacy felt by the Negro male. This is further corroborated in a paper by Elizabeth Herzog:

> ... the man who cannot command a stable job at adequate wages cannot be an adequate family provider; the man who cannot provide for his family is likely to lose status and respect in his own eyes and in the eyes of others – including his family ... A male head of house who is not a breadwinner and provider is a hazard to the happiness of the marriage, and his loss of economic status is so great a hazard to his intrafamily status that he may decamp either to protect his own ego or to make his family eligible for support from AFDC [welfare].[19]

So far the sources we have quoted have been white -- the Negro Problem has been a major segment of sociological studies in the United States. Increasingly, however, black academics and journalists have been expressing their views with regard to the Negro personality. Their concern has been with the reality of the situation, and with the duality of the white myths regarding black sexuality. The latter, as we have seen, fantasize about virility but also, paradoxically, deny masculinity to the male. The official thesis has been that in female-dominated households male children will inevitably suffer from inadequate teaching of male roles. Subsequently in adult life they feel castrated and feminine.

This thesis has been disputed by a number of black scholars. For example, Robert Staples, a sociologist at Howard University, in a paper entitled *The Myth of the Impotent Black Male*, rebuts many of the arguments which are ordinarily advanced in its favour. His main contention is that white standards are not necessarily the appropriate criteria by which to assess black behaviour. For example it is wrong to assume that in households in which the father-husband is absent there will be no adult males present – the contrary is generally the case. In Staples' view the perpetuation of the myth of the castrated black male is not only sexual in its implications but also has political connotations – to reinforce the image of the politically impotent Negro.[20]

Staples also elaborates a theory about black sexuality as opposed to white which helps to explain the stereotype of Negro virility held by many white women:

> In a concrete sense, this means that black men do not moderate their enthusiasm for sex relations as white men do ... The difference between black men and white men in sexual responses may be explained by realizing that for white men sex has to be fitted into time not devoted to building the technological society, whereas for black men it is a natural function, a way of life.[21]

That this is possibly the case is borne out by clinical evidence concerning white America. The stress of urban living causes sexual inhibition. To counter this the last decade has seen the development of movements, such as those based on the psychiatrist Alexander Lowen's theories, concerned with the rediscovery of touch and the body.[22]

As might be expected, there is no general consensus of black opinion with regard to the nature of the Negro personality. Professor Clemmong Vontress of George Washington University, in a paper *The Black Male Personality*, expressed views which caused Staples, whom we cited above, to accuse him of 'slander of the black population'. The paper in question posits a number of components which make up the black personality, among them self-hatred. It was mainly this concept which generated Staple's criticism of a fellow black academic:

> As products of a racist society, we have acquired the same cultural attributes as have whites. Included among these are anti-black sentiments. This helps to account for the desperate attempt to approximate the looks and behaviour of whites. The destructive in-fighting among blacks can also be explained in terms of self-rejection ...'[23]

Vontress goes on to examine the genesis of this phenomenon, and in so doing indicates what he regards as the core of the matter:

> In this country, the white man has been obsessed with black sex. He has possessed black women because he perceived them to be more libidinous than his own ... Having created the myth about the black man's sexual greatness, he then proceeded to punish him for his own figment of the imagination. Thus, it seems clear that the white man's sexual jealousy of the black man is at the heart of the race problem in this country ... Since white hatred for black people, especially black men, is sexually based, and usually unconscious, it is apt to remain intact and become more intense, especially now when black men are moving about in the open with white women hanging onto their arms.[24]

Vontress adduces considerable evidence to support his thesis. Staples, however, maintains that the analysis given merely serves the purpose of further denigrating black people in the eyes of whites. In our view Vontress' paper bears out our contention that the sexual component is the core of black-white relationships in the United States.

Despite concealment, avoidance, and the pudeur born of the whole circumstance of the Negro in the United States, there were individuals who in their writings openly admitted the significance of the sexual factor in race relations. W. E. B. Du Bois in his *Darkwater*, first published at the beginning of this century, wrote of the degradation of black women by white men:

> I shall forgive the South much in its final judgement day: I shall forgive its slavery, for slavery is a world-old habit ... I shall forgive its so-called

'pride of race' ... but one thing I shall never forgive, neither in this world nor the world to come: its wanton and continued and persistent insulting of the black womanhood which it sought and seeks to prostitute to its lust ...[25]

Although black people in the USA have taken tremendous steps in the last twenty years towards the creation of a new self-respect and pride in race, the process in terms of the relationship between the sexes is not yet complete. The historical exploitation of Negro women by the white males has had, and still has, the most profound effect on the erotic lives of black men and women in relation to each other. The role of the male is essentially ambivalent. On the one hand he is thought of by the white society which surrounds him as being the apotheosis of virility, and on the other the same white society denies him the opportunity to fulfil his ordinary male expectations as provider and father to his children. This ambivalence infuses his attitude and behaviour towards his own womenfolk. He is aware that his partner knows that his role is less than male, and at the same time he cannot feel pride in possessing her as she is rejected for her blackness as much as he is.

Clinical evidence from black psychiatrists supports such an analysis. What emerges from such evidence is that black couples are conscious of their belittlement by white society and so are devalued in their relationship to each other. There is, however, a compensatory mechanism by which their actual degradation enhances erotic feeling so that sexual pleasure is increased. The principle at work here appears to be that of turning the accusation of inferiority and animality into a positive force – the couple enjoy the fulfilling of the myth.[26]

The point we have tried to establish above is that the sexual history of the black, and inter-racial sex in particular, has affected sexual relationships between black men and women.

The situation when a black man is involved with a white woman has a very different psychological basis. It appears to be composed of two main elements which at times are opposed to each other. Convention and law put her out of his reach. He *knows* she is forbidden to him which inevitably increases his desire for her. His ego is inflated because she has chosen him instead of a white lover. Co-existing with such feelings are those associated with her whiteness as a symbol of the oppression of black people. In her person he can take revenge for all the humiliations he has suffered in her world. Thus to possess her is to satisfy the desire for a forbidden object and simultaneously to accomplish her humiliation through having intercourse with the despised, rejected Negro.

The white woman's attitude in such a relationship depends in part upon the whole mythology of the black invented by white America. He too is forbidden to her but the attraction he holds for her is greater than this. According to the myth the Negro is outside the ordinary restrictions and conventions which have surrounded sexual activity for the majority of Americans. He represents the 'natural' man, uninhibited and free to invoke all the animality and sensuality she may possess. It is analogous to the experience of the repressed white male with a prostitute.

Historically, as we have seen, the greatest area of miscegenation was that concerned with the white slave-master and the black, female slave. The existence of the 'peculiar' institution of slavery gave opportunity to the development of a special psychological attitude on the part of the black woman. A contemporary commentator, Angela Davis, writes:

> In confronting the black woman as adversary in a sexual contest, the master would be subjecting her to the most elemental form of terrorism distinctively suited for the female: rape. Given the already terroristic texture of plantation life, it would be as a potential victim of rape that the slave woman would be most unguarded. Further, she might be most conveniently manipulable if the master contrived a ransom of sorts, forcing her to pay with her body for food, diminished security in treatment, the safety of her children, etc.[27]

The argument can be taken further. There was not only the amelioration of the individual's immediate circumstance but also the possibility that the children of this enforced union might become free. In one sense it could be said that just as the master manipulated the slave-woman so she manipulated him. In most cases this meant that a relationship initiated through rape led to relatively privileged status for the female slave as against her male counterpart. The latter could do little or nothing to protect his woman. In this way his masculinity was denied. For the woman the white man was supportive both in the economic and psychological sense. In the contemporary context without slavery the black man is still unable to give his mate the protection and economic security she demands.

Thus the white man, the oppressor, is nevertheless, from the point of view of the exploited woman, seen as the embodiment of that which is powerful and protective. That this attitude is still very much operative today is seen from the following cases.

Calvin Hernton in his book, *Coming Together* (NY 1971), relates how he is travelling in a train in the South. With him in the carriage are a group of white college football players. An attractive black girl enters the carriage. Although remaining aloof, her presence disturbs the white boys who clearly wish to get to know her but seem unable to do so. Later that evening Hernton returns to the bar to find great interaction taking place between the white barman and the girl. 'Their relationship was obviously structured according to the old white man dominance and black woman submissiveness – each one knew his and her place, when to smile, when to crack an insinuating joke, etc., just like a white man and a black woman in the South would have acted ten years ago.'[28] Hernton's point is that the black girl preferred acting out the traditional role assigned to her in relation to white men rather than take advantage of the much more open situation which has developed between the races in recent years.

A very different case is cited by W. H. Grier and P. M. Cobbs, two black psychiatrists, in their *Black Rage*:

> An attractive black wife and mother sought out a highly recommended white professional man and in his consultation room began describing in a very businesslike manner the relevant issues which had brought her to his office. After listening to her briefly he got up from his desk, came round, kissed her, took off her clothes, and made love to her. He then told her he would look after her problems and dismissed her.[29]

The authors' comments are of considerable interest. During later treatment she told them that she had been faithful to her husband until this episode when she had felt she had to yield to the white man. What was in her mind was the impressiveness of the man himself, his office and his reputation. 'This type of passive submission, strongly coloured by eroticism, has historically characterized the relationship between black women and white men ...'[30]

By citing such cases we do not mean to suggest that such feelings characterize *all* sexual relationships between black women and white men, but that because of the historical matrix of such relationships an element of the submissive is almost always present. This may be associated with feelings of masochism – the black woman feels degraded that she has submitted to the archetypal oppressor, but it is a degradation with deep erotic overtones. Black women, however, do not have a monopoly of masochistic feelings – they are inherent in the sexuality of many women.

The problem which has to be faced – and the myth of black sexuality has fostered its growth – is that the black individual through the historical, colonial experience, has become imbued with white values. In the sexual expression of that process the white person becomes the desired partner. Despite the reiteration of the greatness of an African past before slavery, despite the upsurge of Black Power, the Negro in the United States is still a victim of this process. Eldridge Cleaver, in the person of his character the old man Lazarus in *Soul On Ice*, has this to say:

> There is no love left between a black man and a black woman. Take me, for instance. I love white women and hate black women. It's just in me,

so deep that I don't even try to get it out of me any more. I'd jump over ten nigger bitches just to get to one white woman. Ain't no such thing as an ugly white woman. A white woman is beautiful even if she's baldheaded and has only one tooth ... It's not just the fact that she's a woman I love; I love her skin, her soft, smooth, white skin. I like just to lick her white skin as if sweet, fresh honey flows from her pores, and just to touch her long, soft, silky hair. There's a softness about a white woman, something delicate and soft inside her. But a nigger bitch seems to be full of steel, granite-hard and resisting, not soft and submissive like a white woman. Ain't nothing more beautiful than white woman's hair being blown by the wind. The white woman is more than a woman to me ... she's like a goddess, a symbol. My love for her is religious and beyond fulfillment. I worship her. I love a white woman's dirty drawers.[31]

Lazarus represents the older generation and Cleaver opposes him to the young Negroes of today. They despise and hate him but in their vehement rejection one can detect their fear that this is also what they feel.

Fanon puts it in a different way:

Out of the blackest part of my soul, across the zebra striping of my mind, surges this desire to be suddenly white.

I wish to be acknowledged not as *black* but as *white*.

Now – and this is a form of recognition that Hegel had not envisaged – who but a white woman can do this for me? By loving she proves that I am worthy of white love. I am loved like a white man.

I am a white man.

Her love takes me on the noble road that leads to total realization ...

I marry white culture, white beauty, white whiteness.

When my restless hands caress those white breasts, they grasp white civilization and dignity and make them mine ...[32]

We have tried to show something of the genesis of the myth concerning Negro sexuality and how it has affected the sexual relationships of black and white. Despite evidence that it is no more than a myth, belief in its validity is still apparent. In the opinion of Gilberto Freyre, the Brazilian sociologist:

Contrary to the general impression that it was for the most part the African who communicated to the Brazilian his lubricity, it is my belief that the former, as a matter of fact, was sexually the weakest of the three elements that united to form our country. In any event, among the Negroes ... erotic dances were more frequent and more ardent than

> among the Amerindians and the Portuguese, and this would appear to indicate a weaker degree of sexuality ...[33]

Whatever facts are made available they will do little to diminish the efficiency of the myth. Its strength lies in the satisfaction it gives those who believe in it – both black and white. The myth was born out of particular historical circumstances. Those circumstances have changed but there still remains for the white American an almost compulsive attraction in the notion and idea of the vast sensuality of the Negro.

No white person, even the most liberal, is immune to the seduction of the myth. Norman Podhoretz, editor of *Commentary*, in an article in the issue of that journal for February 1963 states the case of the liberal with considerable honesty:

> Yet just as in childhood I envied Negroes for what seemed to me their superior masculinity, so I envy them today for what seems to me their superior physical grace and beauty ... They are on the kind of terms with their own bodies that I should like to be on with mine, and for that precious quality they seem blessed to me.
>
> The hatred I still feel for Negroes is the hardest of all the old feelings to face and admit, and it is the most hidden and the most overlarded by the conscious attitudes into which I have succeeded in willing myself. How, then, do I know that this hatred has never entirely disappeared? I know it from the insane rage that can stir in me at the thought of Negro anti-Semitism; I know it from the disgusting prurience that can stir in me at the sight of a mixed couple ...[34]

WHAT MISCEGENATION IS!

WHAT WE ARE TO EXPECT

Now that Mr. Lincoln is Re-elected.

By L. SEAMAN, LL. D.

WALLER & WILLETTS, Publishers,

NEW YORK.

1 The title page of a mid-nineteenth-century racist pamphlet

2 'The Voyage of the Sable Venus, from Angola to the West Indies' (*Stothard*) – the frontispiece to a poem written by an eighteenth-century white Jamaican planter

3 'A Negro Festival drawn from Nature in the Island of St Vincent'
(*Brunyas*)

4 Love – 'A Discovery: That which was white, is now its contrary'
(Hogarth)

5 Times of the Day: Noon (*Hogarth*)

6 'A Planter of Quality with His Wife and Slaves' (from *Voyage à Surinam* by P. Benoit, 1839)

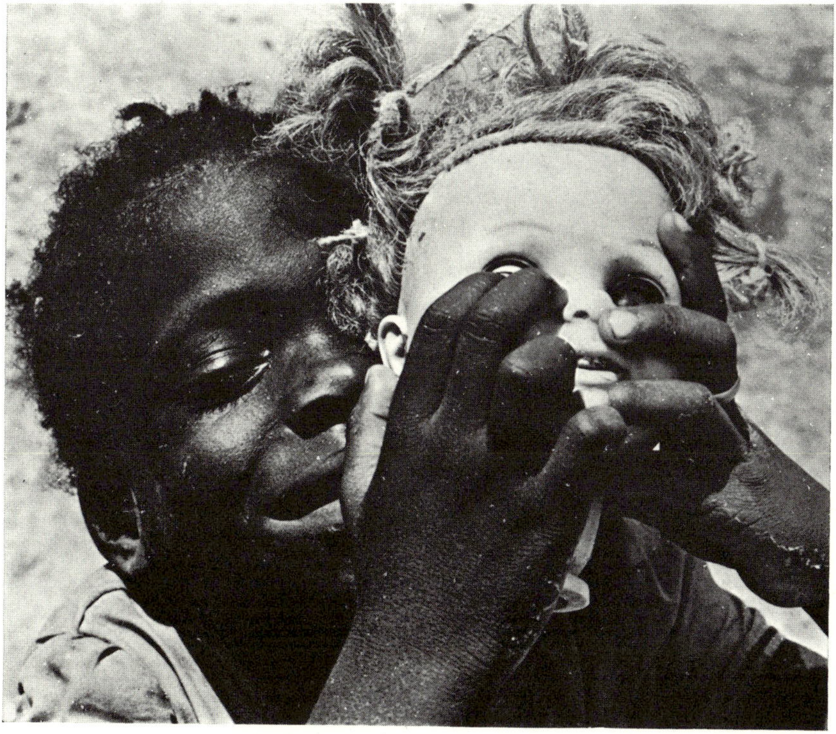

7 Black and White in Arkansas, USA

8 Miscegenation in Kenya: Charles Njonjo, the Kenyan Attorney-General, marries an English schoolteacher, 18 November 1972

CHAPTER 7

The West Indies

Bryan Edwards, the planter-historian, writing of the climate of the Caribbean had this to say: 'The propensity also, which the climate undoubtedly encourages, to early and habitual licentiousness, induces a turn of mind and disposition unfriendly to mental improvement.'[1] Although his remarks concerned Negro slaves they could equally apply to the white population, as we shall see. Edwards was writing in the late eighteenth century; nevertheless, his views would have validity for today. Mental improvement may have advanced but the libido of the contemporary West Indian of any colour is still remarkably active from an early to an advanced age.

The colonial societies which came into being as a result of the territorial ambitions of the major European, maritime powers – Spain, France, Britain and Holland – were all based on the institution of slavery. We have already spoken of the effects of the institution on the dominant group in the chapters devoted to the United States. With regard to the sexual abuse of black slaves by slave-masters and their associates the Caribbean represents an exaggerated form of what occurred in the United States.

Black slavery was introduced into the Caribbean in the early sixteenth century after the decimation of the aboriginal Indian population by the Spaniards and their successors. It is quite clear from contemporary evidence that miscegenation occurred from the inception of slavery. By the seventeenth century this was on such a scale that the government of Antigua, a British colony, felt impelled to pass a law prohibiting 'Carnall Coppullation between Christian and Heathen'.[2] For heathen read Negro or Indian, for Christian read white. The penalties for infraction of the law bore more severely on the heathens. A free white was fined, a bond servant (white) had his term of indenture extended. The black or Indian, however, was flogged and branded. Antigua appears to have been somewhat preoccupied with sexual irregularities as in the same year (1644) the legislature passed a law in which any incestuous act was punishable by death.

The Antiguan legislation is unique in the British Caribbean, unlike similar laws which were passed in a number of the Southern States. Taking the West Indies as a whole it is apparent that miscegenation obtained a kind of social sanction. The fact that other islands did not follow the example of Antigua suggests that this was the case.

An eighteenth-century Spanish source indicates that by this time an elaborate system of nomenclature had grown up to describe the various gradations created by racial intermixture:

> Among the tribes which are derived from an intermixture of the Whites with the Negroes, the first are the *Mulattoes*; next to these are the *Tercerones*, produced from a White and a Mulatto, with some approximation to the former, but not so near as to obliterate their origin. After these, follow the *Quarterones*, proceeding from a White and a Terceron. The last are the *Quinterones*, who owe their origin to a White and Quarteron. This is the last gradation, there being no visible difference between them and the Whites, either in colour of features; nay, they are often fairer than the Spaniards. The children of a White and Quinteron consider themselves as free from all taint of the Negro race. Every person is so jealous of the order of their tribe or cast, that if, through inadvertence, you call them by a degree lower than what they actually are, they are highly offended. Before they attain the class of the Quinterones, there are several intervening circumstances which throw them back; for between the Mulatto and the Negro there is an intermediate race, which they call *Samboes*, owing their origin to a mixture between one of these and an Indian, or among themselves. Betwixt the Tercerones and Mulattoes, the Quarterones and Tercerones, etc. are those called *Tente en el Ayre*, *Suspended in the Air*; because they neither advance nor recede. Children, whose parents are a Quarteron or Quinteron, and a Mulatto or Terceron, are *Salto atras retrogrados*; because, instead of advancing towards being Whites, they have gone backwards towards the Negro race. The children between a Negro and a Quinteron, are called Sambos de Negro, de Mulatto, de Terceron, etc.[3]

The existence of such firm gradations shows that the process of racial intermixing was firmly established. In addition, what had become quite central to the process was the acceptance of the inherent inferiority of the black. That is something which the contemporary West Indies is only now beginning to reject.

In their territories the British, possibly less imaginative, were content in the eighteenth century with a simpler system of gradations:

> I proceed now to persons of mixed blood (usually termed People of Colour) ... all the different classes, or varieties, are not easily discriminated. In the British West Indies they are commonly known by the names of *Samboes*, *Mulattoes*, *Quadroons* and *Mestizes (h)*; but the Spaniards, from whom these appellations are borrowed, have many other and nicer distinctions ...
>
> (*h*) A *Sambo* is the offspring of a Black Woman by a Mulatto Man, or *vice versa*. *Mulatto*, of a Black Woman by a White Man. *Quadroon* of a Mulatto woman by a White Man. *Mestize* or Mustee of a Quadroon Woman by a White Man. The offspring by a White Man are white by law ...[4]

Whatever distinctions and niceties people of colour may have made amongst themselves, these were not recognized by their white masters. To them, the people they had in fact created were regarded as being essentially inferior. 'No property, however considerable, can ever raise a man or woman of colour, not even when combined with education, to the proper rank of a human being, in the estimation of an English or Dutch Creole. They are always kept at a respectful distance; and it would be looked upon as a kind of sacrilege, for a man of colour to sit down in the house of a Barbadian.'[5] Today in Barbados it is still exceptional to find black or coloured people who are welcome in the homes of indigenous white Barbadians.

Clearly there were numerous exceptions to this rigidity of discrimination. In particular this applied to the concubines or mistresses of planters. Some governors of British islands in this period were not above installing their concubines to act as hostesses in their official residences. To consort with black and coloured people in terms of a sexual relationship was acceptable. What was not was the notion that such women could ever aspire to marriage with a white man. Lightness of colour, and a great deal of money, might, however, overcome the barrier: '... no White man of decent appearance, unless urged by the temptation of a considerable fortune, will condescend to give his hand in marriage to a Mulatto.'[6]

The lengths to which European and American academic apologists will venture in order to rationalize the sexual pillage committed by their ancestors in slave societies is sometimes ludicrous:

> The white man in tropical America was out of his habitat. Constant association with an inferior subject race blunted his moral fibre and he suffered marked demoralization. His transitory residence and the con-

tinued importation of Africans debased life. Miscegenation, so contrary to Anglo-Saxon nature [*sic*], resulted in the rapid rise of a race of human hybrids. Planter society was based upon whites and blacks, removed to unfamiliar scenes, and their unhappy offspring. The saddest pages of imperial history relate the heartrending attempts to effect adjustment between these discordant elements.[7]

The poor, unhappy European deprived of his habitat, and a mere transient, devotes his time to the sexual abuse of black women no doubt in an endeavour to forget his unfortunate condition.

In the eighteenth century those Europeans who commented on the situation were more aware and sensitive than their present-day equivalents with their preoccupation with rationalizations of white sexual behaviour. Bryan Edwards, whom I have quoted above, was moved to almost Gibbonesque heights when writing about the condition of the mulatto woman:

> ... unhappily, the young men of their own complexion, are in too low a state of degradation, to think of matrimony ... Thus, excluded as they are from all hope of ever arriving to the honour and happiness of wedlock, insensible of its beauty and sanctity; ignorant of all Christian and moral obligations; threatened by poverty, urged by their passions, and encouraged by example; upon what principle can we expect these ill-fated women to act otherwise than they do?[8]

As was pointed out with relation to slave society in the south of the United States, circumstances which deliver the complete destiny of a human being into the hands of another are apt to produce formidable distortions of character in the individual possessed of such power. This was very much the case in the West Indies. Both men and women slave-owners were guilty of the most extreme acts of sadism directed against the unfortunates that they owned. In some instances white females outshone their male counterparts in their capacity for the exercise of cruelty.

'It will appear extraordinary to the reader, that many women, living in the colonies, should not only *order*, and often *superintend*, but sometimes actually *inflict with their own hands* some severe punishments upon their slaves, and that these should not always be women of a low order, but *frequently of respectability and rank* ...'[9] What is perhaps even more extraordinary is that compatriots of the planters' wives in England were having the vapours or swooning at the merest hint of the indelicate. It says much for the power and atmosphere of the slave plantation that it was able to transform such fragile creatures into monsters of lubricious savagery:

On the subject of women becoming the executioners of their own fury, Doctor Jackson observes that the first thing that shocked him in Jamaica was a creole lady, of *some consequence, superintending the punishment of her slaves, male and female, ordering the number of lashes, and, with her own hands, flogging the Negro driver, if he did not punish properly.*

Captain Cook relates, that two young ladies of fortune, in Barbados, sisters, one of whom was displeased at the pregnancy of a female slave belonging to the other, by the son of the surgeon attending the estate, proceeded to some very derogatory acts of cruelty. *With their own garters they tied* the young woman neck and heels, and then *beat her* almost to death with the heels of their shoes. One of her eyes continued a long while afterwards in danger of being lost ...

Captain Cook states further, that he saw a woman, named Rachel Lauder, beat a female slave most unmercifully. Having *bruised her head almost to a jelly*, with the heel of her shoe, she threw her with great force on the seat of the child's necessary [commode], and *then tried to stamp her head through the hole*, and would have murdered her, if not prevented by two officers. The girl's crime was the not bringing money enough from on board ship where she was sent by her mistress, for the purpose of prostitution.[10] [We have already referred (see p. xi) to Lieutenant Davison's evidence about the clergyman's wife at Port Royal (Jamaica).]

The ingenuity of punishments described suggests that such acts were due to calculation rather than to moments of aberration.

One of the motivations concerned in these acts of sadism was undoubtedly that of jealousy. The pattern of illicit sexual relationships between black and white had been firmly established before the arrival of white women in any numbers. As a wife, to find your husband involved with a mulatto or black concubine, or a prospective lover already attached in this way, was to create a situation in which revenge could easily be exercised against the slave in question, or another.

It must not be thought, however, that the planter's wife had a monopoly of ingenuity with regard to punishment. The slave-master could, and often did, allow his imagination to assist him in the matter:

Mr Dalrymple, in June 1789, saw a negress brought to St George's, Grenada, to have her fingers cut off. She had committed a fault, and ran away to avoid punishment; but being taken, her master *suspended her by the hands*, flogged and cut her cruelly on the back, belly, breast, and thighs, and then *left her suspended till her fingers mortified* ...

Captain Ross has seen a negro woman, in Jamaica, flogged *with ebony bushes* (much worse than our own thorn-bushes) so that the *skin of her back was taken off, down to her heels*. She was then turned round and flogged *from her breast down to her waist*, and in consequence he saw her afterwards *walking upon all fours*, and unable to get up ...

Mr Hercules Ross, hearing one day, in Jamaica, from an inclosure, the cries of some poor wretch under torture, he looked through, and saw a young female *suspended by the wrists to a tree, swinging to and fro*. Her toes could barely touch the ground, and her body was exceedingly agitated. The sight rather confounded him, as there was no whipping, and the master was just by seemingly motionless; but on looking more attentively, he saw in his hand *a stick of fire*, which *he held so* as to occasionally touch her about her private parts as she swung. He continued *this torture* with unmoved countenance, until Mr Ross, calling on him to desist, and throwing stones at him over the fence, stopped it.[11]

The reasons for such punishments varied from the commission of a trivial offence (the breaking of a plate), to the serious (absconding from the estate). It was also a serious matter to attempt to avoid the sexual advances of the master. It is interesting to note that the quotations given above are part of the evidence given before a Select Committee of the House of Commons in 1790 and 1791.

But there were other indignities which the female slave had to suffer. Not all white men owned slaves and had them at their command. Many living in the towns – tradesmen, clerks, soldiers, and so forth – provided a considerable clientele for prostitutes. These women were recruited from black and mulatto slaves whose owners wished to increase their income and from those who had been freed and had no other way to support themselves. Those who were slaves were often owned by white women who trained them for this purpose. 'Mongrel wenches from their youth are taught to be whores: you cannot affront them more than to give any hint of her being dull and unskilled in the magical art ...'[12]

Prostitution also existed on the sugar estates. 'The estate's midwife is employed, as I have been assured, by men who call themselves gentlemen, to be their procuress, and she does her best in the discharge of the hateful duties of her office. Persons on a visit to a friend's house, think it no disgrace to send out for a girl when bed-time arrives, or which is about the same thing, secure one of the female servants for the night.'[13] There were variations in this pattern: '... when a white man is inclined to get a mongrel or black girl for a night the usual mode is to hire a boy or old woman to procure one ...'[14] It is possible that in such cases the master was not above profiting from the occasion by taking part or whole of what was given to the girl for her services.

It is not surprising, granted the general venality of the estate and the sexual corruption of the female slaves, to find that some slave-women set themselves up as pimps and procuresses. Possibly this was done with the connivance, if not the assistance, of their masters. Often they were the mothers of the girls concerned. 'Those gypsies have a wonderful ascendancy over men and have injured many, both powerful and subordinate; the poor slaves on a plantation are obliged to pay them as much adoration as the Portuguese the Hostess or Virgin Mary, for the government of the cowskin [the whip] depends in great measure on their smiles and frowns.'[15]

The white people consisted not only of the planter's family but of men employed as overseers and managers. The general term for them was book-keepers, though in fact they spent most of their time riding around the estate seeing that the work was done. Housing was provided by the planter. It was obviously to his advantage to have single men or at least men who had left their families behind in England. These men formed the group which was most susceptible to concubinage. After the planter had exercised his *droit de seigneur* the book-keeper could exercise his own choice.

An anonymous early nineteenth-century novel, *Marly; or the Life of a Planter in Jamaica*, describes how the newcomer, fresh from England, is introduced to life on the estate:

> The book-keeper was rather taken unawares, and a half-blush overcast his countenance, at being caught by the stranger, in familiar chat with a negro girl. Marly made an excuse, but the other interrupting him said, there was no occasion, for this was only Diana, his sable wife, and on her retiring, Langeby told him that he had a fine girl in his eye, who would answer him well. 'No objections,' added he, 'will I hear, for I know what you will say. It is the same with us all when we first come to the island; but after a little experience, we uniformly fall into the same track, and follow the common custom. Besides, it is of real advantage; for, in the event of your being sick, your girl will be the most attentive of nurses, far more so than what can be expected from strangers. Be you advised, and follow the manners of the country, of which you will never repent, and you know the maxim, that when in Rome, we should do what the Pope does.'[16]

If the girl chosen were a slave, clearly an accommodation had to be reached with the planter. If she were free, then it was a matter for the book-keeper to arrange. The economics of the situation were a reflection of the system of colour gradings of Caribbean society:

> Langeby, you can tell whether black or brown is most expensive – for when you and I were together upon Tadmer, you would not be advised

for your good, but you must have a brown lady, forsooth; but she, I believe, made you repent of your choice, after spending nearly two years of your salary. But since you left the estate, I understand you have grown more wise, and more black in your choice, and ever since you have had more money in your pocket than you formerly possessed.[17]

Black was not only beautiful, it was more economic. The lighter her shade and approximation to the European the more money the girl would demand from her keeper.

The fictional account of *Marly* is corroborated by more serious observers of the West Indian scene. Some were appalled at what they saw:

... if slavery and its attendant abuses did not exist there, no great additional improvement in the state of society could be expected, *while the most gross and open licentiousness continues, as at present, to prevail among all ranks of the Whites ... Every unmarried White man, and of every class, has his Black or his Brown mistress, with whom he lives openly*; and of so little consequence is this thought that his White female friends and relations think it no breach of decorum to visit his house, partake of his hospitality, fondle his children, and converse with his *housekeeper* – as if that conduct which they regarded as disgraceful in their own class, was not so in the female of Colour ... But the most striking proof of the low estimate of moral and religious obligation here, is the fact, that the man who lives in open adultery – that is, who keeps his Black or Brown mistress in the very face of his wife and family, and of the community – has generally as much outward respect shewn him, and is as much countenanced, visited, and received into company, especially if he be a man of some weight and influence in the community, as if he had been guilty of no breach of decency, or dereliction of moral duty.[18]

The condemnation of such behaviour appears almost to be on the grounds of propriety rather than of sexual misbehaviour. In other words the married man who did not flaunt his coloured mistress in his wife's face was a better man than he who did.

Despite their cruelty to the generality of those enslaved, white men were influenced by the sexual relationships formed with black and coloured women. In many instances emotional bonds were created between the couple. Such feelings led to the manumission of concubines and their children. But there were obstacles to this:

White men occasionally give freedom to their mistresses and their children. But this, in all cases where the mistress and her children are not the slaves of the White man, must be effected by purchase, and of course with the owner's consent. But such purchases cannot be effected when the estate is mortgaged, or the owner is a minor. White men often complain that the owner is not compelled to give freedom to their children on being paid their value. In all cases where slaves are made free, a bond must be given that they shall not become chargeable to the parish.[19]

Nothing could demonstrate more clearly that the slave was regarded as a thing, a chattel, rather than a human being.

When such difficulties were overcome the concubine and her children could profit considerably if the father was a man of property. There were many instances of mistresses and children being freed by will. The practice was considered to have reached alarming proportions in eighteenth-century Jamaica. So much so that a law was passed in 1748 limiting the amount of property to £1,200 sterling which could be inherited by a concubine and her issue.[20]

It must be remembered that in West Indian slave society to become a concubine of a white man was the only means for a slave-woman to achieve something approaching freedom. Equally for the free woman of colour such an alliance represented success:

> Few marriages take place among them. Most of the females of colour think it more genteel and reputable to be the kept mistress of a white man, if he is in opulent circumstances, and can afford to indulge their taste for finery and parade, than to be united in wedlock with the most respectable individual of their own class. They view marriage, indeed, as an unnecessary and unnatural restraint ... These are the sentiments of nine-tenths of the females of colour in this island [Jamaica], and accordingly at least that proportion are in the situation of housekeepers, as they are here styled, to white men; while the males console themselves in the same way either with one of their own colour, or with a sable companion. Though some of the females of colour are possessed of considerable property, given them by their white parents, or amassed by their own industry, they never aspire to a conjugal union with a white man; nor if such a union were sanctified by the custom of the country, is it probable that they desire to enter into it. A white man, indeed, according to the ideas of distinction which here prevail would be considered as degrading himself by a matrimonial alliance with a woman of colour, however favoured by fortune or accomplished by education. But the latter gives herself little concern about this, while the most distinguished and opulent of the whites pay an illicit homage to her charms, and even the man of family shall openly and unblushingly

forsake his wife and abandon his children to hold dalliance in her company.[21]

It would appear that the virtue of the Anglo–Saxon male was so profound that although he might love the woman of colour and his children by her he could never bring himself to betray his caste by marrying her.

The sexual freedom of the society has to be contrasted with the rigidity with which social distance was maintained by class and colour. The society was pyramidal in form, with the whites occupying the apex. Within the white group distinctions were made according to class. Thus your rich planter would by no means hob nob with a lowly clerk or tradesmen. But all were united in considering themselves as superior to all others. Below them came the free people of colour. The strength of colour was so strong that a free black felt inferior, and was so considered, to the enslaved man of colour. Next in the hierarchy were the freed blacks. Below them was the general mass of the slave population. As we have seen, the coloured group maintained within itself a series of minute distinctions in terms of colour and physical appearance. The criterion here was the nearer the individual's appearance was to the European the higher his social status. As we shall see this has by no means entirely vanished from the contemporary West Indian scene.

Such a system can only operate if it has the sanction of all the groups which compose it. That is to say the black had to acknowledge he was inferior to the coloured, and the coloured accept the superiority of the white, and so on. Matthew Lewis, visiting his Jamaican estates in 1815–17, made an excellent comment on the situation:

> ... nor can the separation of castes in India be more rigidly observed than that of complexional shades among the Creoles. My black page, Cubina, is married: I told him that I hoped he had married a pretty woman; why had he not married Mary Wiggins? He seemed quite shocked at the very idea. 'Oh, massa, me black, Mary Wiggins sambo; that is not allowed.'

The discrimination exercised by the whites against black and coloured people was entirely on the grounds of colour. Education and money made no difference to the inflexibility of their opinion. They were concerned to maintain the social distance between themselves and everyone not classified white. Their obsession with racial purity has a certain air of unreality about it – to have such beliefs and then dishonour them daily in a clandestine way has all the air of schizophrenia:

> The brown children of the more opulent of the whites are educated in the island, or sent to Great Britain for that purpose. Such as have

> received a liberal education, and do not follow the immoral example around them, are for the most part well behaved, respectable people. Notwithstanding this, they are excluded from the society of the whites, and exposed to many other mortifications, in consequence of the line of distinction which custom and the laws draw between the whites and the browns. A white man, though he lives on a footing of the most perfect familiarity with his brown housekeeper, never sets her down at his table, nor introduces either her or his children to his respectable acquaintance.[22]

Education in Britain frequently meant that the daughters of Europeans were at the same school as their illegitimate relatives. Friendships were formed between them in the somewhat more liberal atmosphere of the mother country. As soon as they returned, however, these ceased overnight. Coloured girls having had this experience – of knowing white people on equal terms – must have been extremely galled to return to their own society and be compelled to assume their allotted position of inferiority.

As a result of these distinctions an interesting duality developed. Coloured people of means created equivalent institutions to those possessed by the whites:

> The more independent people of colour, shut out from the general society of the whites, form a separate society of themselves. They have their own amusements, their parties, their visiting and their balls. The latter are fully as gay and as expensive as those of the whites; and as the brown females are the chief planners and supporters of these, the young and dissipated of the white men, their admirers, form a distinguished part of those meetings of pleasure. On these occasions the men of colour, the brothers, uncles, cousins, and other relations of the women are excluded: though sometimes the brown ladies condescend to attend a ball given by the men of their own colour. The practice of white men giving dances to the women of colour is thought a matter of little consequence, except by the brown men, who, being contemptuously excluded from these entertainments, must feel the indignity; in fact, it is calculated to excite feelings not the most amicable between the two classes. The white gentleman, who tonight leads out the fair creole as a partner in the dance, may tomorrow give his hand, on a similar occasion, to the beauty of a darker shade, who dresses as well, and thinks of herself as lovely and as attractive as the other. The white ladies sometimes resent this behaviour in their male acquaintance with a becoming spirit; but in general it is not thought of much consequence.[23]

Although there must have been considerable satisfaction in imitating the behaviour and manner of white people, coloured people nevertheless suffered great humilitations and indignities. There was no question that they wished to be thought of as white. They despised that part of them which was regarded as Negro. To suffer rejection from those they desired so ardently to accept them must have created feelings of gross anxiety. 'The free people of colour are excluded from many of the privileges of the whites; they are not competent to serve as jurors, they are excluded from all offices, civil, military, and ecclesiastical. These disqualifications are thought necessary for political purposes ...'[24] If they had had the information it might have been some consolation to know that their brethren in the southern United States were even more denied.

Clearly in such a scattered region as the Caribbean, with different metropolitan powers in control, conditions with regard to miscegenation varied a great deal. But whatever the variation there always existed a rigidity of distinctions. The system had become so well established that it survived the great traumatic experience of the plantocracy – the emancipation of the slaves. Mrs Flannigan, a witty and acute Englishwoman, visited the island of Antigua in the 1840s after emancipation.

Mrs Flannigan explains the intricacies of the Antiguan colour grading system:

> The several removes from a black are as follows: The *mongrel*, the offspring of a black and mulatto; the *mulatto*, the offspring of a black and a white; the *mustee*, the offspring of a mulatto and a white; the *fustee*, the offspring of a mustee and a white; and the *dustee*, the offspring of a fustee and a white. This last gradation is the connecting link between the degraded children of Ham, and the descendants of his more honoured brethren. It is to be noted, however, that the *mulatto* is not *always* fairer than the *mongrel*, or the *mustee* than the mulatto; and children of the same parents often exhibit as much, if not more, difference of complexion, as those of Europeans.[25]

This variation in colour within the same family can be considerable – some children may be quite fair while others may be quite dark. This is a phenomenon which is noticeable in the Caribbean today. It can, and does, cause great distress within families as the fairer tend to be more favoured by the parents. The more familiar term for dustee would be octoroon. Dustee seems to have been peculiar to Antigua. The physical appearance of coloured people singled them out from their fellow Antiguans:

> The chief peculiarities in the coloured race are, the extreme pliancy of limbs, attenuation of person, large black eyes, and a profusion of black

curling hair. The men are generally *under* than above the middle size, but in most instances, possessed of good figures. The females are also small and slender, and are noted for an ambling gait, combined in many of them with an extreme affectation of manners.[26]

The disabilities which affected the coloured people of Antigua were no different from those we have mentioned above – they existed in a kind of legal and social limbo. Prejudice against them in Antigua was so intense that it even extended to the grave:

Not only were the coloured people refused interment in the churchyard, but so fearful were the whites of profanation, that the very *bell* which tolled out *their demise* was prohibited from being used to perform that service for those degraded ones through whose veins flowed the least drop of Africa's tarnished blood. Accordingly, a smaller bell (which still hangs in the belfry) was obtained from an estate in the island ... which was regularly kept for the sole use of persons of colour, until within these last few years, when their rights as fellow creatures have been allowed, and those mean and pitiful distinctions of caste, in great measure, done away with.[27]

What occurred in Antigua was a reinforcement of that which existed in the other islands – the acceptance, despite the humiliations inflicted upon them, by people of colour that the ideal in life could only be seen in terms of the European world:

It was not only the soreness of spirit which this state of affairs inflicted on the coloured man, but as Prejudice was the offspring of Slavery, it was consequently the groundwork of that horrible system of licentiousness which rendered Antigua among the West India Islands famous, or rather *infamous*, for so many years. The coloured women participated in the *prejudice* of their masters, and as they became the mothers of female children, they reared them up in the same spirit, and inculcated into their minds that it was more honourable and praiseworthy to inhabit the harem of a white man, than to be the lawful wife of a man of colour. This conduct was, of course, the grave of all domestic peace, the destroyer of connubial love; and by its dire, its *demoniacal* influences, caused the fairest island in the world to become, in a moral point of view, a dreary marsh, exhaling the poisonous miasma.[28]

Even if the hyperbole of the writer is discounted, enough remains to show how embedded the system had become so that it could survive the levelling of emancipation, and continue into our own time.

Many rationalizations have been advanced as to the necessity of white prejudice – the meretricious character of the mulatto, his association with slavery, his being the living proof of the libidinous nature of the white man – but they are not sufficient to explain the positive refusal of the Anglo-Saxon to come to terms with a situation of his own creating. We have mentioned in other chapters the role of the white woman in intensifying the pattern of prejudice. This was certainly the case in the Caribbean:

> It is said, that the white ladies are the strongest upholders of prejudice; but that their refusal to mix with this class of persons is not occasioned from any shade of colour, but on account of their general illegitimacy. This, however, is not the sole cause; for there are illegitimate white people, whom they are in the constant habit of meeting without any aversion; while, at the same time, many of the people of colour, particularly the younger ones, are the offspring of parents who have been legally united within the sacred walls of the temple of God, and whose intellectual attainments fit them for any society.[29]

In relation to both whites and the black slaves the numbers of the free coloured population in some areas were comparatively small. In the last decades of the eighteenth century in the islands of the Leeward group – Antigua, St Kitts, Nevis, Montserrat and the Virgin Islands – there were 8,000 whites, 81,000 black slaves and 2,600 free coloureds.[30] In one island, St Kitts, the proportion of slaves to free persons in its three urban parishes was about three to one. In the rural areas this was about twenty to one.[31] At the beginning of the nineteenth century Trinidad had a white population of some 2,000, and it was estimated that free people of colour numbered three times as many.[32] This would suggest that the rate of racial intermixture in Trinidad was considerably greater than in the Leeward Islands at a similar period. This may be explained in part by the fact that Trinidad had hitherto been both a French and Spanish colony before being ceded to Britain. In the period 1797–1806 the Trinidadian white population rose from 2,086 to 2,274, while the free coloured group increased from 4,466 to 5,401, and the number of slaves increased from 17,643 to 31,133.[33]

A similar pattern was exhibited by the mainland British colony of British Guiana, which in 1829 had a white population of just over 3,000, nearly 70,000 slaves and 6,360 coloured people.[34] Barbados exhibited a different trend. It had always been attractive as an area of white settlement – climatically, from a European point of view, it is extremely mild. Between 1786 and 1829 the white population declined from 16,167 to 14,959 whereas the slave population grew from 62,115 to 82,902. Clearly sexual interaction between white on the one side and black and coloured on the other must have increased in the same period as the number of coloured people rose from 883 in 1786 to 5,146 in 1829.[35]

Jamaica, the largest British possession in the Caribbean, could boast, in 1791, a population of 30,000 whites, over a quarter of a million slaves and 10,000 freed black and coloured people.[36] It is interesting to note that Jamaica, with twice the white population of Barbados, controlled over three times as many slaves. The contrast with the French island of Haiti – the western part of Hispaniola – is illuminating. In 1790 the total population was 519,000, of which 452,000 were slaves. The free coloured, or *Affranchi*, amounted to 28,000, and the whites numbered 40,000.[37] If the figures for Jamaica are compared with those for Haiti it is seen that, comparatively, the rate of sexual interaction between black and white in Haiti was much greater than that of Jamaica.

Hispaniola, the island which comprises today the Dominican Republic and Haiti, was divided by the Treaty of Ryswick in 1697 between France and Spain, France obtaining the western part. In 1685 Louis XIV issued the famous Code Noir which was to govern all relations between masters and slaves. Unlike the equivalent British slave codes, the Code Noir in its Article 59 laid down that if a slave obtained his freedom either through manumission by a parent or master, or bought it, he was to have all the rights of a French citizen. From the beginning of French rule miscegenation began to occur. It was not considered exceptional. Haitian society at this time consisted of grands blancs – the white estate-owners; petits blancs – the clerks and tradesmen of the towns; the black slaves; and the *Affranchi*, or gens de couleur.

In the century after the promulgation of the Code Noir the size and prosperity of the gens de couleur grew considerably. Many, because of their wealth and connections were accepted into the society of the grands blancs. They became completely Gallicized. France was the centre of their universe. They sojourned in Paris like any grand blanc, and sent their children to be educated there. They may have started with the stain of illegitimacy, but overcame it by marrying their sons and daughters to members of French families. Those families who, in the course of time, had rid themselves of the African in them by marriage and association with the whites, were the most cruel to their slaves, and most arrogant towards the petits blancs. They became in fact more prejudiced in terms of colour and class than the pure-bred Frenchman.

Their behaviour aroused the intense animosity of the petits blancs. By the 1750s discriminatory laws began to be passed. The first was a local law of 1758 which denied to the gens de couleur the right to carry arms – the hallmark of a gentleman. It was put about that all white people might be in danger from the growth and influence of people of colour. In the event grands blancs began to side with their white inferiors in their campaign of prejudice. In France Louis XV appeared to be convinced of this danger for he introduced restrictions affecting the free travel of gens de couleur in France. On petition from Haiti in 1771 the king issued *Instructions to Administrators*, which emphasized that people of colour and their descendants must be separated from the whites for all time:

> For the next two decades the affranchi had to face openly avowed discrimination. One by one his rights in the Code were abrogated. He might not fill any responsible office either in the courts or the militia, for that would elevate him above white persons. Certain careers, such as goldsmithing, were closed to him, because they brought wealth; others, notably medicine and the apothecary's art were forbidden on the ground that whites might be poisoned; law and religion were barred to him because of their public and honorific nature. Coloured women were forbidden in 1768 to marry white men. In 1779 began a series of laws designed to humiliate the coloured person in public: his clothes must be of a different material and cut from the white person's; he must be indoors by nine o'clock in the evening; he might not sit in the same section of churches and theatres with whites.[38]

The restrictions imposed sound like a combination of the mediaeval sumptuary laws, which forbade common people to dress like the nobility; the Nazi anti-semitic laws, and the law and practice of the southern States of America. The paradox is that Haiti passes from a period in which the condition of the gens de couleur was vastly superior to that of his counterpart in the British islands to a condition which was far more repressive than anything which occurred in the Caribbean domain of the Anglo-Saxon.

This was a state of affairs which lasted until the French Revolution of 1789, and the Haitian movement for independence in 1791. Thereafter there follows a period in which blacks and gens de couleur struggle for power. In time this is followed by the domination of the blacks. Today the elite of Haiti is no longer white but coloured and black. Caste and colour lines are rigid. The elite is concerned to maintain its position as a bastion of French culture against the black tide of the peasantry with their African affiliation.

Haiti can be used as the exemplar of the French West Indies. Miscegenation occurred in all the territories governed by France – Martinique, Guadaloupe, St Martin, St Lucia, Dominica, Grenada, Trinidad, St Vincent and the mainland colony of Cayenne. The pattern varied but everywhere there was created a category of gens de couleur whose desire was to assimilate with their masters.

It is evident that a process which begins with the advent of the European and black slaves becomes institutionalized in time so that when the basis of the social structure is overthrown by emancipation it possesses the strength to persist. The nineteenth century, despite all the political and social changes which it brought to the Caribbean, left virtually untouched the patterns of prejudice and discrimination which had preceded it.

Restrictions affecting the legal and social position of coloured people in the British islands remained in force almost up to the eve of emancipation. For instance in Jamaica it was only in 1828 that legal disabilities, which had prevented coloured people from holding public office, were rescinded. Writing in 1834, just after emancipation, an English missionary had this to say:

> Relieved from these proscriptions by which they had been enthralled and bowed down, they as a body immediately began to advance in the scale of civilization, intelligence, and virtue, so that at the present time they discover a renovation of character and a degree of improvement in manners, customs, and knowledge, of which history, in a similar space of time, scarcely affords a parallel. In their house, dress, personal appearance (complexion excepted), general deportment, wealth, morals, and religion, many of them are on an equality with the most respectable of the whites. Nor are they less in the higher attainments of the mind. There are now to be found among them men of talent, learning, and accomplishments, who would do honour to any community. They fill the public offices, practise as solicitors and barristers in the courts of law; are found among our tradesmen, merchants, and estate proprietors; are directors of our civil institutions; are enrolled among our magistrates; and have even obtained a seat and influence in the senate.[39]

Even if missionary zeal is discounted – the writer would have attributed such improvement to the spread of the gospel – the fact remains that the people of colour had, at this period, achieved a great deal and had moved away from their depressed state. Sixteen years later, in 1859, Anthony Trollope confirmed the opinion above. He also showed that antagonism still existed between black, white, and coloured:

> Both the white men and the black dislike their coloured neighbours. It is useless to deny that as a rule such is the case. The white men now, at this very day, dislike them more in Jamaica than they do in other parts of the West Indies, because they are constantly driven to meet them, and are more afraid of them.
>
> In Jamaica one does come in contact with coloured men. They are to be met at the Governor's table; they sit in the House of Assembly;

they cannot be refused admission to state parties, or even to large assemblies; they have forced themselves forward, and must be recognized as being in the van. Individuals (whites) decry them – will not have them within their doors – affect to despise them. But in effect the coloured men of Jamaica cannot be despised much longer.[40]

It is clear why white people both despised and feared the coloured man – he represented a threat to their supremacy. In fact in some of the islands, such as St Vincent and Grenada, the white population after emancipation had begun to emigrate on a considerable scale, surrendering the land to the blacks and coloured people. Black antagonism sprang from another source. From this point of view the Negro felt that people of colour wished to adhere to the whites and joined with them in despising the blacks. The whites had reason to feel menaced. The Jamaica census of 1861 gave the total population as 441,264, of which the whites constituted 13,816, the coloured 81,065, and pure Negroes 346,374.[41] The Negro, although the majority, lacked the skills, education and attainments of the coloured people. Thus from a European standpoint he was less of a menace. Events in our own century have proved that the whites in the West Indies had real grounds for their fears.

Whatever criticism may have been made on the part of whites or coloured people, and the former's reiteration of the necessity of maintaining social distance, there is no questioning the fact that the coloured woman maintained a great physical attraction for the European. Towards the end of the nineteenth century Lafcadio Hearn, who became a Buddhist and an authority on Japan, visited the French West Indies. He was enormously impressed by the filles de couleur:

Physically, the typical fille de couleur may certainly be classed, as white creole writers have not hesitated to class her, with the 'most beautiful women of the human race'. She has inherited not only the finer bodily characteristics of either parent race, but a something else belonging originally to neither, and created by special climatic and physical conditions – a grace, a suppleness of form, a delicacy of extremities (so that all the lines described by the bending of limbs or fingers are parts of clean curves), a satiny smoothness and fruit-tint of skin – solely West Indian . . . Morally of course, it is much more difficult to describe her; and whatever may be safely said refers rather to the fille de couleur of the past than of the present half-century. The race is now in a period of transition; public education and political changes are modifying the type, and it is impossible to guess the ultimate consequence, because it is impossible to safely predict what new influences may yet be brought to affect its social development.[42]

Interestingly enough, the dramatic possibilities of the intricacies of miscegenation in the Caribbean had not inspired writers in Britain. An exception, however, was Grant Allen, a fairly prolific novelist and author. Allen had spent some years school-mastering in Jamaica. This no doubt gave him an insight into the colour complexities of the society. In 1892 he published a novel, *In All Shades*. The story deals with the tragic adventures of a young Trinidadian man of colour, who, after his medical training at the University of Edinburgh, returns to the West Indies. Unfortunately on the voyage home he meets, and falls in love with, the daughter of a white planter from Trinidad. The consequences, as can be imagined, are disastrous. The colour prejudice inherent in white women, *pace* Miss Margery Perham, at this time is well expressed:

> 'You oughtn't to speak like that, you know. Of course one feels at once a sort of natural shrinking from black people – one can't help that – it seems so innate in one. But one oughtn't to let them see it themselves, at any rate. Respect their feelings, Nora; do, dear, for my sake, I beg of you.'
>
> 'Oh, it's all very well for you, Marian,' Nora answered, quite aloud, and strumming on the deck with her parasol. 'But for my part, you know, if there's anything on earth that I can't endure, it's a brown man ...'[43]

The contemporary pattern of miscegenation in the Caribbean in part follows the historical pattern I have attempted to describe, and in part has been affected by a number of factors which have developed in the last thirty years. Of these three are of great importance: the struggle for political independence; the development of a black consciousness; and the growth of tourism. The societies still tend to be pyramidal in form with the whites at the apex. This is strongest in Barbados, the Bahamas and Bermuda, and weakest in islands such as Grenada and St Vincent, where there is a much depleted white population – St Vincent with a total population of over 90,000 has 1,804 whites and 17,444 coloured; Grenada, with a similar total population, has under 7,000 whites and a mixed group of over 37,000. In the case of Barbados, of the approximately quarter million people, over 10,000 are whites, and nearly 14,000 coloured. Bermuda is the territory in the region where racial tension is at its worst. With a resident population of something over 40,000, there are nearly 27,000 people classified as coloured – this includes those of pure Negro descent – and approximately 16,000 whites. It is my contention that wherever in the Caribbean the whites are a significant minority, as in the case of Barbados and Bermuda, prejudice and discrimination are at their most intense. Whereas in areas where the white minority is insignificant in terms of the total population racial tension is at its least.[44]

The new-found political consciousness of Caribbean societies, whether in the form of Castroism or independent membership of the British Commonwealth, has led to a new pride in being West Indian. This consciousness is very closely linked to the development of a bias towards Africa and things black. Undoubtedly this has affected miscegenation. A generation ago the coloured or black man always endeavoured to marry a woman lighter than himself – a pattern common throughout the New World wherever the Negro is found. For aspirants in the coloured middle class the best marriage to make was with a European woman. This class is the one which is most intransigent with relation to the surrender of the notion of the inherent superiority of the white. The older male generation in this group is still apt to contract marriage with a European Englishwoman.

The writer propounded the hypothesis some years ago that one of the most active principles in West Indian society was the 'white bias'.[45] The latter we described as the tendency to adulate everything which was European and to denigrate all that was African. In my opinion this was certainly true up to the sixties. There has undoubtedly been a shift in values, particularly among the educated, young black people. But it is debateable how far this has affected the self-image. Research done by Dr Errol Miller at the University of the West Indies suggests that the 'white bias' has moved away from the ideal of the European as such but still approximates much more to a white image than a black one.

Four hundred and seventy-five pupils from three secondary schools in Kingston, the capital of Jamaica, were given an extensive questionnaire to answer including such questions as 'What do you dislike about your body?' 'What parts of your body would you change if it were possible?' and 'What do you like about your body?' The respondents were divided into colour groups – White, Chinese, Fair, Clear, Brown, Dark, and Black:

> Of the total sample, 72·6 per cent report that Fair or Clear is the ideal colour of the handsome boy. The preference for these colours is not only true of the sample as a whole, but it is also true for each colour group within the sample. Of the two colour types, Fair is the one preferred. It is preferred by 53·2 per cent of the total sample as the ideal colour of the handsome boy ... Fair colour would probably be close to the colour one associates with a deeply tanned or sunburnt White person, while Clear is somewhat darker than this but also a little lighter than the coffee colour commonly associated with the typical West

Indian ... One member of the sample said, 'The handsome boy should not be too porky [White]; he should be tanned' ... It seems reasonable to say that the ideal colour in this culture context is one or two shades removed from White, and is accepted by most.[46]

The corollary of the stereotype of the beautiful girl is the same as for the handsome boy. 'The beautiful girl has Caucasian features and is Fair or Clear in colour ...'[47] This research was conducted in 1968–1969, a period when there was a definite reawakening amongst intellectuals in the Caribbean as to the significance of their African heritage. This of course can be paralleled by similar movements in the United States in the sixties. What is difficult to assess is how this has affected the mass of the West Indian population – that is, a black population. Certainly Miller's researches would suggest that adolescents, at any rate in Jamaica, are not turning towards the ideal of the African physical type.

The West Indian population is essentially heterogeneous. While it is true to say that people of African descent predominate there are other ethnic groups of significance – the Chinese and the East Indian. Together with the coloured group they constitute a barrier to the acceptance of a black ethos. Novels, plays, stories and poetry may be written emphasizing the importance of links with Africa but for a considerable minority it is very difficult to identify with a continent which is totally alien in terms of culture and language. At a literary conference in Jamaica two or three years ago East Indian writers experienced difficulty in accepting the notion that African culture was of fundamental importance for the West Indian writer.

The paradox of the situation is that even the most vehement of Black Power leaders in both the Caribbean and the United States tend to have white wives. The tradition, indeed, does die hard.

My own researches over the last ten years in the Caribbean suggest the mythology of the superiority of the white is still being upheld in terms of marriage. That is to say a coloured or black man will generally tend, particularly in the middle classes, to marry a woman who is lighter than himself. This not only improves his own social status but creates greater opportunities for his children. It is in fact the historical pattern.

In the contemporary Caribbean miscegenation not only takes place between white and coloured, and within the coloured group, but between those of African descent and East Indians and Chinese. Both the latter groups are comparative newcomers on the Caribbean scene. East Indians were brought into the West Indies as indentured labour to work on the sugar estates after emancipation and the consequent loss of labour on the plantations. The main areas to which they went were Trinidad, Guyana and Jamaica. Today in the first two islands they constitute almost half the total population. In Jamaica they number some 30,000 in a population of 2,000,000.

On the whole the contemporary East Indian tends to be endogamous – that is he marries within his group. This endogamous pattern is repeated throughout the region – they constitute a minority in most of the islands. Trinidad is probably the society where East Indian endogamy is least marked. Reactions from the coloured black group to marriage with East Indians are generally that the coloured person is marrying down and thus loses status. From the East Indian point of view such an alliance is to break the solidarity of the family and kin group. For neither family is it satisfactory. In Guyana the issue of such a marriage are known as Douglas.

The Chinese are even later comers to the Caribbean, arriving in the eighties and nineties of the last century. At first they were employed on the land but very soon became involved in retail trading of all kinds. Traditionally their pattern was also endogamous. Again, Trinidad is the society where more Chinese–Coloured alliances have taken place. Religion and culture were the historical barriers to miscegenation as in the case of the East Indian.

In both cases, that of the East Indian and the Chinese, political events in terms of former colonies achieving independent status, have produced a different attitude towards intermarriage with the population of African descent. The latter is everywhere in the majority. If the minority wishes to continue to signify it must come to terms with this new situation. In other words the tendency is probably towards a relaxation of the traditional pattern of endogamy.

Another minority is composed of people from the Middle East – the Lebanon. Despite their country of origin they are known throughout the area as Syrians. They are probably the most endogamous group in the Caribbean today. Mainly Christian, they have, having started as itinerant salesmen or peddlers, achieved a dominant economic position in a number of different trades. Their reluctance to intermarry is exhibited in all the areas into which they have gone – most of the former British West African colonies as well as the West Indies.

Tourism is the latest catalyst to affect miscegenation in the Caribbean. The West Indies have become since the 1939 war one of the major regions of European and American tourism. The market is dominated by citizens of the United States and Canada, with the British and South Americans constituting a minor contribution. From an original beginning, in which the Caribbean was a playground for the rich of these countries, the advent of the package-tour has meant the arrival of middle- and lower-middle-class whites. They come into a black society and experience difficulty in making adjustment. For Americans in particular it is a unique experience – being able to interact, in a free situation, with black and coloured people on a level of equality. Again, for many Americans the possibility of having sexual encounters with black people is a new experience. Sexual interaction is mainly between black or coloured men and white women. It appears that American white women feel that the sexual approach of the West Indian is refreshingly free from the inhibitions normally associated with their own menfolk.

The dimension of this type of miscegenation is limited to a particular group in the population. They frequent the beach adjacent to tourist hotels, and are in fact gigolos. Known as beach-boys they have achieved both notoriety and success. Their activities could be taken as a reflection of the economic problems of the Caribbean as a whole. The opportunities for young men are severely limited. To become a beach-boy at least assures that your standard of living improves, and you can taste some of the affluence which the tourist flaunts. For the white typist from the United States or Canada the beach-boy in the Caribbean supplies the glamour necessary for a tropical holiday.

In this chapter we have tried to plot the course of miscegenation in the West Indies. There are similarities with the situation in the United States, but we have tried to point out that the West Indies, because of their special history as a colonial area dominated by a number of European powers, exhibit a unique contribution to the process of miscegenation.

CHAPTER 8

The Case of Africa

It is not our intention in this chapter to make an analysis of the process of miscegenation throughout the African continent but rather to attempt to examine a number of specific instances. Clearly South Africa is the country in which, historically speaking, there has been the greatest contact in terms of the sexual between the European and the African. It is also the only country in Africa where such relationships are expressly forbidden at law. But before examining the South African case it will be helpful, in order to create a perspective, to look at other areas of the continent.

The nature and character of the European powers which controlled a particular African colony obviously had a definite effect on the pattern of race relations which developed. Thus distinction can be made between the Portuguese, the Dutch, the French and the British in this respect. A British example is the colony of Sierra Leone.

Sierra Leone is unique in the history of British colonialism in that it was founded as a haven for the poor black people who lived in England in the eighteenth century. It was through the inspiration of the Evangelical group known as the Clapham Sect, which comprised most of the leading anti-slavery advocates in the country, such as William Wilberforce, Thomas Clarkson and Granville Sharp, that Government was persuaded to organize the settlement of the colony. At a cost of some £15,000, including stores and provisions, a convoy of three transports and a naval sloop, the *Nautilus*, was made ready. In April 1787, after innumerable delays owing to bad weather, the convoy set sail from Plymouth.

Granville Sharp had created a constitution for these new colonists in their new, free land. It was partly based on Anglo-Saxon regulations and Biblical injunctions. The black settlers, some 700, signed the agreement, but many took fright that it might mean a new form of slavery.

By November 1786 the number pledged to sail to Sierra Leone had declined to 259. When, in the following April, the transports left London for Plymouth there were 456 passengers aboard, due to more recruitment:[1]

> ... Vassa records them as 290 black men, 41 black women, 11 black children, 70 white women and 6 white children; the remaining 38 were officials or craftsmen with their families and 1 private passenger. Over 50 died on board; 24 were landed at Plymouth; 23 ran away. But more were sent to replace them. Finally 411 sailed ...[2]

The presence of these white women was of considerable importance as they subsequently were married to the black men on board. Sierra Leone might be said to have been founded on miscegenation. Accounts differ as to the social condition of these women. Mrs Anna Falconbridge, a somewhat colourful author, visited the colony in 1791 and wrote of her experiences. She met some of the female members of the original expedition, and was somewhat appalled by their condition. One of them gave her the following information:

> She said, the women were mostly of that description of persons who walk the streets of London, and support themselves by the earnings of prostitution; that men were employed to collect and conduct them to Wapping, where they were intoxicated with liquor, then inveigled on board ship and married to *Black men*, whom they had never seen before; that the morning after she was married, she really did not remember a syllable of what happened over night, and when informed, was obliged to inquire *who was her husband*. After this, to the time of their sailing, they were amused and buoyed up by a prodigality of fair promises, and great expectations which awaited them in the country they were going to: 'Thus,' in her own words, 'to the disgrace of my mother country, upwards of one hundred unfortunate women were seduced from England to practice their inquities more brutishly in this horrid country.'[3]

There is some doubt as to the accuracy of this report. The main ground of criticism is that it would have been totally out of character for Granville Sharp, a man of deep religious convictions, to have countenanced the recruitment of prostitutes for his great experiment. On the other hand it is very possible that the kind and type of women who 'volunteered' to go to Sierra Leone was kept from him. Again, the Navy, which was supplying transportation, was not particularly interested in the sexual morality of their passengers. The explanation may well be that the Negro settlers, anxious for the companionship of the opposite sex, invited any woman who expressed a desire to travel with them, prostitutes included.[4]

Whatever may have been the moral and social position of the white women concerned it appears that they set a precedent for racial intermarriage in Sierra Leone which has persisted to our own day.

If miscegenation is taken as an index of harmonious race relations then there is little doubt that Sierra Leone in the nineteenth century was overtly well adjusted. The European element in the society was small. They did not live in a segregated area, as tended to occur in the next century. Both Government service and social clubs were integrated. Clergymen of the Church Missionary Society set the example in terms of marriage. A number, such as Gustavus Nylander, Melchior Renner and Charles Wenzel married black women from Nova Scotia. These people were the remnants of families who had remained on the British side during the American War of Independence, and subsequently emigrated to Nova Scotia and from thence to Sierra Leone. Some European traders in the colony, such as John Broadhurst and John Nicol, did the same. This was paralleled on the Creole side, that is the descendants of black settlers not the indigeneous Africans, by prominent individual males marrying English women who they brought out to the colony. It was not always a case of a marital union. Sir Charles MacCarthy, Governor of Sierra Leone from 1816–1844, took as his mistress Hannah Hayes, a mulatto. There appeared to be no prejudice against mulattoes and many achieved success in public life – Charles Heddle, a coloured trader, was a member of the Governor's Council from 1845–1863, John Meheux was Sheriff of the colony from 1855–1886.[5]

Not all Englishmen in high positions in the colony viewed the state of affairs with equanimity. Sir Arthur Kennedy, who was Governor in the middle of the century, expressed his fears to the Colonial Office in a Despatch of 1853:

> The confusion, cabals, heart burnings arising from illegitimacy are indescribable. The following outline which I believe to be strictly according to fact may illustrate the subject. I will omit names, having no desire to do more than justify the foregoing remarks. Mr A., an officer of one of the courts, is the illegitimate son of the former judge of the court by a black woman. Mr B., his junior in the same office, is legitimately born of a white woman by the same father. Mr A. is married to an illegitimate daughter of Mr C. (a white man) by a black woman. Mr C. was a member of the Legislative Council . . . Mr D. in the Secretary's office is the illegitimate son of the new judge in the Colony by a coloured woman. ... Mr D. is married to the illegitimate

daughter of Mr E. (later a magistrate and member of Council) by a black woman which woman is now married to one of the most wealthy and intelligent of the coloured men of the Colony.[6]

A comparison can be made between Sierra Leone and the Caribbean during this period in its ramifications of the relationships of both white and coloured.

There is no question that Sierra Leone is unique, both in its history and in the sphere of race relations, in British Colonial Africa. The Church Missionary Society elsewhere in the continent took a poor view of clandestine sexual relations on the part of their officers. Not only was the unfortunate unmarried missionary subject to long-range scrutiny from home with regard to his behaviour, but he suffered from religious scruples in addition. Neither of these affected the trader or Government official. In addition these men dedicated to dispel the darkness of paganism could not afford to bring out an English wife and maintain her on the pittance they received. Some missionary bodies in Central Africa encouraged and assisted their clergymen to take their wives to the fields of their endeavour rather than submit themselves to the terrible temptations of 'native' women. This, however, had a number of unexpected repercussions.

In the case of other parts of British Africa, as new areas opened up in the nineteenth century, the Europeans were almost entirely missionaries, traders and administrators. There were few white women with them. It is true to say that in these early periods of contact between white and black race relations were not characterized by great animosity. But the advent of European women changed this profoundly. There is '... a general tendency for the presence of white women to arouse a strong protective male instinct closely associated with an abhorrence for the idea of possible sexual relations between black men and white women. The result was an aggressive attitude in the British male which inhibited easy social contact between the races ...'[7]

Even Livingstone, so renowned for his love and affection for the African, at the thought of such contact was moved to passion. 'We would do almost anything to avoid a collision with degraded natives; but in case of an invasion — our blood boils at the very thought of our wives, daughters, or sisters being touched — we, as men with human feelings, would unhesitatingly fight to the death, with all the fury in our power...'[8]

Livingstone displays an almost Sicilian concern at the hypothetical rape of his beloved ones – the thought might even have excited him.

One missionary in Central Africa, A. J. Swann of the London Missionary Society, thought of European women in Africa as 'delicate flowers of civilization growing in the midst of general darkness and cruelty...'

Rape, of course, was the ultimate and unspeakable crime. But there were other dangers to which the delicacy of the English middle-class woman might be, and almost certainly would be, exposed.

> ... think of a modest girl ... hitherto shielded with such jealous care from contact with anything coarse or impure ... in fact, grown up stupidly innocent; think of her suddenly thrust into a barbarous country where the inhabitants are naked and not ashamed (Eden?), and where they exhibit a wanting knowledge of decency which to her English prudery must appear horribly indecent; where too, the women among whom she has to come to minister will ... talk glibly to her of matters that the most depraved of her sex in her own country would hesitate to mention; consider the effect of this ordeal on a mind innocent of evil, and you will realize that this unwholesome experience must necessarily be acquired at the cost of a certain loss of delicacy ... so this rude contact with coarse animal natures and their unrestrained display of animal instincts tends imperceptibly to blunt a modest woman's susceptibilities, and even, in time, to tinge her own thoughts and language with an unintentional coarseness.[9]

The author quoted above, Sir Harry Johnston, the explorer, was writing at a time (1887) when prostitution in London was of immense proportions. Surely he must have been aware that London prostitutes, the compatriots of his 'modest' girl, would certainly have outweighed in vulgarity and obscenity the majority of women he encountered in Africa?

It is of some importance, as a gloss on the situation, that no cases of rape were ever reported at this time before these countries were officially annexed to the empire.[10] Mary Kingsley, that intrepid, lone English traveller in West Africa in the late nineteenth century, would have laughed at Sir Harry's fears.

It can be assumed that the English woman did not make her contribution to the process of miscegenation in Central Africa. It was left to the British male to shoulder this responsibility. He did this with aplomb, and no doubt enjoyment.

Two accounts from Matabeleland in what is now Mr Ian Smith's terrain, Rhodesia, illustrate the process of miscegenation in the late nineteenth century in this part of Africa. It will be noted that neither makes any mention of marriage. The first is by H. Vaughan-Williams, and was published in 1889:

> On entering Matabeleland he was struck with the beauty of the young girls who were 'far from shy' and, he was informed, would offer themselves to any white man for two yards of blue cloth. Young girls

tried to crawl into bed with the visitors. They were 'very persistent and seemed insulted when we cleared them off'. On another occasion Lobengula [the Matabele Chief] sent them three 'young, well set-up Matabele girls ... who looked like bronze statues'. By his own account he seems to have spent much of his time in warding off the attempts of 'these maids' to break down the resolve of the uncooperative visitor. Other whites were more cooperative, and by 1890 miscegenation had so progressed that Lobengula called a meeting at Bulawayo 'of all the men, women and girls to discuss the subject of fornication' as he was concerned about the number of half-caste children. The women when accused of prostitution, were reported to have replied that the men sent them to the whites and 'then collared all the produce of their sins'. Sam Edwards, who had known the Matabele for more than thirty years, felt that the meeting would be of no avail for the girls 'must have limbo and beads and will risk their bodies to have them as per usual'.[11]

The second account is that of J. S. Moffat, a former missionary, who was British agent at Bulawayo for three years in the 1890s. He described the whites in the most caustic terms – 'abominably filthy', 'living almost like natives thinking their thoughts and imitating their ways'. Of individuals he knew he used the same language. 'Utterly demoralized', 'a very low lived man', 'keeps a considerable native harem', 'a moral invertebrate', and so forth.[12] Moffat's strictures are based on what he regarded as the degradation of the white man in the eyes of the 'natives', which hampered his task of spreading the Gospel. That the peers of these same men in England would have consorted with prostitutes of their own colour did not, apparently, occur to him. Clearly it was the white man who was degraded by these sexual relationships. The black women could not *become* so degraded as they were already in that state.

In the two Rhodesias after the First World War a policy of segregation began to develop:

It was not simply the threat of economic competition, or even of political infiltration; it was a combination of these factors together with the shadow of miscegenation, and the presence of a vast mass of people across a cultural gulf which seemed unbridgeable. An abhorrence of miscegenation was general, it clinched the argument, and perhaps sometimes it was even a substitute for thought ...[13]

By this time Lobengula was long dead, as were his maidens, and the European male was dominated by his wife from England.

A familiar argument in favour of segregation was used by Charles Bullock, who became Chief Native Commissioner during this post-war period. 'Hybridization, however gradual, cannot be contemplated with equanimity. Apart from that danger, it is best and right that each race should develop (and, if possible, be given full opportunities of developing) according to the potentialities that lie within its biological inheritance.'[14] In a debate in the Legislative Assembly one member said: '... if we do not face the position today, then I can see that in the future we shall have not a white race but something undesirable to the Maker of humanity...'[15]

There is an odious air of patronage in such statements akin to those of the white Southerner in the States when speaking of the 'progress' of *his* Negroes. Today's supporters of Ian Smith can claim a tradition over fifty years old for their policy directed against the Rhodesian African.

By the 1920s, as we have suggested, the whole atmosphere of interracial sex had changed. There were now a far greater number of European women than there had been in the early days of the colony. Their presence helped the adoption of extremely rigid attitudes akin to those of South Africa:

> According to most Europeans, such relations [sexual] threaten to shake the very foundations of the social system of Southern Rhodesia. The structure of the European family can be maintained only if European women are 'untouchable', only if intimate and permanent relations with African males are discouraged and prevented ... Africans must not try to impinge too closely upon the intimate relations of the European household. African servants, for example, may be allowed to handle and care for European infants and to wash dishes, towels, and diapers; they generally will not be permitted, on the other hand, to use these dishes and towels or the lavatory and bathing facilities ...[16]

Opinions such as the above demonstrate that marriage can be used as an index of true racial equality. The European in Rhodesia was, and is, determined to keep control of political and economic power. The maintenance of their social system – that is the continuing exploitation of the African – is dependent on the refusal to miscegenate. To do that is to give equality to the exploited. The illogicality of the latter part of the quotation is clear. If you allow 'natives' to perform intimate household duties the possibility is always there that a sexual situation may develop. A hypothetical segregation may collapse in the face of domestic intimacy.[17]

The burden of sexual segregation falls more heavily upon the white woman than on the white man. If the latter consorts with an African woman he will meet censure but he will not be totally ostracized. A woman, however, '... who married or was known to have sexual relations with an African would be certain to lose status, and be subjected to the sanctions of European public opinion and law. Should she marry an African, there would be a real possibility that she would have forfeited all the traditional protection and support that surrounds her as a member of the dominant cultural group.'[18] To act in this way is for her to betray the group whose main purpose has been to protect her 'untouchability'. To have sexual relations with an African through *choice* is to destroy the whole *raison d'être* of white supremacy.

Rhodesia remains a society in which the white minority is determined to remain dominant. The corollary of this is that all sanctions, short of legislation prohibiting sexual relations, must be invoked to inhibit such relations. Geographically Rhodesia is a long way from Sierra Leone. It is even further in terms of social distance.

The French experience in Madagascar differs profoundly from the Anglo-Saxon forms of colonialism we have discussed so far. The island only became a French colony in 1896, achieved the status of an overseas territory in 1946, and became independent in 1960. The French presence is thus almost totally a twentieth-century phenomenon. Mannoni, in his study of the psychology of colonialism, *Prospero and Caliban* (London 1956), used the island, in which he had spent long periods, as the basis of his research.

In the initial period of contact between the two races marriages and sexual unions were comparatively frequent. But as French women began to arrive, the archetypal situation developed, and such relationships began to decline. Such unions had hitherto not aroused the resentment of Malagasy men. Families in fact felt such alliances as a source of pride. Galliéni, who was Governor from 1896–1905, encouraged this process for a time. The growth of a half-caste population, it was thought, would bridge the gap between the races. Unfortunately this did not occur. Mannoni makes the point that as a people the Malagasy in their relations with Europeans do not appear to have an inferiority complex. In the case of the half-caste, however, he feels rejected by both racial groups and thus inferior.[19]

The arrival of French women, and the equivocal status of the half-caste, changed the pattern of sexual behaviour:

> The colonial woman is, as it were, the feminine counterpart of Prospero, but – and it is an astonishing fact – in Madagascar the European women are far more racialist than the men. Sometimes their racialism attains preposterous proportions. For instance, at a mass, sung for the souls of some European victims of the rebellion, women from the good Christian community raised an indignant protest against the presence of Malagasy choirboys. No man, however much a racialist and however little a Christian, would have gone that far.[20]

Unions between French women and Malagasy men were very infrequent. This was partly because such women did not satisfy the Malagasy notion of the ideal of woman, and partly because of the ostracism the woman would meet from the European community. A European man on the other hand could contract such an alliance much more easily as he does not enter into the intricacy of familial relationships to the extent a woman is forced to. Also he does not necessarily cut his ties with his own community.

Mannoni explained the phenomenon of feminine racialism in the following way:

> At least one element in this feminine racialism is over-compensation for an inferiority complex similar to that of *nouvelles-riches* in Europe, whose relations with their domestic servants and social inferiors bear the stamp of over-compensation. There is undoubtedly some sexual tinge to it too: the white woman is constantly trying to impress it on the white man's consciousness that there can be no possible comparison between herself and the Malagasay woman. As for her attitude to the Malagasay man, the power of issuing tyrannical orders to him no doubt satisfies her unconscious urge to dominate a male figure.[21]

This analysis could be applied to the European woman in many colonial situations. It is the female component which disturbs the classical stereotype of the Anglo-Saxon being more racialist than the Latin. Portuguese wives in Mozambique behave very much as their French counterparts in Madagascar.

Senegal was under French colonial rule from 1848–1960 when independence was granted. Prior to 1848 – from the first decades of the seventeenth century – the French penetration in the form of trading companies based on Rouen and Bordeaux existed. Later in the century companies, such as the *Compagnie du Sénégal*, obtained their charters from the King and were granted trade monopolies of various kinds.[22] St Louis, at the mouth of the Senegal River, and originally a fort, became the first capital in 1659. At this time a number of company trading posts were spread over the country. The men employed at these posts can best be described as the drop-outs of French society – near-criminals, debtors and so forth.[23]

From the outset miscegenation had taken place between this riff-raff and local women. Their progeny, the *métis*, were frequently employed by the company, as were those Negroes who had been greatly influenced by the French, and who were known as *habitants*. Both had a number of rights and privileges denied to the mass of the African population. From these beginnings developed a positive policy of assimilation through miscegenation. This was partly due to the paucity of European women, and to the hardships of life in trading posts 'up country'. It must not be thought that sexual relationships between the French and Africans were confined to the level of the plebian. Many senior company officials were either married to Senegalese women or had set them up as their mistresses. A number of these came from rich and influential African families. Such women were known as *signares*.

Lower down in the scale French soldiers and petty officials organized their *signares* to run a business in order to augment their income. If they left to return to France the practice was to make over the business to the *signare* and their children. It was felt that the children would provide a cadre of people so Gallicized that their loyalty would be unquestioned. To an extent it worked – both for the benefit of the *métis* and the companies. Some of the former rose to occupy relatively important posts in Government.[24]

In the nineteenth century this process of *métissage* developed even more. In 1879 a General Council for the colony was created on the lines of similar institutions in France at the level of départements. It was an elective body to which a number of *métis* were elected. Here they were in a position to be of service to their masters – the companies – but also to create a financial and political network of great advantage to themselves. As the century progresses the picture emerges of a coloured middle class, Gallicized to a degree, and exercising considerable influence on the affairs of the colony.

This state of affairs began to change about 1900 when Dakar, by then a flourishing city, initiated a plan of segregated living, on the ostensible grounds of health. Other factors, however, can be discerned. Possibly the most important were those concerned with the fact that the European population was now beginning to increase rapidly. The female element of the latter had risen dramatically. The numbers of French families were now sufficient to begin to deprive the old *métis* families of their power and influence. Thus we can say that demographic changes produced changes in the original pattern of miscegenation. The significant period for these changes was the 1930s.

At the end of the decade with the coming of war there was a revival of Franco-African sexual relationships which persisted into the post-war period of Senegalese labour recruitment to France. But the attitude of French fathers to their mulatto children was no longer as it had been traditionally. Tradition had demanded that they should be responsible for their welfare, and in the past this had been honoured. The new phase, however, of black-white sexual relationships was dominated by the casual affaire of short duration. The result was that children resulting from such encounters were often abandoned by *both* parents. This was in great contrast to the heyday of *métissage.*The blame for this change in thought and feeling can be attributed to the growth in number of European families. The community as such no longer gave approval to *signares*. The behaviour in fact began to approximate much more to that existing in British colonies. The actual composition of the French population at this time may also have been significant. Curiously enough, the new dimension here was of people of inferior social status whose arrival coincided with the development of a new cadre of educated Senegalese. A situation was created in which the two ethnic groups began to isolate themselves for the first time in their history of contact.

In 1972 Rita Conor Cruise O'Brien published a study of race relations in Senegal, *White Society in Black Africa*. The author embodied a small survey she made concerning attitudes towards mixed marriages. Her findings are of great interest:

> Mixed couples resident in Senegal are nearly all composed of a Senegalese man and a French woman, while before the war when there were few European women in the colony, the opposite was the case. Since 1945, the number of African students in French universities has risen steadily and they have often sought French wives because there were no African girls of their own level of education. Initially many of them remained in France, but towards the end of the Fifties, as the opportunities for jobs in Senegal became more numerous, this new generation began to return home.[25]

This, we can see, represents a complete reversal of the patterns we have been describing.

In the sample taken of French expatriates sixty per cent were against mixed marriages. Interestingly some of the reasons given for this negative view are very similar to those forthcoming from Anglo-Saxons when similarly questioned.

'I find it entirely distasteful, I have physical discomfort in seeing a white and black together. I could never stand the thought of a black head on white sheets.'[26] The first part of that statement can be compared to the opinion of Norman Podhoretz on the same theme which we quoted in another chapter. The second has considerable Freudian overtones.

The French conception of love played its part in rejection of miscegenation. The following was the view of a banker: 'Love has been a part of European culture since the Middle Ages, but Africans don't know about it. "Dear" doesn't exist in their language [*sic*]. They try to imitate love *à la mode européenne* from what they learn in the cinema, but they return to their original ways. They don't make love the same way we do.'[27]

Overt racist opinions were also expressed:

> The white race diminishes with each mixed marriage. A mixed race is inferior to the white race. It is also a degradation of white women that they should have mulatto children in an underdeveloped society. In so doing, they lose their place in white society. When a white woman marries an African, it is her downfall. It repels me – a woman is an imbecile to mix with blacks. The wife must often work to support her black husband.'[28]

Replies from Senegalese informants to the same question were much more ambivalent. Out of twenty-three respondents six approved, seven disapproved and ten reserved their opinion.[29] The background to this was in part the fears most had for the disapproval of relatives, and for being cut off from African life – they might be 'lost for Africa'.

The mulatto view appeared to differ from the African: 'I approve entirely – if ever I were given the chance to marry a Frenchman, I would not hesitate.' Here is the tragedy and success of Gallicization – the mulatto obviously adhering to the French side of her heritage wishes to become even more French, to identify herself with things European. The same problem, however, can occur with the African woman. The French wife of a Senegalese civil servant made this statement:

> The French are more racist here than in France – they have a colonialist temperament. In France, we were often invited to people's homes, here, we are not. I have been living in Senegal for seven years and have never once been invited to the home of any of the people with whom I work in the bank. Most of the French people we see are technical assistants who work with my husband, and these are few. Contact with the Senegalese is difficult for me because when men come to the house they never bring their wives, and they converse in Wolof which I do not understand.[30]

In the brief survey we have made of miscegenation in Senegal the contrast with British Africa is quite apparent, but at the same time the increasing racism in France has had its repercussions in her former colonies with regard to miscegenation. An even greater contrast is provided when we turn to consider the society which has set its face totally against the idea of miscegenation – South Africa.

Europeans, in the form of the Portuguese, had established contact with the southern part of Africa as early as the fifteenth century. Da Gama touched at Mossel Bay in 1497. In the years that followed the Dutch and the English used the harbours as watering places for their ships. It was not, however, until 1652 that the first permanent settlement of Europeans at the Cape was made by the Dutch. Three years before, a report had been made to the Dutch Government outlining the advantages to be gained from the establishment of a settlement. In it the writers gave their opinion as to the 'native' population.

> ... Others will say that the natives are brutal and cannibals, from whom no good can be expected, and that we will have to be continually on our guard, but this is a vulgar error, as will be shown further on. We do not deny that they live without laws or police, like many Indians, nor that some boatmen and soldiers have been killed by them, but the cause is not generally stated by our people, in order to excuse themselves. We are quite convinced that the peasants of this country [Holland] in case their cattle are shot down or taken away without payment would not be a hair better than these natives if they had not to fear the law ... The killing of our people is undoubtedly caused by revenge being taken by the natives when their cattle is seized, and not because they are cannibals ...[31]

The Report is interesting in a number of ways. Its importance from our point of view is that it describes the Hottentots almost in terms of equality with Dutchmen. This benign view certainly entered into sexual relations for quite a long period. In fact it only came to an end in the middle of the nineteenth century with the settlement of the Transvaal and Orange Free State by the *Voortrekkers*.

Slavery of Africans and of people brought from India and the East Indies appears to have occurred from the first years of the colony. The settlers had few women with them. Inevitable sexual connections were formed with both Hottentots and Indians, both slave and free. The Dutch married these women or kept them as concubines:

> In addition to these illicit or casual relations which might exist in spite of social disapproval, there were also regular unions that took place with full social approval and religious sanction ... These early mixed marriages are all of European men and women of pure blood, either liberated slaves or daughters of slaves from the East, especially from Bengal. On aesthetic grounds there could be no objection to these Bengalese women, and since there was certainly no objection on grounds of skin-colour, they and their children were simply absorbed into the predominantly white community. On the other hand, intermarriage, as distinct from cohabitation, between European men and Hottentot women at the Cape was extremely rare ...[32]

It would seem that these, the first Dutchmen at the Cape, were singularly free from colour prejudice. Their reluctance to marry Hottentots – as physical types they are at a great remove from the European – must not be attributed to aesthetic feelings but rather to the fact that the Hottentots were the indigenous inhabitants of the Cape whom the Dutch had subjugated. Marriage with such women would have affected the status of both partners in the society.

To describe the Cape at this period as merely a Dutch colony would be wrong. The society in fact was a medley of races. It comprised a number of European nationalities – English, French, Italian, Hungarian, German, Chinese as well as a whole range of ethnic groups from the Far East:

> In such an environment, race contacts were more free and less conventional than in a more rigid and stable society. Within the urban zone, in which there was always a large preponderance of men, miscegenation took place on an extensive scale. Commissioner Goske ... was shocked to discover, when he visited the Cape in 1671, that three out of every four children born of slave mothers were of European paternity. In 1678 the Council issued a proclamation forbidding the *practice* of concubinage with female slaves ...[33]

This proclamation was followed by legislation in 1685 which forbade marriage between white men and slave-women. Needless to say the injunction against concubinage was not effective and the institution continued to flourish. Miscegenation was not only a matter of concubinage and marriage, it also comprised a prostitute element:

> Female slaves are always ready to offer their bodies for a trifle; and towards evening, one can see a string of soldiers and sailors entering the lodge where they misspend their time until the clock strikes 9 ... The Company does nothing to prevent this promising intercourse, since, for one thing it tends to multiply the slave population, and does away with the necessity of importing fresh slaves. Three or four generations of this admixture (for the daughters follow their mothers' footsteps) have produced a half-caste population – a mestizo class – but a single shade darker than some Europeans.[34]

What it amounts to is that the headquarters of the Dutch East India Company at the Cape in 1787 was used as a common brothel with the approval of the company itself. The modern equivalent would be if oil companies and other international corporations were to permit their premises overseas to be used for prostitution either open or disguised. Such a situation is of course unthinkable.

The brothel served the needs of *hoi-polloi.* For the middle-class scion of a Dutch family there was no necessity for such a recourse. His sexual pleasures were to be found in his own home:

> Boys who, through force of circumstance, have to remain at home during these impressionable years between 16 and 21 more often than not commit some folly, and get entangled with a handsome slave-girl belonging to the household. These affairs are not regarded as very serious ... the offence is venial in the public estimation. It does not hurt the boy's prospects; his escapade is a source of amusement, and he is dubbed a young fellow who has shown the stuff he is made of.[35]

This form of sexual abuse – the girl was probably punished or sold if she became pregnant – is typical of the slave society. As we shall see, in another chapter, very similar events occurred in colonial Brazil.

The Dutch, perpetually enterprising, were not above profiting from the libidos of each other:

> Female slaves sometimes live with Europeans as husband and wife with the permission of their masters who benefit in two ways: the cost of upkeep of the slave is reduced through the presents she receives from the man, and her children are the property of her master since the children of female slaves are themselves slaves ... In this manner, the slave population is always increasing ...[36]

It sounds an excellent arrangement of benefit to all concerned except the unfortunate slave-girl.

The appetite for miscegenation continued throughout the eighteenth century. The alliance of whites and Hottentots produced a group known as *Bastards.* This at the time was not necessarily a derogatory term but one used to describe biological reality. They constituted the origin of the people termed the Cape Coloured today. A further facet in the chain of miscegenation was the unions of the progeny of white–slave (Malay or Indian) with the offspring of slaves with Hottentots. They also comprise an element in the contemporary Cape Coloured. François Vaillant, who visited the Cape in the 1780s, stated that one-sixth of the population were *Bastards.*[37] Later, in the nineteenth century, these people settled in their own communities along the Orange River.

These halcyon days of inter-racial sex, at any rate from the European point of view, were destroyed by the advent of the *Voortrekkers.* Their character seems to have been bounded by unadulterated Calvinism and colour prejudice. For them a black person was already damned because of his colour. The latter was associated with sin and evil, both anathema to your religious Boer. To him can be attributed the responsibility for modern South Africa's views on race. As a member of God's elect it is a distinction and honour he would welcome.

The effects of this Boer philosophy, or mania, can be seen in the legislation which began to occur in the twentieth century. Its beginning was a law of 1902, passed in the Cape Colony and later extended to other parts of South Africa. This outlawed sexual acts between Africans and white prostitutes. A generation later, in 1927, under Hertzog, legislation was introduced which prohibited all sexual relations between blacks and whites. This was followed in 1949 by an Act of Malan's Government – the Prohibition of Mixed Marriages Act – which made intermarriage between Europeans and *all* non-Europeans illegal. Thus the field of prohibition was extended from blacks to the coloured people.

The most recent legislation on this topic dates from 1950 and 1957. This amended the Immorality Act of 1927 to include 'immoral and indecent acts' between whites and all non-whites. Its full title was the 'Act to Prohibit Illicit Carnal Intercourse between Europeans and Natives and other Acts in Relation thereto'. The lawmakers modestly opined that their object was not to check immorality as such but 'to try to preserve some sort of apartheid in what one might call prostitution . . .'[38] Here we enter the twilight world of the racist laws of the Third Reich.

Sexual acts thus became a criminal activity if performed with the wrong person. The penalties attached for both parties to the crime was seven years' hard labour, and corporal punishment in addition for the male partner.

If marriage is an indicator, prior to the passing of the fifties' legislation the percentage of Europeans marrying outside their group was very small. It declined from 0·47 per cent in 1925 to 0·14 per cent in 1946. In the same period intermarriage between the other racial groups in South Africa increased – that is marriages between African and Coloured, African and Indian, and Indian and Coloured.[39]

Legislation regarding sexual behaviour is always difficult to enforce. South Africa's Immorality Laws are no exception. Marriage, as we have seen, between whites and non-whites can be effectively prevented. Illicit sexual relations, however, are another matter. The actual detection of the offence constitutes a major problem in itself. If the act is discovered by the police many white males – most instances occur between white males and coloured or Indian women – have sufficient means to bribe them so that their cases never come to court. The police themselves are heavily involved in *participation* in the crime as will be seen from the figures quoted below. Thus it is reasonably correct to state that the number of cases before the courts in no way represents the real incidence of illicit miscegenation.

In a paper, 'Miscegenation in South Africa', Pierre Van den Berghe analysed the offences reported in a 'native' newspaper, *Golden City Post*, from January 1958 to April 1960.[40] A hundred and seventy-five cases were reported. Of these 162 involved European men, and thirteen concerned European women. Thirty-five of these cases were dismissed for one reason or another. The great majority, ninety-seven, of the offenders received a four to six months' prison sentence. Twelve whites were given the birch instead of being sent to prison. Only two individuals escaped with a fine.[41] The occupational range of offenders is interesting. As might be expected, black prostitutes constituted the largest category of female offenders. Of white males, sailors and Government servants, including the police, formed the largest section – fifty-six. Twenty-seven people were caught in a police trap. Professional men formed only a small minority – four. Interestingly enough, two of these were a doctor and a Minister of the Dutch Reformed Church. The latter institution is in the forefront of the fight for apartheid.[42]

It has been suggested that illicit miscegenation is more likely to be found amongst highly prejudiced whites than among their liberal compatriots.[43] This would explain the high proportion of Government servants in the figures quoted.

To explain this it is necessary to consider the whole white South African ethos. Having passed from a period in the seventeenth and eighteenth centuries, in which miscegenation was actually socially approved, to an age in which the rigidity of Calvinism has taken over, the European wishes to condemn and reject the permissive past. As part of this process, we would suggest, there remains an unconscious desire on the part of the white man for coloured women. In having sexual intercourse with such a woman he not only satisfies this desire but he acts out the archetypal colonial role of abusing the females of the subjugated group. White women, not having access to black or coloured male prostitutes, are not prominent in the meagre statistics available. But that they are sexually attracted by non-European men is borne out by the behaviour of such women when visiting London – they are apt to seek out the company of blacks and attempt to establish a relationship with them. The emotions, guilt and fear connected with miscegenation are admirably expressed by the white South African author, Alan Paton, in his novel *Too Late the Phalorope* (New York 1953).

South Africa, now that the United States has rescinded its anti-miscegenation laws, remains unique among the nations of the world as the last remaining bastion of white supremacy. In her fight to reduce human dignity she is the pariah of human societies.

CHAPTER 9

Miscegenation In Europe—Britain and France

All the great maritime, colonialist powers in Europe from the time of the discovery of Africa in the fifteenth century imported Negro slaves. Portugal, the pioneer of the African slave-trade, had been the first. In the case of Britain it appears that John Lok, on his return from his voyage to West Africa in 1555, carried with him some five black slaves: 'They brought with them certaine blacke slaves, wherof some were tall and strong men, and could wel agree with our meates and drinkes. The colde and moyst aire doth somewhat offend them ...'[1] The experiment does not seem to have been successful as they were later taken back to their home.[2]

By the end of the fifteenth century the trickle started by John Lok had turned into a sizeable flow. The great majority was employed as servants – possibly unpaid – by the nobility, and also by merchants and traders. Negroes began to be a familiar sight in the seaports of Britain, and in London in particular. But this black immigration as in our own day brought problems. The famine of the 1590s created a situation in which blacks were blamed for the social ills which beset the country. Queen Elizabeth, herself an employer of Negroes, was sufficiently disturbed to make public her feelings on the matter. In a letter addressed to the mayors of the major cities in the kingdom she stated: '... that there are of late divers blackamores brought into this realm, of which kind of people there are already here to manie consyderyng howe God hath blessed this land with great increase of people of our nation as anie countrie in the world ... those kinde of people [blacks] should be sente forth of the land ...'[3]

This exhortation did not have much effect. It was followed in 1601 by a Proclamation which empowered a Hanseatic merchant, Caspar van Senden, to ship Negroes from England to Spain and Portugal.[4]

Unfortunately the Proclamation had no teeth – it required the Queen's subjects 'which be possessed of any such blackamoors that refuse to deliver them ... then we require you to call them before you and to advise and persuade them by all good means to satisfy her majesty's pleasure therein; which if they shall eftsoons willfully and obstinately refuse, we pray you to certify their names to us, to the end her majesty may take such further course therein as it shall seem best in her princely wisdom.' No further course in fact was ever taken, and the black population continued to grow.

Royal sanction on the part of Elizabeth's successor, James I, further increased the black dimension in the country. The King and his wife employed both black entertainers and servants.[5] The patronage of the court and the growth of slavery in the Americas ensured that both demand and supply were satisfied. Advertisements began to appear in newspapers for runaway slaves – these were a commonplace of the times.[6] As the century proceeded so black immigration increased. Black servants began to be employed by anyone who wished to be considered fashionable, and by those who aped their betters. Pepys writes in his *Diary* for 5 April 1669: 'For a cookmaid we have, ever since Bridget went, used a black a moor of Mr Batelier's, Doll, who dresses our meat mighty well, and we mightily pleased with her.'

By the middle of the next century the Elizabethan alarmist views that Britain was to be engulfed by swarms of blacks were revived. As no proper records were kept this allowed the advocates of restriction to make the most exaggerated estimates, from 3,000 to 30,000 were figures quoted by both individuals and contemporary newspapers. This is not totally unlike the situation in Britain today where extremist supporters of the policy of repatriation for black immigrants indulge in fantasy projections which make half the population of Britain black by 2000 AD.

There is little doubt, however, that the eighteenth-century population of black people was sizeable. A German baron visiting London in 1710 could write: 'There are, in fact, such a quantity of Moors of both sexes in England that I have not seen before ...'[7] Later Captain Philip Thicknesse comments: '... nay in almost every village are to be seen a little race of mulattoes, mischievous as monkeys, and infinitely more dangerous ...'[8] After the American War of Independence the Negro segment became swollen through the influx of slaves who had fought with the British. '... the city of London is lately infested with American negroes...'[9] The most prominent of the critics of this blackening of England was the Jamaican planter, Edward Long. In 1772 he published his *Candid Reflections*, which expressed his views, and those of many others, on the iniquity that England was facing through black immigration:

The multiplication of Negroe domestics tends therefore, in a very signal degree, to defeat the wise and good purposes of these laws, since it excludes an equal number of poor white natives from that bread to which they are entitled by a prior claim, and turns them adrift to seek it by whatever means they can devise ... there can be no argument alledged that will prove the expediency, policy, or utility, of encouraging the importation of Negroe domestics; and if they are not necessary here in that capacity, for which alone they seem at all qualified, they cannot be deemed, in any view, as a needful or valuable accession to the people of *England* ...[10]

It is interesting to note that the ideas expressed – that the Negro was becoming a charge on the community, etc. – are not totally unlike those of Enoch Powell. The latter can thus claim a distinguished [*sic*] ideological lineage stemming from the West Indian plantocracy.

Although domestic servants – both slave and free – formed the largest section of blacks in England at that time there was another smaller, but significant, category. This was made up of seafarers. Many were the slaves of ships' masters, others were freemen. A large proportion appear to have served in the navy – untrustworthy estimates in the late eighteenth century give a figure as high as twenty-five per cent.[11] It is of considerable interest that these seamen formed the origin of the later settlements of black people from the West Indies, Africa and elsewhere in the major seaports of Britain. Some of these black 'colonies' have persisted to the present day. The district of Stepney in London near the docks was one of the major areas of such settlement. An Anglican clergyman, Dr Mayo (1733–91), worked amongst these people. The following was written about him:

He was particularly kind to the negroes and uninstructed men of colour, who, employed generally on board a ship, occasionally resided in his parish, which is full of seafaring people. I suppose no clergyman in England ever baptized so many black men and Mulattoes; nor did he ever baptize them without very much previous preparation ... The attachment of these poor people to him was very great. Several of them never came into the Port of London, without waiting upon him, by way of testifying the respect in which they held him.[12]

Whatever category the Negro belonged to, servant, seaman, or student – some few had come from West Africa to be educated and sent back to civilize their compatriots – he suffered under the law. The position was essentially one of confusion. This sprang mainly from the fact that although slavery was legally established in the colonies overseas the notion of slavery itself was unknown to English Common Law. This gave opportunity to the learned judges to offer exceptionally differing opinions. In the early years of the eighteenth century Chief Justice Holt declared that, 'As soon as a negro comes to England he becomes free.' By 1720 Justice Hardwicke declared that the arrival of a slave in the country did not automatically make him free. A later judgement of the same judge in 1749 stated that a runaway slave in Britain could be legally recovered. Just over thirty years later the famous London magistrate, Sir John Fielding, stated from the bench, after deploring the practice of West Indian planters bringing slaves to England, 'It is a species of inhumanity to the blacks themselves, to bring them to a free country.'[13]

The most controversial and misunderstood case was that concerning a Negro boy who had been brought to England and subsequently forced to serve as a slave in the West Indies. He sued and won both his pay and his liberty. This was interpreted then and now – no less an authority than the *Encyclopedia Britannica* supports this view – that Lord Mansfield in giving judgement decided that the mere advent of a slave into Britain was sufficient for him to become free; but an article in the *Law Quarterly Review* (1934) by Eward Fiddes points to the ambivalent situation which Mansfield created: '. . . if the various pronouncements of Mansfield are collated it is clear that he had no thought of proclaiming a complete emancipation of a slave as soon as he touched English soil. As far as a system of slavery could be administered under English law he remained a slave. He could be bought and sold. He had no claim for wages . . .'[14]

It is against this background of settlement, slavery, and legal ambiguity that we must consider the sexual interaction of blacks and whites in Britain in the first three centuries of black immigration. In the earliest period the disproportion between the sexes amongst the Negroes was not excessive – black maidservants were much in evidence in the seventeenth century – but this balance gave way to a considerable excess of males over females in the eighteenth century. In the same way as the white colonizer deprived of his own womenfolk had recourse to indigenous women, so the Negro in England consorted with, and upon occasion married, white women. The latter came from the same section of the population as the blacks, the poor and the depressed. It was similar to the pattern of inter-racial marriage and sex in the American colonies which we refer to in other chapters.

Edward Long, the West Indian planter, whom we have quoted above, was incensed by the racial contagion spread by such activities:

> Upon arriving in London . . . not infrequently, they [the Negroes] fall into the company of vicious white servants, and abandoned

prostitutes of the town; and thus are quickly debauched in their morals, instructed in the science of domestic knavery, fleeced of their money, and driven to commit some theft or misdemeanour, which makes them ashamed or afraid to return to their master ... the major part of those who remain are of the most worthless sort; they care not what becomes of their foreign wife or child, but very soon intermarry here, and fix themselves for as long as they can find support; but when the prospect of an easy substance fails, they make no scruple to abandon their new wife and mulatto progeny to the care of the parish, and betake themselves to the colony, where they are, sure, at least, of not starving. The lower class of women in *England*, are remarkably fond of the blacks, for reasons too brutal to mention; they would connect themselves with horses and asses, if the laws permitted them. By these ladies they generally have a numerous brood. Thus, in the course of a few generations more, the English blood will become so contaminated with this mixture, and from the chances, the ups and downs of life, this alloy may spread so extensively, as even to reach the middle, and then the higher orders of the people, till the whole nation resembles the *Portuguese* and *Moriscos* in complexion of skin and baseness of mind. This is a venomous and dangerous ulcer, that threatens to disperse its malignancy far and wide, until every family catches infection from it.[15]

Poor Edward Long – the behaviour of these blacks was so unlike that of his peers in Jamaica. There the white planters merely abused the black and coloured female slaves while maintaining their status as gentlemen. His horror of miscegenation is so great that he virtually equates it with bestiality. His modern counterparts in Britain at least have not stooped so low. It is possible that Long resented the Negro male, because he was reversing roles and debauching white women as the planters debauched black women.

Unhappily for Long and his supporters the contamination had already reached the 'middle and higher orders'. There were instances of free Negroes, such as Charles Morett, who married a middle-class woman in the Midlands.[16] But the aristocracy itself was not immune. One of the most notorious instances concerned the Duchess of Queensberry and her inordinate passion for her black servant, Soubise, from St Kitts in the West Indies. Soubise was 'adopted' by the Duchess, and educated in all the accomplishments fitted to a gentleman. He appears to have been accepted by 'society' to the extent that he became a member of West End London clubs, visited the opera, and rode in Hyde Park magnificently accoutred. He not only was the Duchess' lover but was in demand by other society women. Soubise also found time, and energy, to frequent brothels. He must have been the incarnation of all the fears of the opponents of miscegenation. His saga of success ends sadly. His extravagance was such that his patroness was eventually forced to set him up as a riding-master in India. For a time he was successful there but soon after died as the result of a fall from a horse.[17]

Soubise was exceptional, and was accepted as such. The same was not the case of one Mingo, a black footman in the employ of the Earl of Craven. He was caught in *flagrante delicto* with the Earl's mistress. Both were dismissed by the irate Earl.[18]

Given the opportunity provided by the mistress-servant relationship it is not altogether surprising that black-white sexual liaisons developed in upper-class households. As we have seen in the case of the United States such occurrences were by no means uncommon in a similar situation. In addition the myths of black sexual prowess recounted in numerous publications of the day must have acted as a stimulant to experiment. The fact that such activity did take place is reflected in contemporary cartoons and broadsheets. One of the most outstanding examples is Hogarth's *Noon* in the series *Four Times of the Day*. It shows a Negro embracing an attractive white woman with his hands on her breasts.

Upper-class liaisons were one aspect of miscegenation in eighteenth-century England, but there were other, perhaps more respectable aspects. Marriage seemed to overcome the prejudices connected with miscegenation. Such marriages appear to have been very largely a middle-class phenomenon. At the level of the working masses, to which most blacks belonged, concubinage or a fugitive relationship was much more the norm. Marriage to a respectable Negro tradesman was not frowned upon. The union of the female licensee of a public house in the city of York to such a Negro was noticed in the local paper with no adverse comment.[19]

The most vocal supporters of such unions were obviously enough those who had been engaged in the great struggle for the abolition of the slave-trade, and later for the emancipation of the slaves. But even amongst them there can be detected a note of equivocation. The conflict seems to be between notions of the brotherhood of man and middle-class sentiments as to the place occupied by menials, white or black. A typical example is that of the dinner given by William Wilberforce in 1816 to celebrate the abolition of the slave-trade. As in the Bible he went into the highways and byways of London to collect his Negro guests. Having done so he insisted that they should dine separately from his friends – presumably they were white. At an appointed time, however, all were gathered together to be presented to a Negro and his white spouse. The couple were accompanied by their 'partly coloured child, the fruit of their mutual loves . . .'[20]

This ambiguity or equivocation in the English attitude towards both black people and miscegenation is still apparent in contemporary England. It tends to disappear when it is a question of an alliance between a prominent coloured male – an Indian prince or a distinguished African politician and a white woman – but is very much to the fore in the case of the new immigrant population. That there is an ingredient in the Anglo-Saxon character which makes him prey to such feelings is not altogether conjectural.

In the first years of the nineteenth century the Negro dimension in the English population continued to be significant. The black was now, at any rate in London, a familiar sight. There appeared to be an acceptance, possibly only superficial, of mixed couples. A visitor from the United States was able to remark in 1805 that, 'It would seem that the prejudice against colour is less strong in England than in America . . . A few days since, I met in Oxford Street a well-dressed white girl who was of ruddy complexion, and even handsome, walking arm in arm and conversing very sociably, with a Negro man, who was as well-dressed as she, and so black that his skin had a kind of ebony of lustre . . .'[21]

Over fifty years later the scene had changed completely. The sight of a black face in most parts of London was uncommon. Andrew Halliday, one of Henry Mayhew's collaborators in his famous survey of *London Labour and the London Poor*, found that amongst the city's beggars there were few Negroes. Interestingly enough a number of these had originated in the United States:

> My father was a slave, so was my mother. I have heard them tell how they got away, but I forgot all about it. It was before I was born . . . We agreed to come to England together. My brother had been living with some Britishers, and he had heard them say that over here niggers were as good as whites; and that the whites did not look down on them and illtreat them, as they do in New York.[22]

Halliday's informant went on to say that this dream exploded when they went to work in England, and eventually they were forced to run away from a travelling circus because of ill-treatment by white grooms.

There are a number of reasons for this decline in the black population as the nineteenth century proceeded. The most important of these concerns the changing attitudes of the West Indian plantocracy, due to the abolition of the slave-trade in 1807, and the emancipation of the slaves in 1833. Slavery in its heyday had permitted the slaveowner the luxury of importing domestic slaves to England while he sojourned in that country.

The end of the slave-trade meant that this supply was virtually cut off. Thus the absentee planters could no longer afford the luxury of the ostentatious display of Negro servitors in London – their labour was required on the plantations. After 1833 the situation was even worse as the freed slaves had no reason to go to England to obtain the freedom they already possessed. The planter bound for home was not inclined to take with him a paid servant whose absence would further deplete an already insufficient labour-force.

We have already spoken of the sexual imbalance in the black population which was one of the main factors in promoting miscegenation. Interbreeding of black and white produced a mulatto group which in turn interbred with whites. This process, coupled with the fact that the supply of Negro immigrants was now cut off, led to the eventual extinction of the Negro as a distinct physical type. This, as Bernard Shaw once said, is the only positive way in which to eliminate racial antagonism in a society with a black minority – amalgamation through miscegenation.

A minor bar to any increase in the black section in England had been the passing of an Act of Parliament in 1832 which effectively prevented the introduction of West Africans. Shipmasters were prohibited from carrying Negroes from West Africa and landing them in a British port under penalty of £100 fine in the money of the day. As a result of this legislation African settlement became negligible.[23]

We do not mean to suggest that the black population of England became extinct by the middle of the nineteenth century but that the greater part of it had become absorbed in the host population. Permanent pockets remained in the major seaports of the country such as Liverpool, London and Bristol. These formed the points of growth for the black colonies of seafarers which began to form in the twentieth century. These was, and is, a specialist group forming a kind of ghetto complex.

Underlying the attitudes and behaviour of the English towards the black presence in their midst was a sexual fear and a sexual fascination. This comes out again and again in contemporary accounts from Elizabethan times onwards. It had died down as the black population began to be absorbed but reappeared in a virulent form at the advent of Africans who were part of international exhibitions which became a feature in London in the first years of the twentieth century. Some extracts from both the popular press and more serious publications illustrate this point:

> To anyone who has spent some years in Africa, the familiarity which exists between certain white women visiting the Kaffir kraal at Earl's Court Exhibition and the blacks on show there, is a peculiarly revolting spectacle. From the hour this 'savage' side-show is opened until late at

night, the kraal is besieged by crowds of females who hustle each other in their rivalry to obtain personal association with the Matabele and other coloured men on view. Some of the women use all their arts of fascination to please these sons of the African wilderness. But lately we saw a European girl detach flowers from her bosom to adorn the person of these niggers and we have seen grown women not only shake hands with them but stroke their limbs admiringly. Nothing is left undone by certain misled English females to gratify the vanity of these miscellaneous African natives in whose delightful manners and customs this show is presumed to instruct us, The Kaffir Exhibition at Earl's Court has in fact degenerated into an exhibition of white women visitors, and a very disgusting exhibition it is. These raw, hulking and untamed man-animals are being unwillingly and utterly corrupted by unseemly attention from English girls.[24]

That was an account from 1889. It must have made the blood boil of those English counterparts of Southern gentlemen whose function in life was to protect the flower of Southern womanhood. One might say that the might of the British Empire in its full glory was based on the corruption of 'native' women by the British male, and their protection of the English female from the horrors of sexual contact with unspeakable black males.

More general racist overtones are apparent in the following extract from an English popular magazine (1917):

Some years ago we used to have large bodies of natives sent from Africa on military service or in some travelling show, and it was a revelation of horror and disgust to behold the manner in which English women would flock to see these men, whilst to watch them fawning upon these black creatures and fondling them and embracing them, as I have seen dozens of times, was a scandal and a disgrace to English womanhood. How then is it possible to maintain as the one stern creed in the policy of the Empire the eternal supremacy of the white over black?[25]

For the average Englishman at this time knowledge of the Empire was, to say the least, exiguous. One fact, however, he did know – that white people had created dominion over the black. Thus the writer was making explicit what the silent majority felt.

At a different level – that of the serious journal – articles lamented that the British public at home, unlike those who upheld the flag overseas, did not know how to behave towards the lesser breeds. 'For many years white colonials have shuddered at witnessing repulsive Ethiopians intimately, almost maritally consorting with beautiful British girls in streets, in restaurants, in theatres, in night clubs, lodging houses and hotels. There was no concealment of the affectionate attitude of a certain type of white female toward the brown, black and yellow male.'[26] Unfortunately this is an attitude which still causes antagonism, not so much in Britain but in ex-colonial territories where the 'natives' have pretensions to equality with their former masters.

After the 1914 war the enclaves of black people in the seaport cities of Britain were swollen by numbers of coloured seamen, both West Indian and African, who had been recruited during the war to serve in the Merchant Navy. They had decided to make Britain their home base. Unfortunately bad economic conditions in the years after 1918 caused a slump in shipping with consequent unemployment. Amongst these cities Liverpool had another dimension besides that of black seamen. These were factory workers, some 5,000, who had been attracted by wartime jobs in industry. Most of them were unemployed due to the general economic depression which affected the country. It was in Liverpool in 1919 that race riots occurred for the first time in the history of England, and from there spread to other seaports:

> The race riots here [Liverpool] have developed to such an extent, and the bitterness displayed by the Europeans towards the Negro colony has become so acute, that the local authorities have sought the aid of the Government. The strife is the outcome of the Negro familiarity with the white woman, which in some cases has been legalised by marriage, and the fact that Negroes are holding jobs which demobilised men contend should be theirs ... There [are] about 2,000 Negroes in the city, and they are afraid to be in the streets; they have been discharged from their employment. Others have been refused shelter by lodging-house keepers. In such cases military are interning Negroes until they can be repatriated to houses which were wrecked. During the riot in the South End of the city last night furniture was stolen, and in some cases the hooligans broke into the premises and stole. The furniture of innocent people formed fuel for bonfires. (*Daily Express*, 19 June 1919)

Liverpool provided the perfect scapegoat situation – economic distress, a highly visible minority, and the component of sexual jealousy. Very similar conditions existed in Cardiff in South Wales. There the emphasis was very much on the sexual association of black and white as a cause of provocation:

> Some of the more sober-minded citizens of Cardiff consider that the coloured men are not alone [*sic*] to blame for the disturbances, although

> at the same time they deplore the familiar association between white women and Negroes, which is a provocative cause ... His [that is the Negro's] chief failing is his fondness for white women ... (*The Times*, 13 June 1919)

Even in smaller towns, such as Newport in South Wales, the fervour of antagonism existed:

> Three men, including two well-known Rugby footballers, Jeremiah Shea and Will Haley, and a woman appeared at Newport police court yesterday on charges arising out of colour riots. Evidence was given by the white wives of coloured men that their houses were entered by furious mobs. One witness named Martinez said that the female prisoner shouted at her 'you ought to be burnt because you are a black man's wife'. John Davies, a coloured man, said the crowd shouted 'Come out you niggers.' They burst open his door but he ran away. His wife identified Shea and Haley as alleged leaders in the riot. They, she said, entered her house after breaking the door open with a chopper. She was not aware that the disturbance arose because the blacks insulted a white woman, or that Haley struck a black who had made certain remarks. (*Daily Herald*, 17 June 1919)

There is little doubt that sexual jealousy of the Negro has played a major part in the development of the racialist attitudes of the English people. Coloured people, obviously enough, provide an easy target for this resentment. This is true not only of Britain but, as we have seen, of the United States as well. What must also be taken into consideration in the case of Britain is the high degree of general xenophobia which uses sexual jealousy as its expression. This was manifested against *European* minorities in the country after the war, such as Poles and refugees from the Baltic. In Yorkshire, an area noted for its conservatism, the introduction of Italian miners, with the consent of the local unions, led to severe tensions which were sexually based. The xenophobia may even be turned against their own kind. Again in Yorkshire, boys from one village seeking girls in another are liable to be attacked for molesting [*sic*] females who are regarded as the property of the local males. This suggests that advanced societies can, and do, react in a manner which is ordinarily associated, by them, with 'primitive' tribal groups.

After their indulgence in the passion of race rioting in the immediate period after the 1914 war, English society settled into a period of tolerance of the black groups in their midst. This was possibly because the economy became so depressed in the inter-war period that people were too preoccupied with survival to worry about racial differences.

The black population at this time could be divided into seamen and semi-skilled workers, entertainers and students from the colonies. Their overall numbers were comparatively small. It could be said that the great majority of white people was not aware that Britain possessed a black minority.

This state of affairs was abruptly changed by the coming of the 1939 war. For the first time the majority of the population became conscious of the presence of blacks. There were two sources – West Indians who came over to join the armed forces and to work in factories, and American servicemen. The policy of segregation then current in the United States Army caused a considerable number of incidents concerning competition for English girls. On occasion near-riot conditions prevailed. American Negroes, considerably better-off in terms of pay than their British equivalents, proved most attractive to English girls. This aroused resentment both from the English and the Negroes' white compatriots. That this was the case was demonstrated by the numerous scenes which occurred when black US troops began to leave the country in 1945. Local girls surrounded their departing sweethearts crying and screaming. The authorities both military and civil were confronted with a serious problem.[27]

The war accustomed the British people to the presence of black people. But those they saw, and interacted with, were essentially transients. It was different when migrants from the West Indies, Pakistan and India began to arrive with the intention of settling. We do not intend to give either a detailed analysis of the pattern of immigration to Britain, or to examine in detail the total pattern of black–white relationships which have been built up since 1948 – a considerable literature already exists on these topics – but to emphasize certain aspects which are of concern to the present study.[28]

Two events stand out in the twentieth century with relation to the black invasion of Britain after the 1939 war. One was the arrival of a former wartime troopship, the *Empire Windrush*, in 1948 with the first group of West Indian immigrants; the other was the passing of the Commonwealth Immigrants Act in 1962. The period between saw the flow which was to create the largest black population which has ever existed in Britain. The 1966 census gives a total of approximately 925,200 people originating from the coloured Commonwealth resident in Britain. The two largest groups are the West Indians – 453,300, more than half of whom are from Jamaica – and Indians and Pakistanis – 343,400.

The sexual patterns exhibited by the two groups are quite different. The West Indian tends to seek sexual comfort on the whole from his own kind. In this he has been lucky, for although to begin with there was a sexual imbalance in favour of the male the subsequent arrival of women recruited as nurses has facilitated both marriage and concubinage with women from his homeland. Thus intermarriage with females of the host society has never featured as a characteristic of people from the Caribbean. The availability of compatriot mates, however, has not prevented a minority of both men and women contracting marriage with English people, or entering into some form of sexual liaison. Of this minority most of such unions have taken place at the working-class level to which the majority of immigrants belong. Such unions tend on the whole to arouse some resentment on the part of the host population. This varies in intensity from the immediate neighbourhood of the couple, where it generally meets with acceptance, to active hostility if the couple moves into a predominantly white neighbourhood. Ordinarily this does not occur as the white woman gravitates to the coloured community, where she is accepted. Relationships between white men and coloured women are on the whole minimal.

With the mounting hostility against immigrants which panicked the Government into passing the Commonwealth Immigrants Act (1962) restricting the entry of immigrants, the mixed family became at hazard. The propaganda of racialist groups, especially in the area surrounding the city of Birmingham in the Midlands, not only stated that blacks were taking away jobs which should go to the native population, and that migrants were a burden on the social services, but that they were also debauching white womanhood. The theme was both familiar and obvious, and had been so since Elizabethan times. The riots of Notting Hill and Nottingham in the fifties reinforced the general opinion of the immigrants that the economic refuge of the mother country also meant maternal rejection. The effect on those who had contracted liaisons or marriage with white individuals was to create insecurity even within the coloured community. In some areas special clubs have sprung up to cater for the interests of such families. They help to reduce the feelings of insecurity.

It is important to appreciate that the xenophobia exhibited against coloured people at the present time is taking place within the context of what is probably the most class-ridden society in the world. Thus if there can be an equation between the social status of the black and the white people with whom he interacts antagonism may diminish. A black professional man if he marries a white girl from the middle class is less likely to meet with hostility from the predominantly white community to which he will attempt to adhere. Common interests, common use of language, similar education all help to smooth the path of the West Indian who attempts to penetrate, through marriage, the barriers erected by the middle class against invasion by those considered inferior. In the case of the upper class the task is even easier. There recognition, despite colour, of a community of background can be the passport to acceptance. A Peggy Cripps, the daughter of the late Sir Stafford Cripps, can marry a Joe Appiah from a distinguished Ghanaian family and still be accepted by her circle. A white clergyman can marry a Trinidadian television star, and a picture of the couple is published in the press, with a factual caption and no comment. A generation ago the headlines would have been startling.

It is difficult to distinguish the actual degree of acceptability of mixed marriages in the seventies. It is reasonable to assume that the majority of the host population still has strong emotional reactions against such unions. Part of the basis of this can be attributed to the persistence of the image that black people are more virile than Europeans – the ancient myth – and thus are more animal-like. Michael Banton in the course of his researches discovered that thirty per cent of his sample of whites interviewed were of the opinion that, 'Coloured people have stronger sexual urges than white people . . .'[29] The rationalization of this view would be the fact that immigrant families tend to be larger than those of the English.

The change in views of intermarriage on the part of the host population is seen in two surveys conducted by Social Surveys (Gallup Poll) Ltd in 1958 and 1961 for the *Daily Telegraph* newspaper:

INTERMARRIAGE

	1958 Percentage	*1961* Percentage
Approve	13	7
Disapprove	71	68
Don't Know	16	25

It should be noted in this context that for the vast majority of respondents the question is entirely hypothetical. It took the form of 'Do you think that marriage between a white person and a coloured person, is, or is not, advisable?' In 1954–5 Clifford S. Hill, an English clergyman, conducted a survey of his own. In it he put the question: 'Would you approve of your sister, or your daughter, marrying a coloured person?' Ninety-one per cent disapproved, seven per cent approved and two per cent were undecided:

> On the whole women were slightly less prejudiced than men. There was only one group over the whole age range of both sexes that

showed a marked degree of tolerance and this was young women under the age of 25. On the other hand all the men in our sample under the age of 25 and nearly all the men under 40, were prejudiced. At the other end of the age and sex scale, all the women over 60, and nearly all the women over 40 were prejudiced.[30]

These are interesting figures, and they demonstrate that it is the more nubile of females, those under twenty-five, who are in fact attracted by black men. This can be seen night after night in Caribbean discotheques in the major areas of immigrant settlement. Sexual associations are formed in the atmosphere of pop music and dancing. These tend to be romantic and temporary in most instances. After twenty-five, girls are more interested in marriage, and begin to see the disadvantages of a coloured marital partner, or so it would seem.

It could be said that housing and miscegenation are the two areas in which the hostility against immigrants is seen in its most virulent form. The emotionalism which the idea of intermarriage generates, for reasons which we have suggested, at times assumes gigantic proportions. Middle-class opinion is the most articulate about miscegenation. The working class, amongst which such unions are more frequent, does not express its opinions so freely. After a broadcast to the Caribbean, in which he said that he would be happy for his daughter to marry a coloured man if he were compatible, and which was subsequently reported in the British press, the Reverend Clifford Hill received a deluge of abusive letters. These indicate the depth of feeling aroused by the idea:

I consider you are not fit to bring up your daughter with your ideas of mating her to a Negro. I sincerely hope that God will cut short your life and that you will *die soon* so that dear little white girl may be saved from the hideous fate you plan for her. A black blubber lipped Negro on top of her and unending half castes year after year. You are not fit to be a father at all. You should not put your love of niggers before your duty of protecting your innocent daughter. Poor unprotected little thing.

That was from a woman living in Brighton. Interestingly enough Brighton, a town which has a minute immigrant population, was also the home of one of the pioneer racialist societies of Britain – the Sussex Racial Preservation Society – inspired by a somewhat different kind of clergyman than Clifford Hill.

Another letter was from a gentleman resident in Switzerland:

Your statement in a newspaper that you would not mind your daughter marrying a black man seems to me so indicative of the low social conditions in England at present that I feel I must expostulate. Even horses, cattle, dogs, and cats are mated and bred to be of a pure race. How much more should man 'made in God's image' be strict in preserving our *white* heritage! Why lay the possible onus and curse on your child of breeding mongrels and half-castes and bastard children . . .

Both these effusions with their extravagant emphasis on the sexual aspect of the hypothetical relationship appear to indicate the presence of feelings quite contrary to those expressed by the writers. In other words the protestations are so vehement that they suggest covert desires on the part of the authors to indulge in such sexual activity themselves. There is evidence of a similar kind in the notorious anti-semitic magazine of Julius Streicher, *Der Sturmer*.

What always comes out in discussions about inter-racial marriage is the question, what about the children? Many English people whose knowledge of biology is on a par with their intelligence are firmly convinced that inter-breeding is a 'biological' sin. It is a view common to both men and women as the following extracts from the same postbag show:

We can integrate fellow Europeans, the Irish and even certain [*sic*] oriental races who have light skins, or 'European-type' features. But God chose to make the Negroes distinctive so that they cannot be integrated. It is not for you to tamper with God's handiwork!

The correspondent in question was a man living in Middlesex. A Manchester woman wrote:

Interbreeding is evil and nobody could be proud of half-caste children. You've got a decent English heritage yourself, why encourage your poor little lassie to breed children everyone is ashamed of? The idea of everyone being a wretched khaki colour with thick lips and flat noses in the future is abhorrent to all right-thinking Englishmen. You and your black friends will succeed in promoting race riots if you go on. All men are *not* born equal. There are centuries of evolution behind the whites and you cannot expect the blacks to attain in a few years an equality which isn't there.[31]

The failure to grasp the notion that children of mixed marriages are not at an inherent disadvantage, but that their disadvantages spring from the intolerance of the very people who condemn them, is typical of the illogicality of your true racialist. At a more intellectual level English people will argue that if the black person returns with a white bride to the Caribbean or West Africa she will be rejected by his people. This betrays a profound ignorance of both areas. An acquaintance with either biology or of cultures other than their own has never been an exactly prominent part of many Englishmen's mental equipment.

It is difficult to make any proper estimate of the incidence of mixed marriages in Britain in the absence of any statistical study, covering the major areas of black settlement, specifically related to this question. By and large it is a problem which has been ignored in the greater part of the now, quite extensive literature on immigrants in the United Kingdom. One survey, however was made, concerning London. In this, 1,000 parish priests in areas of immigrant concentration were asked to make a return of such marriages solemnized in their churches for the year preceding March 1963. The figure of eighty-four marriages between people from the coloured Commonwealth and whites was returned.[32] It is unlikely that civil marriages at Registry Offices would be any greater. West Indians and West Africans for example would tend to be married in church as almost all in Britain are practising Christians. Thus it would be reasonable to assume that the total incidence for London would be of the order of 200 mixed marriages a year. By extension the assumption for the whole country might be between 1,500 and 2,000. Ordinary observation would confirm that the incidence is low. In the face of the lack of intensive investigations to this end any statistics remain inspired guesses. What is needed is a number of enquiries covering the country as a whole geared to elicit not only statistical information but also information in depth about such marriages.

At present while the figures for incidence remain largely guesswork, those for cohabitation between white and black cannot even be guessed. Again, there is no indication of the number of black prostitutes catering for a white clientele. In the case of marriages it should be noted that the overwhelming majority are those in which the female spouse is white – few white working-class men contract marriage with a coloured girl.

The pressures which the average mixed couple undergo in contemporary Britain are considerable. Some of these are brought out by an article in the *Guardian* (13 March 1964) by Nadine Asante, an English girl who married a West African:

> We started our married life together in Britain, where my husband is studying at his government's expense, and were shocked to have five consecutive doors slammed in our faces in our first week of marriage and house-hunting. I am resigned to having people label me as 'cheap' when I walk down the street with the man I love. He is resigned to having people believe he married me to 'better himself'. One becomes resigned to these erroneous ideas but one never gets to like them.

A number of comments can be made on the above. The writer betrays a naïvety in expressing surprise at slammed doors. In 1962, before the passing of the Race Relations Act and the setting up of the Race Relations Board, the advertisement boards of newsagents' shops were full of notices for accommodation specifying that no Jews or coloureds need apply. It was also known at the time that house agents practised a hidden form of discrimination against black applicants. A mixed couple ought to have been aware of this situation. Mrs Asante was lucky in the sense that her distress was only for the time they lived in this country – presumably at the end of her husband's studies they would return to West Africa to live – unlike those who are permanently settled in Britain. Her reactions to being labelled cheap were well-founded as in the eyes of many English people any white girl who consorts with or marries a black is either a prostitute, or, as the popular phrase goes, no better than she should be. The rationalization is that she was unable to obtain a white spouse. It would be unthinkable that she acted from choice. That the husband should be regarded as having bettered himself – again, a universally popular notion – stems back to the folklore of empire in which the white is always the superior of the blacks he subjugated.

In most instances the familial and public antagonism which the white girl who marries a man of colour experiences can be formidable. There are cases in which there is no personal animosity to the man, who may have shown his suitability as a husband, but parents are terrified of the reaction of their neighbours. The ancient argument about children is used as a weapon to prevent the marriage. If the neighbours are forgotten, the dimension of ignorance regarding the behaviour of West Indians and West Africans leads parents to suggest there are unspeakable horrors awaiting their daughter. An extreme case, which came to the notice of the author as an undergraduate at Oxford, concerned an upper-class girl who wished to, and eventually did, marry a Turk. Her mother's first reaction to the news was to expatiate at length on the terrible experiences of the harem. What can complicate the situation apart from antagonism of this kind is that the English girl may not, despite experience to the contrary, realize fully that differences in background may cause tension between the couple. This is not a matter of ethnic difference, for it is to be found in intra-class marriages in all societies.

The most sensitive area undoubtedly is that concerning the white female teenager. Here the father feels that it is his duty to protect his daughter from the licentious machinations of her coloured counterpart. It is also the area in which friendships are first formed between the ethnic groups. The West Indian boy coming from a background of miscegenation in the Caribbean does not altogether understand the violence of white parental reaction. He and the girl are sharing the same experiences at school. Their interests are the same – pop music, films and dancing. So she too is bewildered by parental disapproval. Many of the girls succumb to the disapprobation meted out and cease such friendships. It is, in our view, only where the attraction between the two is extremely powerful that these initial obstacles are overcome and the relationship persists.

What has now begun to occur in the seventies is the coming into being of a new generation of British-born 'immigrants' who have been educated and socialized in the society in which they live. These youngsters no longer speak in the accents of the Caribbean or India as their parents do, but express themselves in Cockney, pure Yorkshire or Brummagem and Scouse (Liverpool) as the case may be. It is this generation, totally English but black, which will very likely succeed in overcoming the barriers we have discussed in relation to inter-racial marriage. This in part depends on the continuance, or not, of the demagogic efforts of the Enoch Powells of this country, and in part on improvements in housing, employment and education.

Sexual relationships between the Indo-Pakistani community and the host society take a somewhat different form from that of the West Indian and West African groups. Two basic considerations provide for this difference. One is membership of the village-kin from which the immigrant comes, and the other is his inclusion in an immigrant household in Britain which is virtually a form of extended family. Membership of both ensure that the newly arrived immigrant is cared for and found work. Marriage is to be sought within the framework of these two institutions. To act counter to their demand for such marriage, and to seek union or sexual relations with a European woman is to court expulsion from the group. For the Sikh and Hindu the penalties are very severe – becoming outcaste and ritually impure. For a Muslim, whose religion permits alliances with Christians, it may mean only severance from his family.

Thus the sanctions against inter-marriage are very strong from the immigrant side. The extended family is an economic unit as well as a social one. To be deprived of membership means a loss of the contributions the individual may have made to the common purse both in Britain and in his homeland, as well as a share of the common property. The family itself does all it can to prevent such unions taking place. Not only does the offending party suffer but disgrace is brought upon the family as a whole. If they continue to interact with him after the event they too will be outcasted. As there are not sufficient numbers to constitute proper caste groups in Britain the immigrant community where the individual resides acts in their place. In this connection it means that the wrongdoer is expelled from the community when outcasted.

From the point of view of prohibitions and sanctions a distinction is made between marriage and a sexual liaison. A sexual liaison may be tolerated, particularly if no children are born from it, and the community is sustained by the hope that it is merely ephemeral. With regard to marriage, even after it has taken place the household does not give up all hope of reclaiming the errant spouse. Some contact may be maintained with him and pressure brought to bear on him to divorce. If all else fails, and the individual persists in the error of his ways, then he has to accept the penalties. What this means is that he is now thrown on his own resources, or those he may obtain from the host society, few of which are at his disposal. He cannot travel elsewhere and re-establish himself as his spouse or mistress is the permanent badge of his disgrace. His workmates will ostracize him, and he is cut off from all the social activities of the community. It is not surprising that in these circumstances inter-racial marriage amongst Hindu and Sikh communities is minimal, and very little higher amongst Muslims.[33]

For most people from the Indian sub-continent the sacrifices demanded in order to marry a European are too great to make. It must be remembered that there is a considerable imbalance between the sexes – there are far more men than women – in some areas of Indo-Pakistani settlement. An individual would come from home without his wife but bringing his teenage sons and join an already almost totally male household. The palliative of the situation is recourse to the white prostitute. In one area – the city of Bradford in Yorkshire – where the woollen mills are mainly dependent on Pakistani labour the local prostitute population has grown considerably in order to meet this exotic demand. No prejudice appears to exist on the part of white prostitutes.

There are some other factors which affect sexual relations between such immigrants and the host society. Unlike West Indians, many Indians and Pakistanis regard their sojourn in this country as being essentially temporary. This may not actually occur in practice but the belief is sufficiently strong to inhibit any desire to enter into a relationship with a European girl. Again, unlike people from the Caribbean, there is frequently a language barrier which prevents communication with the white group. Ultimately there is the hostility *all* immigrants experience in sexual matters from the white majority. If all these are considered then the extremely low rate of inter-marriage and other sexual contacts, apart from prostitution, is understandable.

The situation, however, is changing. As more and more youngsters of Asian origin go through the educational process in Britain and acquire fluency in the language there are bound to be departures from the pattern we have attempted to describe. Presented with the manifestation of the nuclear family from an early age in opposition to the extended family, in time the values of the former, with its emphasis on individual freedom, may prevail. In the same way religious adherence may decline. The future may see a considerable increase in the sexual interaction between the English and the peoples of India and Pakistan in their midst.

The history of France and that of Britain are not dissimilar with regard to black people – both were colonial, slave-holding powers, and both were indebted to Portugal for introducing them to the slave-trade and its economic advantages. Yet the history of the Negro in France differs in a number of ways from the British experience.

That there were black soldiers recruited by the Moors in their warfare against Christian Europe seems to be attested. In later centuries some of their descendants found their way to France.[34] In terms of slavery the first real evidence is that of the importation of a number into Bordeaux in 1571. The local *parlement* of that city ordered their release on familiar grounds – that slavery was unknown to the laws of France.[35] Twenty-three years later Negroes were reported to be living in the country.[36] As France developed her expansion overseas, and the slave-trade increased, the flow of Negroes into France also increased. Planters from Martinique and Guadaloupe on their return to their mother-country brought slaves to form part of their household, and so impress the public with their wealth.

As early as 1685 it became apparent that miscegenation was taking place on a considerable scale. In March of that year a law was passed prohibiting the marriage of blacks and whites.[37] This was not rescinded until 1820. By the eighteenth century it was felt that the only way to stop the sexual interaction between black and white was to deport all the Negroes in the country. Louis XV issued such a decree:

> An order from the king has instructed all the Negroes, male and female, to retire into the possession of their masters in America; those who are free will be shipped to Cayenne. The cause of this expulsion is the desire, too marked, of the white men for the Negro women, and of the white women for the Negro men. There is so much of this mixing that there are nearly 1,500 mulatto foundlings. It is this which has awakened the attention of the government, which is afraid that the French nation will lose the whiteness, beauty, and purity of blood.[38]

There appears to have been both practical and chauvinistic reasons for this anti-miscegenation decree. What is also of interest is that contrary to the popular belief of our own day that the French are relatively unprejudiced against black people, the decree shows that their racialist feeling has as long a history as that of the Anglo-Saxon.

After the revolution of 1789 the Negroes in France appear to have prospered. In 1799, fomented no doubt by the fact that Napoleon had re-introduced slavery in Haiti and as a result many Negro army officers had revolted, Parisian blacks were attacked. The grounds of the accusations against them are interesting. It seems that they had ideas above their station, were in fact driving about in splendid carriages accompanied by white footmen and servants. And of course the inevitable cry of the dilution of the pure Caucasian blood of France. 'There will be soon no other than mulattoes in France.'[39]

It is impossible to arrive at any accurate estimate of the numbers of Negroes in France in the eighteenth century – the first official census for the country as a whole only took place in 1800. An American historian of the Negro in France was of the following opinion:

> That there were perhaps less than a thousand in France at any time before the Revolution makes the fear of a Negro problem seem a bit strange. Could there have been grounds for alarm that the blood of France would be altered . . . Reports of 1777 and later years did reveal that two or three score Negroes and mulattoes were intermarried with whites, more commonly Negro men being married to white wives and in numerous instances their union had been fruitful with children. The revelation might have been disturbing to the officials at Paris, but in the provinces it was clearly regarded without concern . . . everywhere the mixed couples seem to have faced no hostile public.[40]

Official fear, xenophobia, and acceptance form the ambivalent pattern of French attitudes towards miscegenation in the eighteenth century.

In the nineteenth century the pattern of recruitment of Negroes to France as slaves changes. One instrument of this change was the army. A black presence in the army dates back to the previous century. Marshal de Saxe created a black brigade formed of Negroes from Senegal, Guinea, the Congo and the Caribbean, as well as Arabs and Indians, to fight in the War of the Austrian Succession (1743–48).[41] The tradition thus established was continued after the Revolution. In 1792 the famous Black Legion of the French Army was raised. It was under the command of a mulatto from Guadaloupe, Joseph de Boulogne, Chevalier de Saint-Georges. The Legion comprised some 1,000 men, two hundred of whom were cavalry. It is, however, his second-in-command who claims our attention. This was Alexandre Dumas, the founder of the famous literary dynasty. He too was a mulatto. His father was the Marquis de La Pailleterie, who brought his bastard son to Bordeaux from Santo Domingo to be educated. His mother was a Negro woman, Marie Cessette Dumas. Dumas entered the French Army when he was twelve. His career by any standards was brilliant – he became a general of division in 1793, and later had a number of commands as a full general. Dumas married a Frenchwoman, Marie Elisabeth Labouret. His death occurred in 1806.[42]

General Dumas is of special interest because he typifies one part of the French attitude towards colour and miscegenation. He himself was much aware of the subtleties and niceties of French 'society'. It is said that he joined the army in disgust because his father contracted a mésalliance in France.[43] It is possible that a revolutionary situation made it easier for a mulatto to be accepted in the army and to reach high office. There were other mulattoes, such as L'Islet Geoffroy, who achieved eminence in official circles. Geoffroy was an artillery officer who was distinguished as a cartographer and became a member of the Academy of Sciences. Dumas represents the beginning of a long line of Negroes and people of colour who rose to prominence in France, and were accepted for the contribution they made to the country. It is sometimes forgotten that Gaston Monnerville, a black French West Indian, was President of the French Senate from 1946 until quite recently. Interestingly enough, if General de Gaulle had died in office Monnerville would have succeeded him until another head of state had been elected.

The careers of such people demonstrate a very important facet of French race relations. Despite the latent racist feelings of individuals, French colonial policy in the nineteenth century was always concerned with promoting assimilation, almost on the model of the Roman Empire. Anyone in the colonies who demonstrated his loyalty to and involvement with France by his command of the language and assimilation of the culture was assured of acceptance in the metropolitan country. This meant in practice that the half-breed or the mulatto was favoured at the expense of the 'native' or black:

> Last century saw in French territories the beginning of a movement, which acquired increasing momentum and which is today [1932] very strong and everywhere widespread, to give the half-breed the status of a French citizen, or at least the presumption that he is a citizen . . . this presumption being founded on facts that can be proved, in particular what is called the possession of civic status: the fact that he has been educated and taught in French schools in the French manner; the fact that he has been reared and supported; and many other facts which constitute possession of civic status and which therefore raise in his favour the presumption that he is a French citizen . . .[44]

After the 1939 war and the beginning of the period of decolonization this process underwent a further change. The French West Indian colonies were by law created an integral part of metropolitan France, thus ceasing to have colonial status and becoming départements of France. All the inhabitants of these territories irrespective of their ethnic background were now full French citizens. The black Martiniquan who travels from his land to the metropolitan country in theory is merely moving from one part of France to another.

An important and illuminating comparison can be made between French and British colonial policy as it affected miscegenation. Britain has always attempted to rule through separation of the Anglo-Saxon from those ruled. In the colonial situation clearly this was not always possible. Inevitably there were sexual contacts between coloured and white. All members of the empire were British citizens but were not encouraged to come to Britain to reside. The half-breed or mulatto was in no way specially favoured, in fact the opposite prevailed – his status was more that of a pariah than a citizen. No black person has ever attained high office in Britain nor is likely to do so. Involvement with things English may be given grudging approval but it was, and is, no passport to acceptance of equality. There never has been a policy of assimilation either socially, or culturally, or sexually. Margery Perham, a noted English authority on Africa, attempted an explanation:

> The Germanic-speaking Europeans – the British, the Germans, the Americans, the Dutch – share a deep bias against inter-marriage with the Negro race. It is no good our trying to avoid this granite-hard fact. It lies at the very heart of our present problem in Africa. This conscious, or sometimes sub-conscious, fear of race-mixture accounts both for the white man's innermost ring of defence and also for all his outer ring of political, social and economic ramparts . . .'[45]

Miss Perham's remarks demonstrate a kind of lacuna in her knowledge of what actually occurred in terms of race mixing between black and white in the Americas and the Caribbean. The acceptance of marriage is one thing – bound up with the denial of equality in a colonial situation – but to imply that there is actually 'fear of race-mixture' on the part of the Anglo-Saxon is contrary to all the known facts. It is possible of course that the slave-masters of America and the West Indies were inherently masochists for whom sex was not enjoyable unless fearful.

The above quotation has a nineteenth-century ring. Actually Miss Perham's thesis was even more cogently put in that century. John Crawfurd, President of the Ethnological Society of London in the 1860s, felt that the gap between the Negro and the Anglo-Saxon was so great that their mating could only produce degenerates. 'In a society consisting of these discordant elements, no substantial equality is possible; since, whether in a free or servile condition, the inferior race would be certain to be viewed by the superior as a degraded class, with whom it is impossible to amalgamate ...'[46] Crawfurd's opinion was a reflection of both the real and imagined conditions in the British Empire at that time. The reality was that marriage between black and white was officially disapproved, and in some cases actually forbidden. Officialdom, on the other hand, turned a blind eye to the existence of extra-marital sexual relationships.

This difference of outlook and policy between these two great colonial powers – France and Britain – affected profoundly the process of miscegenation in the metropolitan countries.

Throughout the nineteenth century the flow of coloured people continued into France. A considerable dimension consisted of those who came in search of education. Thus in the middle of the century a Negro was still a familiar sight in the streets of Paris unlike those of London. A new element, however, was introduced in the 1914 war. Recruitment began in the colonies of black troops to defend the motherland. The largest component of these came from the French West African colonies such as Senegal. Their identification with the cause of France caused them to have great popularity both social and sexual.

The effects of the continuing black presence on French opinion with regard to race mixture can be seen in the responses to a competition organized by the French woman's magazine *Eve*, a precursor of the contemporary *Elle*. *Eve*, in February and March 1920, offered four prizes for the best essays written on the theme of 'Would you marry a Coloured Man?'. In addition three questions on this topic were sent to prominent figures in France. Altogether 2,040 essays were sent in. A majority, 1060, were negative and 980 accepted the idea. As may be imagined many of the reasons given by those who rejected the idea of inter-marriage were fairly obvious. Some, however, were unusual – revulsion at the colour of possible offspring; objection to the colour of the interior of the Negro's hand; and the shape of Negroid lips. Affirmative reasons were much concerned with the athletic qualities of black people which, in the opinion of the women, would lead to healthy, strong children.

The most interesting essay was that of an eleven-year-old girl which won the fourth prize:

> ... I do not know whether I'd find it agreeable with a Negro before me at breakfast. In any case I would not like him to eat without white gloves on because I would always have the impression that his hands

were dirty, and that he would soil the napkin and the table-cloth. Apart from that if I loved him I do not see why I could not be happy with him. I could very likely wipe my cheeks after he had kissed me . . .

Such views are not entirely unknown amongst *adults* in both France and Britain today.

Questions were sent to thirty-three distinguished French personalities. Nineteen were in favour of miscegenation, eight were against, five did not answer, and one was undecided.

Henri Barbusse, the writer, replied: 'One cannot approve, in principle, a union between persons of different races. The persons, themselves, must be the sole judge.' Professor Charles Richet of the Faculty of Medicine at the Sorbonne and a Nobel Prize winner: 'A white woman should by no means marry a Negro. Even if the signs of his ethnic inferiority is little apparent, they will appear in the children . . . All race mixture is detestable. Alexandre Dumas was an exception.' It is interesting to note that the Research Centre in Paris which bears Richet's name today is engaged on research – unbiased – into the relationships of black and coloured in contemporary France. A poet, Hugues Delorme, replied in verse, and illustrated the effect of black troops on his views:

If a quadroon presents himself
Well-made and of good manners
The white woman who refused him
Would reveal herself as stupidly proud,
But yesterday, the blacks, marvellous soldiers,
Showed themselves free from fear and sans reproche
Therefore to choose a black is better far
Than to have as husband a Boche.

J. H. Rosny, of the Académie Goncourt: 'I am hardly in favour of marriage between blacks and whites, and whites and mulattoes.' A more distinguished figure, Pierre Benoit of the Académie Française, was both favourable and witty: 'Mixed marriages do not seem monstrous to me at all. If I were a woman I would much prefer an amiable mulatto to President Wilson, who it seems to me must not be too droll in intimacy.' Jean Finot, the anthropologist: 'All radical measures taken with the aim of preventing marriages between whites and blacks, or what is more grave, whites and mulattoes, become a crying injustice . . .' André de Lorde, a playwright, expressed the archetypal reaction common both in Europe and America: 'The eyes, the odour, the touch of the Negro place between him and us a barrier that all the fine laws of the world and the most eloquent pleading cannot overthrow.'

The enterprise was an interesting one for it not only gave the responses of a cross-section of the French female public – the readers of *Eve* – but also those of savants and littérateurs. One can only guess at what the responses would be in a similar exercise today.

Between the wars another black group was in evidence in France. This consisted of Negro-American writers and artists who found Paris a sympathetic city which did not exhibit race prejudice in an overt manner. The contrast between their homeland and French society in this respect must have been dramatic. They started a vogue which has continued up to the present time. Many distinguished black writers from the States have lived in Paris over the years, such as James Baldwin and Richard Wright.

It was again a war, that of 1939, which led to a further influx of Negroes into France. The pattern of 1914 was repeated – black troops were recruited in the colonial territories. Their advent was, as before, greatly welcomed. But by far the most significant phenomenon was the movement of peoples after the war from the French West Indies to France. This was consequent on the region becoming part of the metropolitan area. This group was further enlarged by a migration of Haitians from their country – political refugees as well as students. The elite of Haiti has always traditionally regarded France as the source of their culture. The third component in this post-war immigration was that of labourers, often specifically recruited, from the former French colonies in Africa. Elaborate training schemes for professionals from these areas increased the extent of the flow.

Some research has been done on the motivations which activate French West Indians to come to France. These are very similar to those which promote people from the British Caribbean to come to England and are basically economic. But in addition there are other factors:

> Apart from economic factors, particularly unemployment, which favour emigration, there are strong ideological and cultural reasons why people would choose to move to France. Here, perhaps, more than anywhere else in the Caribbean area, the idea of the 'mother-country' is potent . . . Thus West Indians often come to France with an idealised and unrealistic vision of what they are to find and with high expectations of the 'mother-country', a situation not unlike that of early immigrants from the West Indies into British society. They have aspirations, however vague, of bettering themselves socially and economically, and they assume that, as Frenchmen, the adventure of moving will be rewarding. Many unconsciously feel that the ambiguity of status deriving from the underlying hierarchy of the islands, where skin colour

and hair texture play their part in determining status, will disappear in France, with its well-known adherence to the creed of equality. They come, therefore, as convinced black Frenchmen, little aware of the complexities of the society into which they are to move . . .[47]

It should be emphasized that the French Government has encouraged this immigration by giving nominal or assisted passages to Europe. Britain has never adopted this policy. French policy was a direct response to the chronic labour shortage in the country which has a very high proportion of its labour-force coming from Europe and overseas.

From the point of view of the French public the arrival of some 200,000 blacks (*Cahiers d'Outre-Mer*, Paris 1971) in their midst aroused a variety of reactions. Most of the immigrants are concentrated in the capital, and in industrial cities such as Strasbourg, Lyons, Marseilles and Clermont-Ferrand. Thus the reactions are urban ones. Hostility on the part of the host society is expressed in a number of petty ways – waiters not paying regard to black customers in cafés, lack of attention in shops, and so forth. Many experience difficulty in getting somewhere to live, but this may in part be due to the general housing shortage in French urban areas.

While the French West Indians tend to be widely dispersed in Paris the African labourers are generally concentrated in specific working-class districts. A curious phenomenon occurs amongst them. While involved in French society in a work situation their solution to the problem of social living is to attempt to reproduce in the places where they live the pattern of life in an African village. This acts as a bulwark against the real or imagined hostility of the host society.[48] Few, if any, contract sexual relationships, except through the brothel, with white people. Choice apart, there is the question of a language barrier – their knowledge of French is mainly elementary.

The black, professional elite, relatively affluent, do not experience the same problems as the other two groups. Like their labourer compatriots they are transients. Unlike them their command of French may be perfect. They seek, and often obtain, sexual relationships with white females. This does lead in many instances to a pathological reaction if they are rejected – it must be because of their colour. This may take the form of delusions that they are being persecuted by white people. In recent years considerable research has been conducted into this and allied phenomena at the Centre Charles Richet in Paris by Professor François Raveau and Dr Françoise Morin.

The approach used by these researchers is based on the belief that in mentally ill people tensions which are latent in normal people are magnified and are therefore easier to study. French West Indians appear to have a higher percentage of delusions relating to colour than do Africans. Africans suffer far less persecution delusions since the establishment of the independent black Republics of former French Africa, but mental disorders have increased. Haitians, as opposed to French West Indians, although subject to the same indignities and frustrations, are sufficiently confident in their status as citizens of an independent black country to attribute this to the general French xenophobia rather than to colour prejudice.[49]

The situation of the French West Indians is distinct from that of the other black groups. As we pointed out, their assumption, backed by the law, is that they are Frenchmen although black. When they experience rejection or hostility, psychologically considered this is as if their mother had rejected them. These feelings are even more intensified when the individual concerned has spent the greater part of his life in France. In a novel by René Maran, *Un Homme pareil aux autres* (Paris 1947), the black hero put his dilemma, over marriage to a French girl, to his white French friend. The latter replies:

> In fact you are like us – you are 'us'. Your thoughts are ours. You behave as we behave, as we would behave. You think of yourself – others think of you – as a Negro? Utterly mistaken! You merely look like one. As everything else, you think as a European. And so it is natural that you love as a European. Since European men only love European women, you can hardly marry anyone but a woman of the country where you have always lived, a woman of our good old France, your real and only country ... [pp. 152–3]

In another passage the hero speaks to the woman he loves about the motives for marrying white:

> The majority [coloured people] of them including those of lighter skin who often go to the extreme of denying both their countries and their mothers, tend to marry in Europe not so much out of love as for the satisfaction of being the master of a European woman; and a certain tang of proud revenge enters into this.
>
> And so I wonder whether in my case there is any difference from theirs; whether by marrying you, who are European, I may not appear to be making a show of contempt for the women of my own race and, above all, to be drawn on by that desire for white flesh that has been forbidden to us Negroes as long as white men have ruled the world, so that without my knowledge I am attempting to revenge myself on a European woman for everything that her ancestors have inflicted on mine throughout the centuries ... [p. 185]

The writer, René Maran, exhibits considerable insight in relation to the state of mind of the coloured man who chooses to marry a white woman. The dilemma has been put in a more scientific form but the facts remain the same – that the heritage of colour and the colonial experience may produce in the individual who embarks on inter-racial sexual relationships profound feelings of insecurity which in the event may become pathological:

> Insofar as truly inter-racial marriage is concerned, one can legitimately wonder to what extent it may not represent for the coloured spouse a kind of subjective consecration to wiping out in himself and in his own mind the colour prejudice from which he has suffered so long. It would be interesting to investigate this in a given number of cases and perhaps to seek in this clouded motivation the underlying reasons for certain inter-racial marriages entered into outside the normal conditions of a happy household. Some men or some women, in effect, by choosing partners of another race, marry persons of a class or a culture inferior to their own whom they would not have chosen as spouses in their own race and whose chief asset seems to be the assurance that the partner will achieve denaturalization and (to use a loathsome word) 'deracialization'. Among certain people of colour, the fact that they are marrying someone of the white race seems to have over-ridden every other consideration. In this fact they find access to complete equality with the illustrious race, the master of the world, the ruler of the peoples of colour . . .[50]

CHAPTER 10

The Anglo-Indians

One of the most interesting instances of miscegenation concerns the sexual relationships of the European and the Indian in the sub-continent of India. Its special interest lies in the fact that it is outside of the classical slave-colonial situation of sexual exploitation. From a European point of view India was never an area of colonial settlement – the size of the country, density of population and the climate were all inhibiting factors. The European presence was concerned primarily with the development of trade, which led eventually, owing to the disunity of the Indian states, to political control and domination.

As in so many other instances, the Portuguese can claim to be the first Europeans to establish themselves in this part of the non-European world. As early as AD 1500 trading posts or 'factories' were created on the Malabar coast in South India. A formula came into being, which was to be followed by all the successors of the Portuguese – Dutch, French and British. Essentially simple, it proved to be extremely effective in action. In return for military assistance against his enemies, the local King or ruler granted concessions and facilities to the European traders. In the case of the Portuguese in Malabar, this led to a fruitful alliance which lasted for over 150 years – from 1501-1663.

The Portuguese 'colonization' of India was concerned not only with trade, but with an anxiety to convert the heathen to Christianity. Both endeavours required considerable manpower. Owing to the rule of celibacy within the Catholic Church, the absence of European women did not necessarily constitute a problem for those engaged in this admirable work. This might be said to have given them an advantage over their Anglican successors in the field of missionary activity. For the traders it was otherwise. A beneficent Government, realizing the necessities of the case, took it upon itself to send out annually from Portugal groups of women who had failed to achieve matrimony in their homeland.[1] Unfortunately this proved expensive, and a new policy was initiated.

This provided an exceedingly practical solution to the problem of the womanless Portuguese. They were encouraged to marry local Indian girls. This not only solved the difficulties of sex and loneliness, but provided a means for penetrating Indian society in the interests of trade. Endeavours were made to ensure alliances between Portuguese men of standing and influential Indian families. The Governor of the Portuguese settlement in the early sixteenth century, Albuquerque, involved himself personally in the prosecution of this policy. 'Albuquerque himself presided at their weddings, and he gave dowries to those who married as he dictated ... and he divided among the married ones the lands, houses, cattle and everything else there was, to give them a start in life ...'[2]

The needs of sex and trade were thus satisfied, but religion was not neglected, as the Church refused to perform such marriages unless the Indian spouse was converted to Christianity. The convert girl was very likely to suffer ostracism from her family and caste for becoming a Christian. This familial and caste rejection extended to the offspring of such unions. It was particularly so in the case of male children. Indians refused to employ youths of this description. Thus they were forced to seek employment with their fathers' trading companies. Two other alternatives existed. One was to join the Portuguese Army or militia as sepoys – soldiers in the ranks. The other was to adopt the profession of arms but on their own account. In other words to become pirates.

These people, the result of the initial process of miscegenation of Indian and Portuguese, were known as Luso-Indians. '... the Luso-Indians learnt poverty and distress. But, born and bred as soldiers, they turned to arms for a living. Lusitanian pirates infested the seas of the Bay [of Bengal]. Others became mercenaries ...'[3] To give credit to the Portuguese they did seek to further the interests of their coloured descendants. But such patronage ceased with the termination of their influence in India. Goa was handed over to the Dutch in 1662, and although provision was made in the articles of capitulation to safeguard the position of those of mixed race, in the event the Luso-Indian lost his comparatively privileged status at the accession of the new European power.

The point to note regarding this initial phase of miscegenation in India is that the mixed group thus created had no alternative, because of the rejection extended by Indian society, but to adhere to the white group. This enforced decision, was, as we shall see, of great historical importance for their descendants and successors.

In time the English succeeded the Dutch in the rape of India. Their rule was to persist into our own time. In their initial period the English, like the Portuguese, faced with the same problems of an exclusively male colony, resorted to the special importation of European women. Again, like the Lusitanian colonists, the policy was abandoned because of the expense of such importations. A directive of the East Indian Company of 1684 shows that they came to the same conclusion as those who preceded them. 'The soldiers' wives shall come to their husbands, if they can find means to satisfy, or pay the owners for their passages, and for such soldiers as are single men, if you could prodently induce them to marry Gentues [Hindus], in imitation of ye dutch pollitcks, and raise from them a stock of Protestant Mestizees ...'[4] The Anglo–Saxon concern for religious proselytization may not have been of the proportions of their Roman Catholic counterparts but it existed nevertheless.

An interesting aspect of miscegenation in this period was the intermixture of Anglo-Saxon men with women of Luso-Indian descent. In Madras such people were known as *Feringhees* or *Topasses*.

The Anglo-Saxon in India in the seventeenth and eighteenth centuries exhibited considerable variation in the kind of sexual and marital alliances he formed. As the interests of the East India Company increased, India began to be looked upon by the penniless females of the English gentry as a potential marriage market. Those who managed to find the fare to India were instructed by their families to make as good a marriage as possible. Potential husbands were selected from the Company's ambitious senior servants. Junior members of the Company, and soldiers, were dependent upon the attractions of either Indian women, or those of mixed descent. The Englishman in India was, however, not only a servant of the East India Company. Frequently he was to be found in the employ of rulers and princes. Such men, whose emoluments were considerable, tended to emulate the life style of their patrons. That is to say they lived in great luxury complete with harems of Indian girls. This style of living was probably at its peak in the middle years of the eighteenth century but continued to persist for another century.

Another process can be distinguished. Depending upon the area, the British soldier might find that his only available sexual companion would be an Indian girl. On the other hand, as the mixed community developed there was a trend for relationships to be formed with the women of this group. Eventually it became rare for an alliance between an Englishman and a pure-bred Indian girl to occur.

While the Portuguese had utilized the services of the Luso-Indians it was left to the Anglo-Saxon to really demonstrate the advantages of a mixed group for those who ruled India. There was no question as to the unswerving loyalty of these people to the Europeans who had sired them.

It was a loyalty which was to outlast the lifetime of the Company and be transferred to the British Raj:

> Their swarthy skins, their faultness knowledge of Indian tongues, modes of dress, habits and religious practices, enabled them to take on a perfect disguise ... and return with important intelligence regarding the enemy's strength, position, and plans. Nor was their usefulness restricted to any one part of the country. Born of Indian mothers wherever the Company had struck its roots, they had in part the external characteristics of the Indian races from which their mothers had been derived ...[5]

It should be remembered that India throughout the greater part of the East India Company's existence had been the prey of internecine conflict on the scale of mediaeval Europe. The Company, despite its concern for trade, had been drawn into these disputes so that its role became military and political as well as commercial. It was in these circumstances that the Anglo–Indian, as he must now be termed, became of great value to its activities.

It is of great significance that although many Anglo-Indians had never seen England their identification with that country was profound. In this they can be compared to the black and coloured middle classes of the West Indies who today, despite the traumatic rejection experienced in the process of emigration to Britain, are still immensely proud of and loyal to the idea of that which is Anglo-Saxon. In 1973 a black professional man, a lawyer and classicist, in Barbados can still speak with nostalgia of a Scottish forebear. This indicates that miscegenation is not only a bio-social process – it is also concerned with states of mind.

The worth of the Anglo-Indian was recognized by the British in India for a long period. To a degree and extent he was accepted socially:

> They had suffered no disabilities. If their fathers could afford it, they had been sent to England for their education, and had generally returned to India in the Covenanted and Commissioned services of the Company. Those who could not proceed to England had been educated locally, and occupied the great majority of positions in the uncovenanted civil service, and in the Company's army ...[6]

This honeymoon of nearly 200 years was, however, destined to be shattered. In the spring of 1786 the first of a series of repressive and restrictive measures against the Anglo-Indians was enacted.

The first of such legislation appears to have been of a minor order but was in fact of a crucial nature. The Upper Orphanage School had been founded in Calcutta under the patronage of the East India Company for the education of orphans of British Army officers. In March 1786 the school was forbidden to permit its pupils to go to Britain to finish their education. At that time the only method of entry into the senior ranks of the Company was through the 'covenanted' services. Such entry was only possible from England. Thus the act of the Company effectively prevented the recruitment of Anglo-Indians for these coveted positions.

This was followed in April 1791 by the closing of another important avenue of employment. 'No person the son of a Native Indian henceforth be appointed by the court in employment in the Civil and Military forces of the Company.' Four years later by a resolution of the Governor-General in Council, '... all persons not descended from European parents on both sides are disqualified for service in the army except as fifers, drummers, bandsmen and farriers ...' By such acts the relatively privileged position of the Anglo-Indian *vis-à-vis* the native Indian, in relation to the European community, began to be eroded.

It has to be understood that from its inception in the seventeenth century the East India Company acted, and was so regarded, as an independent state. Government in England had virtually no control over its activities. This was a state of affairs which persisted until 1772. In that year an Act of the British Parliament did away with a number of political anomalies arising from the autarchic status of the Company. Prior to 1772 it could be said Britain was not directly responsible for any policies adopted with relation to Anglo-Indians. From that time, however, such policies were the joint responsibility of the Company and the British Government in India. The Acts of 1786 and those which followed were initiated with the full knowledge and consent of all concerned with the administration of India.

It is difficult to understand the motivations of the English in adopting a course of action designed to alienate the group which had been so loyal to them. A number of reasons have been advanced – fear of the growing size of the Anglo-Indian community and the possibility of its rebelling against British rule despite evidence of its loyalty; the anxiety of the shareholders of the Company to reserve appointments for their friends and relatives.[7] There are other explanations. It is possible to suggest that towards the end of the eighteenth century racial attitudes began to harden in India. The increasing power and influence of the British presence, the advent of larger numbers of white women, and jealousy of the wealth and ability of the Anglo-Indians all combined to create a situation in which racial prejudice was easily fostered. The role of the Englishwoman in assisting this process cannot be underrated. As in all European colonial situations sexual relationships between her menfolk and 'native' women were regarded as a threat to her status.[8]

Some authorities, such as Philip Woodruff, are of the opinion that Anglo-Saxon indifference rather than racial prejudice was the key to English behaviour. 'Professor Spear believes there was a golden age when Englishman and Indian met as friends and equals and that this ended when political power brought racial arrogance and contempt. My own impression is that from the earliest days most of the English kept to themselves, more from idleness than anything else.'[9] Perhaps the 'idleness' was interpreted by others as arrogance. But in fact the explanation is a trifle simplistic. Is it really possible that men who cohabited with Indian and Anglo-Indian women could be said to have avoided other contacts through idleness?

Despite the rejection they were now beginning to suffer, when, during the Mahratta and Mysore Wars at the end of the eighteenth century, the Company called upon the Anglo-Indians to rejoin its army, the response was immediate: 'They heard the call of the blood, and obeyed it with alacrity . . . To a man they remained true to their fathers' people, preferring death to lifting the sword against England . . .'[10]

Once again the Anglo-Indian had demonstrated his misguided if unswerving loyalty to the European. Incredible as it may appear no sooner had the crisis of the Company ended in 1808 than the former regulations were again enforced, and Anglo-Indians were discharged from the army. This can only be interpreted as an arrogance, and manipulation, of race of splendid proportions. Unfortunately in race relations manipulation is frequently taken as a sign of recognition by those thus abused. This is as true of the West Indies as it is of India.

So far we have used the term Anglo-Indian to denote the community in India which was of European and Indian descent. The use of the term itself, however, only dates from the last years of the nineteenth century. An examination of the varied nomenclature used to describe the community gives considerable insight into the status and attitudes of both the Anglo-Indians and the English:

> The interactions of prejudice are interestingly reflected in the evolution of Eurasian attitudes towards communal nomenclature. In the early days of the British insinuation into India, they were referred to as 'half-castes', 'mixed-bloods', 'country borns' and 'members of the mixed races', and appeared to have accepted these terms without protest. By the beginning of the nineteenth century, these names definitely acquired the value of epithets rather than descriptive terms, and in 1825 the community therefore organised a meeting in Calcutta, which resolved that

'East Indian' was the 'most appropriate and applicable designation'. It was not universally used, however, the term 'Indo-Briton' being more popular as it suggested blood relationship with the ruling class.

A few years previously (1813–1823) the term 'Eurasian', attributed to the Marquess of Hastings, had been sporadically used, and in fifty years it had become so general that the Association founded by E. W. Chambers in 1876 adopted it as a communal designation. Unfortunately, it soon came to have a derogatory implication, which the Eurasians sought to elude by appropriating the label 'Anglo-Indian' from the resident Britishers who had invented it for themselves. In 1897, the Secretary of State for India was petitioned by a deputation, led by J. R. Wallace, to give official recognition to the filched cognomen, but that dignitary remained unimpressed. Undeterred, the energetic doctor founded on his return 'The Imperial Anglo-Indian Association', rhetorically declaring that 'Britishers we are and Britishers we must ever be. Once we relinquish this name (Anglo-Indian) and permit ourselves to be styled "Eurasians" or "Statutory Natives of India" we become estranged from our proud heritage as Britishers.'

The reward of these patriotic exercises was the publicly expressed sarcasm of Lord Curzon, the then Viceroy of India, and the neglect of the euphuistic appellation outside the community itself. But Lord Hardinge authorised its use for the Indian Census of 1911, and it is now (1937) officially employed without being universally recognised, though it is beginning to find favour in print, often with the satirical qualification 'new style'. Moreover, it has not released the Eurasians from their statutory definition as 'Natives of India', nor their occupational definition as 'European British Subjects'. The political subtlety of these terminological anomalies exposes 'Anglo-Indians' to utilisation according to official convenience. As natives they are excluded from certain British privileges, while as European British subjects they enlarge the British electoral and military strength, and are prevented from orienting themselves to complete acceptance of their statutory position.[11]

The writer, Cedric Dover, from whom we have quoted extensively, was himself an Anglo-Indian. In our opinion he expresses the significance of nomenclature for his community prior to the independence of India. It is interesting to note that the term Asiatic, which was current before the 1939 war, and which was used to describe any inhabitant of Asia, has been superseded by Asian. This was because it had acquired pejorative overtones as in the case of Eurasian. In the new climate of political independence after the war it was felt invidious to continue its usage. Anglo-Saxondom in its role as colonial power, and its ethnocentrism, built up a vocabulary of derogation to describe those unfortunate enough to have been deprived of the racial purity (*sic*) of the English.

For the Briton at home, and the expatriate, the inhabitants of the Third World are popularly all known as Wogs. The people of Britain's colleague in the European Common Market, Italy, are either Eyeties or Wops. The peoples of Southern Europe and South America are comfortably disposed of as Dagoes. The arrogance of ethnocentrism invariably expresses itself in a vocabulary of derogation. Popular literature in the form of novels, stories and plays is of great assistance in its dissemination. The European masses do not on the whole read 'scientific' racist literature – they take their ideas from the descendants of Sax Rohmer's Dr Fu Manchu and John Buchan's heroes.

The importance of language as an indicator of social attitudes cannot be over-emphasized. In Britain, for example, vocabulary, intonation, accent, pronunciation and usage are all used to delineate and chart the bewildering ramifications of the class structure.

In the case of the Anglo-Indian his method of pronouncing English led to the invention of a specific word – *chee-chee* – to describe this. The definition in the *O.E.D.* is: 'a word applied disparagingly to the "minced English" of Eurasians or half-breeds in India, and so the class themselves ... Chee-Chee is the general designation the half-cast ladies receive in India.' A more authentic source for the term – the *O.E.D.* bases the main part of its entry on it – is *Hobson-Jobson: being a glossary of Anglo-Indian colloquial words and phrases and of kindred terms: etymological, historical, geographical and discursive*. This work, by H. Yule and A. C. Burnell (London 1886), is a treasure-store of information as to the social behaviour of the English in India – Anglo-Indian is used by the authors in that sense.

The entry in *Hobson-Jobson* is as follows: '*Cheechee*, adj. A disparaging term applied to half-castes or *Eurasians* (q.v.) (corresponding to the *lip-lap* of the Dutch in Java), and also to their manner of speech. The word is said to be taken from *chi* (Fie!), a common native (S. Indian) interjection of remonstrance or reproof supposed to be much used by the class in question. The term is however, perhaps, also a kind of onomatopoeia, indicating the mincing pronunciation which often characterizes them (see below). It should, however, be added that there are many well educated East Indians who are quite free from this mincing accent.

'1781 "Pretty little Looking Glasses,
Good and Cheap for *chee-chee* Misses."
Hicky's Bengal Gazette, March, 17

'1873 "He is no favourite with the pure native, whose language he speaks as his own in addition to the hybrid minced English (known as *chee-chee*), which he also employs."

Fraser's Magazine, October, 437

'1880 "The Eurasian girl is often pretty and graceful ... what if upon her lips there hung the accents of her tchi-tchi tongue."

Sir Ali Baba, 122

'1881 "There is no doubt that the 'Chee-Chee twang', which becomes so objectionable to every Englishman before he has been long in the East, was originally learned in the convent and the Brother's school, and will be clung to as firmly as the queer turns of speech learned in the same place."

St James's Gazette, August 26th'

It could be suggested that the minced, or *chi-chi*, English became distasteful to the English in India because it was a permanent reminder that they had quite literally created the people who spoke it. In other words it was a symbol of their sexual guilt and exploitation. The rules which determine whether a particular English accent is attractive or not to the speaker of standard English seem somewhat unpredictable. In England some regional accents are acceptable, others are not. Antipathy may be determined by association of the accent with undesirable social connotations. Theories of this kind, however, fail to explain the greater acceptability of West Country accents against Northern ones.

As linguistics is not our field it is with some hesitancy that we suggest that quite apart from *chee-chee* the English spoken by Indians is of a distinctive order. The intonation sounds as if it were of Hindi or Urdu origin. It is to be found even amongst East Indians in the West Indies who speak the local English patois.[12]

Fluctuations in the fortunes of the Anglo-Indians continued throughout the nineteenth century. At no time, however, did they recover to the position of acceptability experienced in the sixteenth and seventeenth centuries. The introduction of the telegraph in 1851, and of the railway in 1853, created new opportunities for employment as the number of Indians qualified to fill such posts was limited. In the Mutiny of 1857, or as it is now termed the War of Independence, they once again demonstrated their loyalty to the Anglo-Saxon. The closing of the lower ranks of Government service to Englishmen from overseas also provided them with greater opportunity. But the tide was against them, and political developments in India only served to emphasize their equivocal status.

A recent study of the community sums up their position as they moved into the twentieth century.

> Due to their domestic duties at the houses of the ruling whites where they picked up European ways, and because of their nearness in appearance to them, the Anglo-Indians thought themselves to be one with the whites and tried to imitate them in every walk of life. However, for the majority of the community it always remained a poor imitation due to a lack of money and the absence of actual contact with England. Europeans never treated them as their equals but only favoured them slightly; thus the Anglo-Indians got very little sympathy from the whites 'to whose coat-tails they made desperate efforts to cling'. On the other hand, Indians resented their claims to racial superiority, and with the rise of the patriotic movements and the development of a definite antagonism to the British, looked upon these loyal progeny of the whites with contempt and indifference . . .[13]

Political and social insecurity led to a kind of schizophrenia. One of the historians of the community could write from his heart the following:

> If England is the land of our Fathers, India is the land of our Mothers. If to us England is a hallowed memory, India is a living verity . . . If England is dear as a land of inspiring traditions, India is loved for all that she means to us in our daily life . . . If we lean so heavily to our fathers' side, it is because the creeds and customs of our mothers' people so ordained it. Themselves the victims of a tyrannical caste system and religious orthodoxy, as they have in the present, so they had in the past, no option but to repudiate our consanguinity . . . We naturally identify ourselves with the social, economic and political development and aspirations of our mother country. We would live amicably and on terms of mutual trust and respect with our Indian fellow-countrymen, and would have them reciprocate our sentiments . . . In truth we are England's hostages to India, and they who give and receive hostages are bound to regard them as trust. If only Indians realized this, our economic and political position would not seem to us so desperate as it now appears . . .[14]

That was written in 1926. The position today in the new, independent India is not so very different. Under the 1949 Constitution of Independent India, the Anglo-Indian community was given special representation in both the local and national legislative bodies. With the independence of India these concessions were swept away, but were later renewed so that at the present time the community has special representation in the Indian Parliament. In both practice and theory all employment avenues are open to Anglo-Indians. Many, for example, have risen to senior positions in the armed forces. Despite these changes it would be true to say that the position of the Anglo-Indian in contemporary India is essentially one of uncertainty and equivocation.

It is of some significance to consider how the Anglo-Indian appeared to the European – that is to say how he was viewed physically. Edgar Thurston, who wrote what is possibly the most authoritative work on the castes and tribes of India, gave an account of their appearance in an article – *Eurasians of Madras and Malabar* (1898):

> ... In colour the Eurasians afford, as is natural in a mixed race, examples of the entire colour-scale from sooty-black, through sundry shades of brown yellow, to pale white and even, as a very rare exception, florid or rosy ... The products of alliances between British men and Eurasian women show the least signs of physical degeneration, and possess broader shoulders, hips and hands, greater chest-girth, wider forehead, and more muscle as the result of re-vivification of the stock by direct British intervention ... amid wholesome surroundings, the Eurasian (especially of British Paternity) is capable of developing into being a good physique, such as is required for the hardships of Military services ...

Thurston was writing at the turn of the nineteenth century and, although an anthropologist, was a prey to the prejudices of his time. It is almost as if against his better judgement he has to concede that the Anglo-Indian was not a degenerate type. The popular Anglo-Saxon point of view was that the hybrid by definition must represent the worst qualities, both mental and physical, of the races concerned. Others, less objective than Thurston, gave way to their prejudices. 'Physically the Eurasians are slight and weak. They are naturally indolent ... They are lacking in independence, and are forever begging favours ... They recklessly resign from any and every post when, for some reason or without reason, their feelings are hurt.' 'Their greatest pride is that they are descended from Europeans ... there is nothing that the Anglo-Indian deplores more than his dark skin. He would give anything in the world to become as fair as a European ... He would rather see his daughter married to a low, vulgar European and be ill-treated afterwards than see her marry one of her own kind. The Anglo-Indians have great disdain for the Indians, whom they treat with contempt.'[15]

Biased as these views may be they indicate a kind of reality. Because of the uncertainty of their status and their conflicting loyalties, their behaviour does tend to be equivocal. A comparison with the coloured West Indian suggests that in the case of the Anglo-Indian he has two reference points – India and Britain; in the case of the West Indian,

Africa has not the same validity as India for the Anglo-Indian. In other words the process of miscegenation in the Caribbean has not created a situation of crisis as in India.

The Constitution of India defines an Anglo-Indian as '... a person whose father or any of whose male progenitors was of European descent, but who is domiciled within the territory of India, and is or was born within such territory of parents habitually resident therein, and not established there for temporary purposes only ...'[16] The emphasis for the purposes of definition is entirely on the ability to trace European descent through the male line. The actual community in relation to the total Indian population is very small. The latest census does not, unfortunately, have a separate category of Anglo-Indians. The 1951 census, however, lists 111,637 individuals as belonging to this category.[17]

The contemporary Anglo-Indian is essentially an urban figure. Households reflect the same pattern that is characteristic of Indian society as a whole. That is to say the Anglo-Indian community is stratified in terms of socio-economic class. An interesting linkage, however, is provided by ancillary furnishings in the home. The majority, irrespective of the economic status of the family, will have a pet animal of some kind, an array of flower pots, and some musical instrument.[18] In Bombay, where there are some 3,000 Anglo-Indians, individuals are mainly engaged in a variety of activities, but few have businesses of their own. They are mainly to be found in tailoring, hair-dressing, and the sale of cosmetics, wine and meat. In addition a number are employed on the railways, and a few with European trading firms. Females tend to be office workers, nursery teachers, models and air hostesses. Security of employment is more assured for women than for men as there is increasing competition for male jobs.[19]

The adherence of the Anglo-Indian to that which is English is demonstrated by their dress. In general this is almost invariably European. In urban centres, such as Bombay, this does not serve to distinguish them from the mass of the Indian population which tends to dress in the Western style – shirt and trousers rather than the dhoti or kurta of traditional India. Women avoid the sari, and the pattern of their clothes is very much influenced by their reading of European fashion magazines. They do not affect the jewellery and ornaments typical of the ordinary Indian woman, and attempt to curl their hair artificially to make it appear more European.[20]

The same affiliation is exhibited in terms of religion. The majority belong to one or other of the Christian denominations – well over half are Roman Catholic, and a small minority are members of Jehovah's Witnesses or the Salvation Army. It must be remembered that the Anglo-Indians have little choice in the matter as by definition they are outside the religious and familial complex of Hinduism. But it is doubtful, even if the option existed, that any Anglo-Indian would wish to give religious adherence to Hinduism.[21]

The norm for the Anglo-Indian family is that of the European, Christian monogamous unit. Marriage tends to be endogamous, and associated with the religious affiliation of the family – only a minority of marriages are inter-denominational. At the same time the contemporary picture shows that economic factors are affecting this pattern. That is to say a middle-class Anglo-Indian family is not averse to welcoming a rich Indian boy as a suitor for their daughter. The age of marriage is late – nearly fifty per cent of males marry between twenty-five and twenty-nine. This is due to economic factors as financial security comes comparatively late. Because of this, in the lower income groups a considerable proportion of boys tend to marry lower-class Indian Christians. In general Anglo-Indian marital patterns reflect those of European society, in which class and income affect the choice of partner.[22]

Separateness of the community from the mass of Indian society can be seen in terms of entertainment in the home. This is not necessarily confined to Anglo-Indians. It includes Christian Indians, Muslims and Parsees. While choice is naturally exercised in the matter, both dietary and religious sanctions affect the possibility of social interaction with Hindus.[23]

As occurs in Jewish communities Anglo-Indians make a distinction between those regarded as 'good' and those considered 'bad'. The latter are individuals who refuse to accept identification with the community. They have in fact opted out, and have adhered either to the Indian or European community. Their choice may be on personal grounds, or because of their inability to prove their status legally.[24]

What emerges from a study of contemporary Anglo-Indian society is that it feels at hazard. It has never lost its emotional ties with Britain, but in the India of independence increasingly there is pressure to identify with the greater society. From the heyday of their privilege in the seventeenth and eighteenth centuries they have come to occupy an extremely marginal position. The growth of education in India as a whole has deprived them of their last vestige of superiority. In a recent survey concerning attitudes within the Anglo-Indian community well over half the respondents felt that their situation was worsening, less than a quarter felt they were well-treated, and just over forty per cent thought that they would be happier in Britain.[25]

It should be noted that the miscegenation between Europeans and Indians which created the Anglo-Indians concerned all levels of society, and that many distinguished families on both sides were involved. For example, Job Charnock, the founder of Calcutta, married the widow, whom he saved from suttee (the obligatory self-immolation of a Hindu wife at the death of her husband), of a notable Indian. Skinner of Skinner's Horse, one of the most famous of Indian regiments, was an Anglo-Indian. Lord Liverpool, a nineteenth-century British Prime Minister, was of Anglo-Indian descent on his mother's side. Many aristocratic families in England could, if they wished, claim a 'Eurasian' connection. Unfortunately the record is obscure, as according to their appearance, many Anglo-Indians have 'passed' into the domain of the Anglo-Saxon.[26]

We have attempted very briefly in this chapter to examine some aspects of an unique social group. The facts suggest that the Anglo-Indians are amongst the most unfortunate of the children of conflict.

Notes and References

CHAPTER 2

The European Image of the Non-European

1. Lord Bryce, *The Relations of the Advanced and the Backward Races of Mankind*, Oxford 1902, p. 18.
   E. E. Sikes, *The Anthropology of the Greeks*, London 1914, p. 88.
   T. J. Haarhoff, *The Strangers at the Gate*, Oxford 1948, p. 299.
   C. Kluckhorn, *Anthropology and the Classics*, Providence 1961, pp. 34 and 42.
   H. C. Baldry, *The Unity of Mankind in Greek Thought*, Cambridge 1965, p. 4.
2. Herodotus, *History*, translated and edited by G. Rawlinson, London 1880, Book III, Sections 99 and 101.
3. Ibid., footnote p. 493.
4. Ibid.
5. Ibid., Book II, 58, 77, 84.
6. Further references to the reputation and skill of Egyptian doctors will be found in footnotes 4 and 5 on pp. 136–7 Vol. II in Rawlinson, op. cit.
7. See Rawlinson, op. cit. Footnote pp. 170–71.
8. *Germania*, 20.1.
9. *Annales*, 1.64, 2.14 & 21,
   Agricola, 11.2.
10. Caesar, *De Bello Gallico*, Book 1, 39.1.
11. *Geography*, Book IV.5.2.
12. Suetonius, *Julias*, 80.2.
    Strabo, *Geography*, 3. 2. 15.
    Pliny, *Naturalis Historia*, 3.31.
13. Agatharchides, *De Mari Erythraes*, 16 GGM 1. 118.
    Frontinus, *Strategemata*, 1.11.17–18.
14. Book III, 20.
15. Hans Licht, *Sexual Life in Ancient Greece*, London 1932, pp. 369–70.

16. A. J. B. Ware, *British School of Athens Journal*, Vol. X 1903–4, p. 110.
17. Many of these are reproduced in J. Marcade, *Roma Amor*, Geneva 1961.
18. Herodotus, op. cit., Book II. 30.
19. Apollodorus, *Bibliotheca*, 2.1.5.
20. Ovid, *Amores*, 1.8. 3–4 and 1.13. 33–34.
21. Pausanias, *Description of Greece*, 10.6. 3–4.
22. Josephus, *Antiquities of the Jews*, Book II, Chap. 10.
23. Juvenal, VI, pp. 599–602.
Martial, *Epigramis*, 6.39. 6–7.
24. Aristotle, *De generatione animalium*, 1.18. 722a,
Pliny, *Naturalis Historia*, 7.12. 51.
25. Menander, *Plays and Fragments*, translated by Philip Vellacott, Penguin Classics, London 1967, p. 242.
26. *Kings*, X, 1–10, *Psalms*, 68.31,
Jeremiah, XXXVIII, 7–13.
27. H. Baudet, *Paradise on Earth*, New Haven and London 1965, p. 18.
28. Ibid.
29. Leo Africanis, *The History and Description of Africa*, translated by J. Pory, Hakluyt Society, 1st Series 1895.
Pierre d'Ailly, *Imago Mundi*, translated by E. F. Keiner, Wilmington, NC 1948.
Jacobus de Voraigne, *The Golden Legend*, London 1878.
30. Palladius, *Historia Lausiaca*, and Rufinus of Aquilea, *Historia monachorum, de Apollonio.*
31. Sozomen, *Historia ecclesiastica*, 6.29.
32. Vita S. *Moyris Sethiopis.*
V. Latyšer, *Menologium*, Fase. 2, pp. 330–34.
33. C. S. Coon, *The Living Races of Man*, London 1966, pp. 115–19.
34. Ibid., pp. 115 and 116.
35. S. Lane-Poole, *The Moors in Spain*, London 1897, p. 48.
36. *Song of Roland*, translated by Dorothy Sayers, London 1937, Verses 113, 143 and 144.
37. Sheihl Anta Diop, *L'Unité culturelle de l'Afrique Noire*, Paris 1959, pp. 91–2.
38. C. Brockelman, *Geschichte der arabischen Literatur*, 2nd Edition, Leiden 1943, Vol. I, pp. 13 et seq.
39. C. R. Boxer, *Race Relations in the Portuguese Colonial Empire 1415–1825*, Oxford 1963, pp. 9 and 10.
40. A. F. C. Ryder, 'An Early Portuguese Trading Voyage to the Forcados River', in *Journal of the Historical Society of Nigeria*, Vol. I, p. 298.
41. S. F. de Mendo Trigoso (ed.), *Viagem de Lisboa à ilha de Sãn Tomé ...*, Lisbon ND., pp. 51–2.
42. Quoted by C. R. Boxer in *Race Relations in the Portuguese Colonial Empire 1415–1825*, Oxford 1963, pp. 60–61.
43. Quoted by C. R. Boxer, op. cit., p. 63.
44. C. R. Boxer, 'Fidalgos Portugueses e Bailadeiras Indianas, Séculos XVIL e

XVIII', in *Revista de Historia*, No. 56, Sao Paulo 1961; and Fernando Henriques, *Prostitution and Society*, Vol. I, Chaps IV and V, London 1962.

45. See in particular, Eldred Jones, *Othello's Countrymen*, Oxford 1965, Chap. I, 'The African Image in Sixteenth-Century England'.
46. Anon, *The History of Titus Andronicus*.
47. Eldred Jones, op. cit., p. 80.
48. Ibid., p. 85.
49. *Cook's Voyages*, Everyman edition, London 1906, p. 38. For an admirable assessment of the influence of the Pacific on European notions of the non-European in this period see Bernard Smith, *European Vision and the South Pacific 1768–1850*, OUP 1960, Chap. 5, pp. 96–116.
50. For an account of the settlement of Pitcairn see T. Boyles Murray, *Pitcairn*, London ND.
51. For an analysis of racist thinking in this period see Michael Banton, *Race Relations*, London 1967, Chaps 3 and 4.
52. *The Inequality of Human Races*, paperback edition, Los Angeles 1966, footnote p. 151.
53. Robert Knox, *The Races of Men*, London 1862, p. 287.

CHAPTER 3
The Bastion of Racial Purity

1. Opinion of the presiding judge in the case *Loving* v. *Virginia* in which a Negro-white couple were convicted of contravening the miscegenation statutes of the State of Virginia. They had contracted a marriage outside the State and had returned to reside in Virginia. Quoted by Chief Justice Warren of the Supreme Court of the United States when the appeal from conviction came to that Court. (Cases Adjudged in the Supreme Court of the USA, October Term, 1866, No. 395, *Loving et ux* v. *Virginia*. Decided 12 June 1967.)
2. Judgement in *Loving et al.* v. *Commonwealth of Virginia*, Supreme Court of Appeals of Virginia, 7 March 1966. (*147 South Eastern Reporter, 2d Series.*)
3. This case was concerned with the marriage of a white to a Mongolian in Virginia.
4. The information which follows is based on the report of the case in *147 South Eastern Reporter, 2d Series*. Quotations in the text are taken from that report.
5. *Stare decisis* – governed by a previous decision of principle.
6. Friends of the court.
7. H. Pleckerm, 'The New Family and Health Improvement', *17 Virginia Health Bulletin Extra No. 12*, at 25–26. (*New Family Series*, No. 5, 1925.)
8. The interested reader can follow the whole romantic saga in *Pocahontas*, London 1929 by David Garnett There are a number of eighteenth-century instances of American Indians of both sexes marrying white spouses in Europe.

9. A. E. Estabrook and I. E. McDougle, *Mongrel Virginians: The Win Tribe*, Baltimore 1926, p. 14 and p. 19.
10. The information given here is taken from the record of the *McLaughlin* Appeal before the Supreme Court of the US October Term 1964, 379 US.
11. H. M. Applebaum, 'Miscegenation Statutes: A Constitutional and Social Problem', in *The Georgetown Law Journal*, Vol. 53, p. 49 and p. 52, 1964.
12. *Jackson* v. *City and County of Denver*, 109 Colorado 196, 124 P. 2d 240 (1940).
13. *Hopkins* v. *Bowers*, III North Carolina 175, 16 S.E. I (1892), and *Bennett* v. *Bennett*, 195 South Carolina I, 10 S.E. 2d 23 (1940).
14. *State* v. *Miller*, 224 North Carolina 228, 29 S.E. 2d 751 (1944).
15. The information in this and subsequent paragraphs is based on that given in Applebaum, op. cit., pp. 53–56.
16. *Barker* v. *Carter*, 180 Oklahoma 71, 56 P. 2d 85 (1937).
17. This and subsequent quotations are taken from the Supreme Court Record (No. 395) of the *Lovings* case.

CHAPTER 4

Race Mixture in the United States – The Historical Background, New England and Pennsylvania

1. *Journals of the Provincial Congress of Massachusetts in 1774 and 1775*, Boston 1838, p. 755, and J. C. Ballagh, *A History of Slavery in Virginia*, Baltimore 1902.
2. For examples of this see G. F. Dow (ed.), *Records and Files of the Quarterly Courts of Essex County, Mass. 1636–1692*, Vol. XVIII, Mass. 1911.
3. *Acts and Laws of His Majesties Colony of Connecticut in New England*, Boston 1702, pp. 12–13.
4. G. A. Sheldon, *A History of Deerfield, Massachusetts*, Mass. 1895, p. 59.
5. W. Updike, *History of the Narragansett Church*, 2nd Edition, Boston 1907, p. 217.
6. *Reports of the Record Commissioners of Boston, Mass.*, Boston 1881–1909, 'Boston Marriages, 1700–1809', Vol. XXVIII, p. 29.
7. 'Diary of Samuel Sewall', *Massachusetts Historical Society Collections*, 5th Series, Vol. VI, p. 22.
8. F. W. Bailey (ed.), 'Early Connecticut Marriages as found on Ancient Church Records Prior to 1800', *Bureau of American Ancestry*, New Haven 1896–1906.
9. G. E. Howard, *A History of Matrimonial Institutions*, Chicago 1904, Vol. II, pp. 225–6.
10. J. H. Temple, *History of Framingham, Mass., Early Known as Danforth's Farms, 1640–1880, with a Genealogical Register*, Mass. 1887, p. 236.
11. See *New England Weekly Journal*, 21 February 1738, *New England Weekly Chronicle*, 25 April 1776, *Boston News Letter*, 25 August 1718, and 1 May 1732.

12. *Continental Journal and Weekly Advertiser*, (Boston) 21 December 1780.
13. G. H. Moore, *Notes on Slavery in Massachusetts*, NY 1866, p. 209.
14. *Boston Gazette and County Journal*, 16 March 1767, and *Records of the Courts of Assistants of the Massachusetts Bay in New England, 1630–1692*, Boston 1901–04.
15. *Massachusetts Historical Society Collections*, 5th Series, Vol. III, pp. 432–433.
16. Moore, op. cit., p. 57n.
17. 'Boston Marriages', op. cit., 1700–1751, p. 5.
18. Elizabeth Donnan, *Documents Illustrative of the Slave Trade to America*, Washington DC 1930–35, Vol. III, p. 4n.
19. A. W. Lauber, *Indian Slavery in Colonial Times*, NY 1913, pp. 126 and 127.
20. N. B. Shurtleff (ed.), *Records of the Governor and Company of the Massachusetts Bay in New England, 1628–1641*, Boston 1853, Vol. I, p. 246.
21. *Massachusetts Historical Society Collections*, 2nd Series, Vol. III, p. 93.
22. *Plymouth Church Records, 1620–1854*, Vol. XXIII, pp. 492–493, *Boston Weekly Post Boy*, 14 September 1741, *Journal of Negro History*, Washington 1923, Vol. VIII, p. 159.
23. J. H. Temple, op. cit., p. 255.
24. *Massachusetts Historical Society Collections*, 2nd Series, Vol. III, pp. 95–97.
25. Ibid.
26. Donnan, op. cit., Vol. III, p. 69.
27. F. W. Bailey, op. cit., Vol. I, pp. 7 and 8.
28. B. Brawley, *A Social History of the American Negro*, NY 1921, p. 242.
29. Samuel Dexter writing to Dr Jeremy Belknap, *Mass. Hist. Soc. Colls.*, 5th Series, Vol. III, p. 386.
30. T. M. Cooley, *Sketches of the Life and Character of the Rev. Lemuel Haynes, A.M. ...*, NY 1839, pp. 28 and 70.
31. G. F. Dow (ed.), op. cit.
32. Ibid., Vol. II, p. 247, Vol. V, pp. 316 and 411, Vol. VIII, p. 41, Vol. VII, p. 411.
33. G. E. Howard, op. cit., Vol. II, p. 193.
34. William Bradford, *History of Plimouth Plantation*, Boston 1889, pp. 476–7.
35. Ibid., pp. 474–5.
36. St Jerome, *Ad Furiam*, p. 10.
37. Bradford, op. cit., pp. 463, 469, 466 and 465.
38. *Diary of Cotton Mather*, NY 1911, p. 58.
39. E. Oberholzer, Jr, *Delinquent Saints*, NY 1956, p. 127.
40. H. W. Laurence, *The Not-Quite Puritans*, Boston 1928, pp. 175–6.
41. *Pittsfield Records*, Boston 1853, Vol. II, p. 175.
42. W. B. Weeden, 'The Early African Slave Trade in New England', *Proceedings of the American Antiquarian Society*, New Series, Vol. V, Worcester, Mass., 1889, p. 310.
43. Records of the Suffolk County Court, 1671–80, *Colonial Society of Massachusetts Publications*, Boston 1933, Vol. XXX, Pt II, p. 809.

44. *Massachusetts Archives, Domestic Relations 1643–1774*, Vol. IX, pp. 349–52.
45. Ibid., Vol. IX, pp. 393–4.
46. *Acts and Resolves, Public and Private of the Massachusetts Bay*, Boston 1869–1886, Vo.l I, p. 578.
47. Ibid.
48. Ibid.
49. *Mass. Hist. Soc. Colls.*, 5th Series, Vol. III, p. 390.
50. S. Sewall, 'Selling of Joseph', *Mass. His. Soc. Colls.*, 6th Series, Vol. VI, p. 18.
51. J. R. Barlett (ed.), *Records of the Colony of Rhode Island and Providence Plantations in New England, 1636–1792*, Providence 1856–65, Vol. IX, p. 653.
52. U. B. Phillips, *American Negro Slavery*, NY 1940, p. 112.
53. A. W. Calhoun, *A Social History of the American Family*, Cleveland 1917, Vol. I, p. 205.
54. Ibid., p. 210.
55. Ibid., p. 209.
56. Ibid., pp. 314–15.
57. Ibid., p. 209.
58. Ibid., pp. 210–11.
59. E. R. Turner, *The Negro in Pennsylvania*, Washington 1911, pp. 29–31.
60. Calhoun, op. cit., p. 211.
61. E. R. Turner, op. cit., pp. 194–5.
62. T. Branagan, *Serious Remonstrances*, quoted by E. R. Turner, op. cit., p. 195n.
63. E. R. Turner, op. cit., pp. 195–6.
64. R. R. Wright, *The Negro in Pennsylvania*, Philadelphia 1912, (Reprinted NY 1969), pp. 174–5.
65. Ibid., p. 175.
66. Ibid., p. 212, and A. H. Stone, *Studies in the American Race Problem*, NY 1908, pp. 62–3.
67. A. H. Stone, op. cit., p. 62.
68. F. L. Hoffman, *Race Traits and Tendencies of the American Negro*, American Economic Association 1896, p. 199.

CHAPTER 5
Race Mixture in the United States – The Ante-Bellum South

1. Ann Maury, *Memoirs of a Huguenot Family*, NY 1872, pp. 349–50.
2. H. Pleckman, 'The New Family and Health Improvement', *17 Virginia Health Bulletin Extra*, No. 12, *New Family Series*, No. 5, 1925, pp. 25–26.
3. A. W. Lauber, *Indian Slavery in Colonial Times, within the Present Limits of the United States*, NY 1913, pp. 207–8.
4. J. S. Bassett (ed.), *The Writings of Colonel William Byrd*, NY 1901, pp. 8–9.

5. A. Beveridge, *Life of John Marshall*, NY 1919, Vol. I, pp. 239–41.
6. J. F. D. Smyth, *Tour in the United States of America*, London 1784, Vol. I, p. 191.
7. Maury, op. cit., p. 360.
8. J. R. Brodhead, *Documents Relating to the Colonial History of the State of New York*, Albany 1858–87, Vol. VI, p. 647; Gilberto Freyre, *The Masters and the Slaves*, NY 1946, and *New World in the Tropics*, NY 1963, pp. 72–3.
9. Office of Indian Affairs, Osage Tribe, (Letters Received) 25 January 1824.
10. W. W. Hening, *Statutes at Large; Being a Compilation of All the Laws of Virginia from the First Session of the Legislature in the Year 1619*, etc., Richmond, Va., 1810–23, Vol. III, pp. 86–88.
11. Ibid., Vol. I, pp. 146 and 552.
12. Lauber, op. cit., p. 250.
13. Father William, *Recollections of Rambles in the South*, NY 1854, pp. 122–30.
14. J. G. Pollard, 'Pamunky Indians of Virginia', *Bulletin 17, 1894, Bureau of American Ethnology*, Washington DC 1894, p. 10.
15. Archives of Virginia, Legislative Papers, Petition 13733, King William, 20 January 1843.
16. Ibid., Petition 1230, Northampton, 26 November 1784.
17. Office of Indian Affairs, Letter Book, No. 2, (Letters Sent) p. 303.
18. See B. Berry, *Almost White*, NY 1969.
19. W. G. Simms, 'The Morals of Slavery', *The Pro-Slavery Arguments*, Philadelphia 1822, pp. 237–8.
20. See H. Hoetink, *Two Variants in Caribbean Race Relations*, London 1969.
21. J. H. Johnston, *Race Relations in Virginia and Miscegenation in the South 1776–1860*, Amherst 1970, p. 217.
22. Quoted by Franklin Frazier, *The Negro Family in the United States*, revised and abridged edition, Chicago 1966, p. 53.
23. John Brown, *Slave Life in Georgia*, (ed.), L. A. Chameroozow, London 1855, pp. 132–33.
24. See Ivan Bloch, *Sexual Life in England Past and Present*, London 1958.
25. Moses Grandy, *Narrative of the Life of Moses Grandy; Late a Slave in the United States of America*, Boston 1844, p. 18.
26. S. Northrop, *Twelve Years a Slave; Narrative of Solomon Northup, A Citizen of New York, Etc.*, Auburn 1853, p. 65.
27. Helen T. Catterall, *Judicial Cases Concerning Negro Slavery*, Washington 1926, Vol. III, pl 228; and Frederick Douglass, *My Bondage and My Freedom*, NY 1855, pp. 85–88.
28. Numerous cases are quoted by Frazier, op. cit., pp. 61–69, and Johnston, op. cit., pp. 219–236.
29. Catterall, op. cit., Vol. II, p. 451.
30. Ibid., Vol. I, p. 318.
31. R. B. Flanders, *Plantation Slavery in Georgia*, Chapel Hill 1933, p. 142.

32. See Catterall, op. cit., Vol. I, pp. 227–8, 302; Vol. II, pp. 375 and 451; Vol. III, pp. 655–56.
33. J. H. Russell, *The Free Negro in Virginia*, Baltimore 1913, p. 127.
34. F. L. Olmstead, *A Journey in the Seaboard Slave States*, NY 1856, pp. 594–7.
35. Quoted by A. W. Calhoun, *A Social History of the American Family*, Cleveland 1917, Vol. I, p. 323.
36. See the *David Gavin Diary* in the Southern Historical Collection, University of North Carolina, and G. Freyre, *The Master and the Slaves*, NY 1956.
37. Archives of Virginia, op. cit., Petition 4594, Norfolk, 7 December 1803.
38. Ibid., Petition 4472, Fluvanna, 13 December 1802.
39. Ibid., Petition 5321, Loudown, 22 December 1808.
40. Ibid., Petition 5370, Amherst, 6 December 1809.
41. J. H. Johnston, op. cit., pp. 257–8.
42. Archives of Virginia, Executive Papers, 27 May 1807.
43. Peter Neilson, *Recollections of a Six Years Residence in the United States of America*, Glasgow 1830, p. 297.
44. John Rankin, *Letters of Slavery*, Newburyport 1836, p. 69.
45. Manuscript Returns, *United States Census 1830*.
46. Archives of Virginia, Executive Papers, 13 July 1801.
47. See Marquis de Chastellux, *Travels in North America in the Years 1780, 1781 and 1782*, (ed.) H. C. Rice Jr, Chapel Hill 1963, Vol. II, p. 585; Johan D. Schoepf, *Travels in the Confederation* (1783–1784), translated and edited by A. J. Morrison, Philadelphia 1911, Vol. I, p. 357; and *Military Journal of Lieutenant William Feltman, May 26, 1781–April 25, 1782*. Entry of 22 June 1781, Historical Society of Pennsylvania.
48. Feltman, op. cit. Entry of 22 June 1781.
49. C. L. Masters and Virginia Johnson, *Analysis of Human Sexual Response*, NY 1966, p. 191.
50. See for example E. W. Bovill, *The Golden Trade of the Moors*, London 1958, p. 92n; and 'The "Cantino" Planisphere 1502', in A Cotesão and A. Teixeira Da Mota, *Portugaliae Monumenta Cartographica*, Lisbon 1960–, Vol. I, Plate 5.
51. T. Bendyshe (trans. and ed.), *The Anthropological Treatises of Johan Frederich Blumenbach*, London 1865, p. 249.
52. John Jacobus, *Untrodden Fields of Anthropology*, Brussels ND.
53. John Dollard, *Caste and Class in a Southern Town*, 3rd Edition, NY 1957, pp. 160–1.
54. Ibid., p. 161.
55. W. M. Cobb, 'Physical Anthropology of the American Negro', *American Journal of Physical Anthropology*, Vol. 29, 1942, pp. 158–9; C. S. Coon, S. M. Garn and J. B. Birdsell, *Races: A Study of the Problems of Race Formation in Man*, Illinois 1950, pp. 63 and 91.
56. Archives of Virginia, Petition 6300c, Augusta, 12 October 1814.
57. Ibid., Petition 7546, Dinwiddie, 13 December 1820.

CHAPTER 6
Black and White Sexuality

1. James Weldon Johnson, *Along This Way*, London 1941, p. 80. First published in 1933.
2. *Daedalus*, 'The Negro American', Fall 1965, Boston.
Charles E. Silberman, *Crisis in Black and White*, London 1965.
In E. C. & H. M. Hughes, *Where Peoples Meet: Racial and Ethnic Frontiers*, Illinois 1952, there is a single paragraph, p. 111.
There are three comparatively minor references in Allan H. Spear, *Black Chicago*, Chicago 1967.
There is no mention of miscegenation in Harold R. Isaacs, *The New World of Negro Americans*, London 1964.
3. E. C. & H. M. Hughes, op. cit., p. 111.
4. Jessie Bernard, *Marriage & Family Among Negroes*, New Jersey, 1966, pp. 84–5.
5. M. J. Herskovits, *The American Negro*, NY 1928, p. 64.
6. It is apparent in Brazil as it is in the Caribbean.
7. Franklin Frazier, *Brown Bourgeoisie*, NY 1965, p. 117.
8. L. J. Ragatz, *The Fall of the Planter Class in the British Caribbean, 1763–1833*, NY 1963, p. 31.
9. A. W. Calhoun, *A Social History of the American Family*, Cleveland, 1919, Vol. III, p. 43.
10. W. H. Thomas, *The American Negro*, NY 1901, pp. 182–3.
11. W. H. Masters and Virginia Johnson, *Human Sexual Response*, Boston & London 1966, p. 191.
12. A. W. Calhoun, op. cit., Vol. III, pp. 294–6.
13. Frank Harris, *My Life and Loves*, NY 1963, pp. 202 & 205.
14 *Sexuality*, Vol. 2, No. 1, January 1972, pp. 62–3.
15. Ibid., pp. 63–4.
16. Abram Kardiner and Lionel Ovesey, *The Mark of Oppression*, Cleveland and New York 1964 – first published 1951.
17. See *inter alia* the studies of Allison Davis, Burleigh Gardner, Horace Cayton, St Clair Drake and John Dollard.
18. Sources US Dept of Commerce, Bureau of the Census, *Current Population Reports*, p. 20, No. 125; and Bureau of Labour Statistics.
19. Elizabeth Herzog, 'Is there a "breakdown" of the Negro Family?' in Lee Rainwater and W. L. Yancey, *The Moynihan Report & the Politics of Controversy*, Massachusetts, 1967, pp. 345–6 and 349–50.
20. Robert Staples, 'The Myth of the Impotent Black Male', *Intellectual Digest*, Vol. II, No. 3, Nov. 1971, pp. 20–22.
21. Ibid., p. 22.
22. Alexander Lowen, *The Betrayal of the Body*, NY 1967.
23. Clemmont Vontress, 'The Black Male Personality', *The Black Scholar*, Vol. 2, No. 10, June 1971, p. 12.

24. Ibid., pp. 12–13.
25. W. E. B. Du Bois, *Darkwater, Voices from Within the Veil*, NY 1969, p. 172.
26. See W. H. Grier and P. M. Cobbs, *Black Rage*, NY 1969, Chap. V.
27. Angela Davis, 'Reflections on the Black Woman's Role in the Community of Slaves', *The Black Scholar*, Vol. 3, No. 4, December 1971, p. 13.
28. Calvin Hernton, *Coming Together*, NY 1971, pp. 45–7.
29. Grier and Cobbs, op. cit., p. 81.
30. Ibid., p. 82.
31. Eldridge Cleaver, *Soul On Ice*, London 1969, p. 159.
32. Frantz Fanon, *Black Skin, White Masks*, London 1968, p. 63.
33. Gilberto Freyre, *The Masters and the Slaves*, NY 1946, pp. 94–5.
34. Norman Podhoretz, 'My Negro Problem – And Ours', in *Commentary*, February 1963.

CHAPTER 7
The West Indies

1. Bryan Edwards, *History of the West Indies*, London 1801, 3rd Edition, Vol. II, p. 15.
2. *Leeward Islands MSS Laws, 1644–1673*, Colonial Office, 154/1/49–51.
3. Juan y Santillana and A. de Ulloa, *A Voyage to South America*, 3rd Edition, London 1772, Vol. I, pp. 32–3.
4. Bryan Edwards, op. cit., p. 18.
5. John A. Waller, *A Voyage to the West Indies*, London 1820, p. 95.
6. Edwards, op. cit., p. 26.
7. R. J. Ragatz, *The Fall of the Planter Class in the British Caribbean, 1763–1833*, 2nd Edition, NY 1963, p. 5.
8. Edwards, op. cit., p. 26.
9. *An Abstract of the Evidence Delivered before a Select Committee of the House of Commons in the Years 1790 and 1791; on the Part of the Petitioners for the Abolition of the Slave-Trade*, London 1791, p. 73.
10. Ibid., pp. 74–5.
11. Ibid., pp. 68 and 71.
12. J. B. Moreton, *Manners and Customs in the West Indies*, London 1793, p. 129.
13. Thomas Cooper, *Facts Illustrative of the Condition of the Negro Slaves in Jamaica*, London 1824, p. 42.
14. Moreton, op. cit., p. 132.
15. Ibid., p. 127.
16. *Marly*, Glasgow 1828, p. 56.
17. Ibid., p. 83.
18. John Stewart, *An Account of Jamaica and its Inhabitants*, London 1823, pp. 173–4.
19. Cooper, op. cit., p. 23.

20. E. Long, *History of Jamaica*, London 1774, Vol. II, pp. 321–3.
21. Stewart, op. cit., pp. 180–81.
22. Ibid., p. 184.
23. Ibid.
24. Ibid., p. 186.
25. Mrs Flannigan, *Antigua and the Antiguans*, London 1844, Vol. II, p. 165.
26. Ibid., p. 166.
27. Ibid., p. 179.
28. Ibid., pp. 180–81.
29. Ibid., p. 181.
30. Elsa Goveia, *Slave Society in the British Leeward Islands ...*, New Haven and London 1965, p. 203.
31. Ibid.
32. Lionel Mordaunt Fraser, *History of Trinidad*, London 1891, Vol. I, p. 308.
33. Ibid., p. 287.
34. Robert H. Schomburgk. *A Description of British Guiana*, London 1840, p. 42.
35. Robert H. Schomburgk, *The History of Barbados*, London 1848, p. 86.
36. Bryan Edwards, op. cit., Vol. I, p. 284.
37. L. E. Moreau de Saint Méry, *Description ... de la partie française ... de Saint Domingue*, Philadelphia 1797, Vol. I, p. 285.
38. J. G. Leyburn, *The Haitian People*, New Haven 1941, pp. 19–20.
39. J. M. Phillipo, *Jamaica: Its Past and Present State*, London 1843, p. 150.
40. Anthony Trollope, *The West Indies and the Spanish Main*, London 1859, p. 73.
41. *The Handbook of Jamaica for 1890–91*, Kingston 1890.
42. Lafcadio Hearn, *Two Years in the French West Indies*, NY 1890, pp. 328–9.
43. *In All Shades*, London 1892, p. 65.
44. The figures quoted are based on those given in *The West Indies and Caribbean Year Book*, London 1972.
45. See Fernando Henriques, *Family and Colour in Jamaica*, 2nd Edition, London 1968.
46. Errol Miller, 'Body Image, Physical Beauty and Colour Amongst Jamaican Adolescents', in *Social and Economic Studies*, Vol. 18, No. 1, March 1969, p. 81.
47. Ibid., p. 86.

CHAPTER 8
The Case of Africa

1. C. Fyfe, *A History of Sierra Leone*, Oxford 1962, pp. 16–19.
2. Ibid., p. 19.
3. Mrs Anna Falconbridge, *Two Voyages to the Sierra Leone River*, London 1967, pp. 53–54.

4. See Richard West, *Back to Africa*, London 1970, pp. 24–26.
5. C. Fyfe, 'The Sierra Leone Administration in 1885', *Sierra Leone Studies*, NS June 1955, p. 227.
6. *Colonial Office, Despatches and Reports*, Series No. Co. 267/233, 1 August 1883.
7. H. A. C. Cairns, *Prelude to Imperialism*, London 1965, pp. 59–60.
8. David Livingstone, *Narrative of an Expedition to the Zambesi and its Tributaries*, London 1865, p. 416.
9. A. J. Swann, *Fighting Slave Hunters*, London 1810, p. 137.
10. Cairns, op. cit., p. 60.
11. Ibid., pp. 56–57.
12. Quoted by Cairns, op. cit., p. 57.
13. Richard Gray, *The Two Nations*, Oxford 1960, p. 19.
14. *Central African Archives, Salisbury, ZAH*, 'Evidence to the Morris Carter Land Commission, 1925', pp. 1625–1628.
15. *Legislative Assembly Debates, Southern Rhodesia (Salisbury)*, 27 May 1929, col. 1167.
16. C. A. Rogers and C. Frantz, *Racial Tension in Southern Rhodesia*, New Haven and London, p. 284.
17. See Doris Lessing's short stories – they make this point.
18. Rogers and Frantz, op. cit., p. 285.
19. O. Mannoni, *Prospero and Caliban*, London 1956, pp. 114 and 118.
20. Ibid., pp. 114–15.
21. Ibid., p. 116.
22. See André Delcourt, *La France et Les Éstablissements Français au Sénégal*, Dakar 1952.
23. Ibid., pp. 95 and 131.
24. J. Hargreaves, 'Assimilation in 18th-Century Senegal', in *Journal of African History*, Vol. XI, No. 2, 1965.
25. Rita Conor Cruise O'Brien, *White Society in Black Africa*, London 1972, p. 265.
26. Ibid., p. 268.
27. Ibid.
28. Ibid.
29. Ibid., p. 271.
30. Ibid., p. 272.
31. H. C. V. Liebbrandt, *Précis of the Archives of the Cape of Good Hope 1651–53*, Letters and Documents Received, No. 1, 'A Short Exposition of the Advantages to be derived by the Company from a Fort and Garden at the Cape of Good Hope', pp. 3–11.
32. I. D. MacCrone, *Race Attitudes in South Africa*, London 1937, pp. 42–3.
33. Ibid., p. 68.
34. O. F. Mentzel, *A Description of the Cape of Good Hope, 1787*, Cape Town 1944, Vol. II, p. 125.
35. Ibid., p. 109.

36. Ibid., p. 130.
37. Jacques Boulenger, *Voyage de François Vaillant dans l'Interieur de L' Afrique, 1781–1785*, Paris 1932, pp. 160–62.
38. E. H. Brookes, *Apartheid*, London 1968, p. 184.
39. Pierre Van den Berghe, *Race and Ethnicity*, NY 1970, pp. 232–3.
40. Ibid., pp. 224–43.
41. Ibid., p. 247.
42. Ibid., p. 248.
43. J. Lewin, 'Sex, Colour, and the Law', in *Africa South*, No. 4, pp. 63–6.

CHAPTER 9

Miscegenation in Europe – Britain and France

1. 'The Second Voyage of John Lok 1554–5', in Richard Hakluyt, *The Principal Navigations, Traffiques and Discoveries of the English Nation*, Glasgow 1904.
2. Basil Davidson, *The African Slave Trade*, Boston 1961, p. 42.
3. *Acts of the Privy Council*, XXVI, 1596–7, 16.
4. 'Licensing Caspar von Sendon to deport Negroes', 1601, in (eds) J. L. Hughes & J. F. Larkin, *Tudor Royal Proclamations, 1588–1603*, Yale 1969, p. 221.
5. J. A. Rogers, *Nature Knows No Colour-Line*, NY 1852, p. 161.
6. See the *Mercurius Politicus*, 11 August 1659 for one such advertisement.
7. Z. C. von Uffenbach, *London in 1710*, edited and translated by W. H. Quarrel, London 1934, p. 88.
8. Quoted in C. Dover, *Hell in the Sunshine*, London 1943.
9. Anon, *A Letter to Philo-Africanus*, London 1787, p. 17.
10. Edward Long, quoted by J. Walvin, *The Black Presence*, London 1971, pp. 70–71.
11. Norman Leys, *Kenya*, London 1924, p. 367.
12. *The Orthodox Churchman's Magazine*, Vol. II, 1802, p. 30.
13. Quoted by M. Dorothy George, *London Life in the 18th Century*, London 1924.
14. For an interesting survey of the legal complexities see Nan Wilson, 'Legal Attitudes to Slavery in 18th-Century Britain; English Myth; Scottish Realism and their Comparative Context', in *Race*, Vol. XI, 4, 1970.
15. Edward Long, op. cit., pp. 67–8.
16. *Notes & Queries*, December 1878, p. 453.
17. *Reminiscences of Henry Angelo*, London 1828, Vol. I, pp. 446–52.
18. *Confessions of Julia Johnson*, London 1828, p. 28.
19. *York Gazette*, 16 June 1832.
20. Joseph Marryat, *More Thoughts ...*, London 1815, p. 10
21. Benjamin Silliman, *A Journal of Travels in England, Holland and Scotland*, Yale 1810, p. 272.

22. Henry Mayhen, *London Labour and the London Poor*, London 1862. Extra Fourth Volume, *Those That Will Not Work*, pp. 425–6.
23. James Walvin, *Black and White*, London 1973, p. 194.
24. J. A. Rogers, *Sex and Race*, NY 1940, Vol. I, pp. 206–7.
25. R. Blathwayt, *Tit-Bits*, 21 July 1917.
26. Stephen Black, *The English Review*, October 1919.
27. *Sunday Pictorial*, 25 August 1945.
28. See for example Sheila Patterson, *Dark Strangers*, London 1963, S. K. Ruck (ed.), *The West Indian Comes to England*, London 1960; Nicholas Deakin *et al.*, *Colour, Citizenship and British Society*, London 1970; R. B. Davison, *Black British*, London 1966.
29. Michael Banton, *White and Coloured*, London 1959, p. 204.
30. Clifford S. Hill, *How Colour Prejudiced is Britain?*, London 1955, pp. 38 and 40.
31. Ibid., pp. 218–20.
32. Ibid., p. 222.
33. Rashmi Desai, *Indian Immigrants in Britain*, London 1963, p. 125.
34. Charles Mangin, 'Soldats Noirs en Europe', in *Questions diplomatiques et coloniale*, année 13, Oct. 1909.
35. Charles de la Roncière, *Nègres et négriers*, Paris 1933, p. 16.
36. Ibid., pp. 14–20.
37. *Bull. et Mem. Soc. D'Anthropologie de Paris*, Vol. I, 13 November 1886, p. 661.
38. Anisson du Perron, *Nouvelles à la Main*, Paris 1898, p. 29.
39. A. Aulard, *Paris Sous le Consulat*, Paris 1902, Vol. I, p. 341, Vol. II, pp. 789–90.
40. S. T. McCloy, *The Negro in France*, Kentucky 1961, p. 53.
41. J. Mathorez, *Les Etrangers en France sous l'Ancien Régime*, Paris 1919–21, Vol. I, pp. 185 and 403.
42. André Maurois, *Les Trois Dumas*, Paris 1937.
43. *Encyclopedia Britannica*, 1969 Edition.
44. René Maunier, *The Sociology of Colonies*, London 1936, Vol. II, pp. 610–11.
45. Margery Perham, *The Colonial Reckoning*, London 1963, p. 64.
46. *Transactions of the Ethnological Society of London*, Vol. I (1861), p. 81f.; Vol. III (1865), pp. 102–3, 110–11, 121; Vol. IV (1866), p. 223.
47. Joyce Edmund-Smith, 'West Indian Workers in France', in *New Community*, Vol. I, No. 5, autumn 1972, pp. 441–51.
48. Unpublished research material of the Charles Richet Centre, Paris.
49. See Paul-Hassan Maucorps, 'Les Problèmes d'acculturation réciproque en recherché interethnique', and 'Les Haïtiens en France: étude préliminaire', in *Proceedings of the Anglo–French Conference on Race Relations*, Sussex 1968; *Ethnies*, Vol. I, 1971, Mouton.
50. Louis Achille, *Rythmes du Monde*, Paris 1949, p. 113.

CHAPTER 10

The Anglo-Indians

1. D. Kincaid, *British Social Life in India, 1608–1937*, London 1939, p. 22.
2. H. A. Stark, *Hostages to India*, Calcutta 1926, pp. 2–3.
3. G. W. Deroze, 'The First Century', in *Clarion*, Vol. I, No. II, Calcutta 1945.
4. J. Rhodes (ed.), *Political India*, London 1932, p. 148.
5. Stark, op. cit., p. 43.
6. Ibid., pp. 50–51.
7. C. N. Weston, *Anglo–Indian Revolutionaries*, Bangalore 1938, p. 103.
8. Percival Spear, *The Nabobs: A Study of the Social Life of the English in 18th-Century India*, London 1963, pp. 62–4.
9. Philip Woodruff, *The Men Who Ruled India: The Founders*, London 1953, Endnote.
10. Stark, op. cit., p. 86.
11. Cedric Dover, *Half-Caste*, London 1937, pp. 138–40.
12. A socio-linguistic analysis of Anglo–Indian speech is to be found in John Spencer, 'The Anglo–Indians and their Speech: A Socio-Linguistic Essay', in *Lingua*, Vol. 16, No. 1, 1966.
13. V. R. Gaikwad, *The Anglo-Indians*, London 1968, pp. 27–8.
14. Stark, op. cit., pp. 31–2.
15. E. B. Reuter and M. Macmillan, quoted by K. E. Wallace, *The Eurasian Problem*, Calcutta 1930.
16. *Constitution of India*, Article 366 (2).
17. *Census of India*, Vol. I, Part IV, 1953, p. 27.
18. D. K. Battacharya, 'The Anglo-Indians in Bombay', in *Race*, Vol. X, No. 2, October 1968, p. 165.
19. Ibid., p. 165.
20. Gaikwad, op. cit., pp. 136–7.
21. Battacharya, op. cit., pp. 165–6.
22. Ibid., pp. 166–7.
23. Ibid., p. 170.
24. Ibid., p. 171.
25. Gaikwad, op. cit., pp. 215, 225 and 226.
26. See Cedric Dover, op. cit., pp. 118–22.

Index

[redacted]